THE CHARLTON
STANDARD CATALOGUE OF

Volume Two: Decorative Ware
Second Edition

By
Pat Murray

Publisher
W. K. Cross

The Charlton Press
Birmingham, Michigan • Toronto, Ontario

COPYRIGHT NOTICE AND TRADEMARK NOTICE

Canadian Cataloguing in Publication Data
Murray, Pat.
The Charlton standard catalogue of Wade
2nd ed.
Previously published under title: Pre-war and more Wades.
Contents: v. 1. General issues — v. 2. Decorative ware —
v. 3 Tableware.
Includes index.
ISBN 0-88968-139-2 (v. 1). - ISBN 088968-181-3 (v. 2)
 ISBN 0-88968-183-X (V. 3)
1. George Wade and Son - Catalogs. 2. Figurines - England -
Catalogs. 3. Miniature pottery - England - Catalogs.
I. Title. II. Title: Pre-war and more Wades.

NK8473.5.W33M8 1996   738.8′2   C95-932732-0

**Printed in Canada
in the Province of Ontario**

The Charlton Press

**Editorial Office
2010 Yonge Street
Toronto, Ontario M4S 1Z9
Telephone: (416) 488-4653 Fax: (416) 488-4656
Telephone: (800) 442-6042 Fax: (800) 442-1542**

CONTENTS

Editor	Sandra Tooze
Assistant Editor	Jean Dale
Graphic Technican	Patrick Glassford

ACKNOWLEDGEMENTS

Corporations

Many thanks to Bill Walker for his help with information regarding early Wade Heath models and backstamps, to Derek Dawe for his help with all Wade products, to Cynthia and Jenny for answering my questions, to J.A. Stringer for his assistance with Wade Ireland products and to Mark Oliver of Phillips Auctioneers and Valuers.

Institutions

I am grateful to the following institutions for their research assistance:
The British Newspaper Library, the Metro Toronto Reference Library and the Stroud Public Library.

Contributors

Thanks also to the following collectors for their photographs and data:
Jenny Chinnery, Ada Davidson, Tom Fish, Ann Glatzel, Marion and Gareth Hunt, P.M. McNicholl, Joanne and Don Mandryk, K Norton, B. and P. Powell, Janet Robinson, Kim and Derek Watson, Carol and John Woolner, Sandy Wright and those who wish to remain anonymous.

HOW TO USE THIS CATALOGUE

The Listings

On the pages that follow Wade models are listed, illustrated, described and priced.

The measurements of the models are given in millimetres. Most items are measured according to their **height**. For relatively flat objects—ashtrays, dishes and some plaques—the measurement listed is the **diameter** of a round item, the **side** of a square or the **longest length** of a rectangle or oval. For a few items, such as boxes, some candle holders, some plaques and posy bowls, both height and width are provided.

Although the publisher has made every attempt to obtain and photograph all models listed, several pieces, naturally, have not come into the publisher's possession.

A Word on Pricing

The purpose of this catalogue is to give readers the most accurate, up-to-date retail prices for Wade models in the United States, Canada and the United Kingdom.

To accomplish this The Charlton Press continues to access an international pricing panel of Wade experts who submit prices based on both dealer and collector retail price activity, as well as current auction results in U.S., Canadian, and U.K. markets. These market figures are carefully averaged to reflect accurate valuations for the Wade models listed herein in each of these three markets.

Please be aware that prices given in a particular currency are for models in that country only. The prices published herein have not been calculated using exchange rates—they have been determined solely by the supply and demand within the country in question.

A necessary word of caution. No pricing catalogue can be, or should be, a fixed price list. This catalogue should be considered as a guide only, one that shows the most current retail prices based on market demand within a particular region.

Current models, however, are priced differently. They are priced according to the manufacturer's suggested retail price in each of the three market regions. It should be noted, however, that it is likely that dealer discounting from these prices will occur.

The prices published herein are for items in mint condition.

Collectors are cautioned that a repaired or restored piece may be worth as little as 50 percent of the value of the same model in mint condition. Those collectors interested strictly in investment potential must avoid damaged items.

All relevant information must be known about an item in order to make a proper valuation. When comparing auction prices to catalogue prices, collectors and dealers should remember two important points. First, to compare "apples and apples," be sure that auction prices include a buyer's premium, if one is due. Prices realized for models in auction catalogues may not include this additional cost. Secondly, if an item is restored or repaired, it may not be noted in the listing, and as a result, the price will not be reflective of that same piece in mint condition.

The Numbering System

All models are numbered consecutively in the section in which they appear. Each section has the following letter prefixes:

AL:	Ashtrays and Lighter
BA:	Basketls
BO:	Bowls
BX:	Boxes
CH:	Candles and Candle Holders
D:	Dishes
FL:	Flowers
JA:	Jars
JU:	Jugs
LA:	Lamps
MD:	Miscellaneous Decorative Ware
PF:	Planters and Flower Pots
PW:	Plaques and Wall Decoration
PB:	Posy Bowls and Logs
V:	Vases and Urns

One mould may produce more than one variation of model. The difference may be in colouring or lettering on the item, as long as it does not affect the mould. When more than one variation of a model occurs, one style number is assigned to the mould and the varieties produced from that mould are indicated by a lower-case letter. For example, model PW-44 was produced in four variations, resulting in PW-44a to PW-44d.

When a derivative of an item is produced, it is indicated by the number 1 following the model number from which it was made. Thus the number of the derivative V-21cl indicates it was produced from model V-21c.

INTRODUCTION

History

In the early 1930s, Wade consisted of three potteries—A.J. Wade Ltd., George Wade & Son Ltd. and Wade Heath and Co. Ltd.—with Wade Ulster (Ireland) being acquired in the mid 1940s. At first the company mainly produced gas burners for domestic lighting, although a small amount of gift ware was made as well. Later, Wade's chief output was insulating products, bobbins, thread guides and tiles. The company even made cone heads for guided missles in the early 1960s.

At the onset of World War II, the government permitted the production of essential ceramics only. All gift ware production came to an end, with parts of the potteries being used as emergency food stores for the duration of the war. Afterwards the potteries were engaged in replacing the essential ceramics that had been destroyed by bombing. By the early 1950s, the George Wade Pottery began producing small collectable figures and animals.

Between 1955 and 1969 Wade Heath and Company Limited worked with Reginald Corfield (Sales) Ltd., of Redhill, Surrey (under the trademark of Regicor London), to produce a range of promotional and point-of-sale advertising ware. These earthenware products were produced by Wade Heath at its Royal Victoria Pottery in Burslem.

In 1958 the three English Wade potteries were restructured under the name Wade Potteries Ltd., later renamed Wade PLC. Wade (Ulster) Ltd. was renamed Wade Ireland in 1966.

The association with Reginald Corfield was discontinued in October 1969, and Wade Heath formed its own product, design and marketing company, called Wade PDM (PDM also stood for point of sale, design and marketing). This company specializes in advertising products for the distilling, brewing and tobacco industries, although it is not limited to those areas. It has become one of the leading suppliers of advertising products in the U.K.

In 1989 Wade PLC was taken over by Beauford PLC and renamed Wade Ceramics Ltd., which is still in operation today. Wade Ireland was renamed Seagoe Ceramics and continued to manufacture domestic tableware until 1993, when it reverted back to the production of industrial ceramics.

The Production Process

The earthenware and Irish porcelain items in this book are made from a hard, solid china, sturdy enough to stand up to regular domestic use. They are produced from a mixture of ball clay, used for its plasticity, china clay, which gives the item a white body and plasticity, and china stone, used as a bonding agent.

Wade's porcelain, or bone china, items differ from earthenware in that they are of a lighter weight, thinner and are translucent. For these models a mixture of china clay, china stone and animal bone, which gives strength and transparency to the pieces, is used.

These materials are mixed in large vats of water, producing a thick sludge or "slip." The slip is passed into a filter to extract most of the water, leaving large flat "bats" of porcelain clay, approximately two feet square and three inches thick. The clay bats are dried and then ground into dust ready for the forming process. Paraffin is added to the dust to assist in bonding and as a lubricant to remove the formed pieces from the steel moulds. Once pressed into the required shape, the clay articles are allowed to dry, then all the press marks are removed by sponging and "fettling," the scraping off of surplus clay with a sharp blade.

One or more ceramic colours is applied to the model, which is then sprayed with a clear glaze that, when fired, allows the colours underneath to show through. This process is known as underglaze decoration. On-glaze decoration—which includes enamelling, gilding and transfer printing—can also be done after the article has been glazed and fired.

Insuring Your Models

As with any other of your valuables, making certain your models are protected is very important. It is paramount that you display or store any porcelain items in a secure place, preferably one safely away from traffic in the home.

Your models are most likely covered under your basic homeowner's policy. There are generally three kinds of such policies—standard, broad and comprehensive. Each has its own specific deductible and terms.

Under a general policy your models are considered part of the contents and are covered for all of the perils covered under the contractual terms of your policy (fire, theft, water damage and so on). However, since some models are extremely delicate, breakage is treated differently by most insurance companies.

There is usually an extra premium attached to insure models against accidental breakage by or carelessness of the owner. This is sometimes referred to as a "fine arts" rider. You are advised to contact your insurance professional to get all the answers.

In order to help protect yourself, it is critical that you take inventory of your models and have colour photographs taken of all your pieces. This is the surest method of clearly establishing, for the police and your insurance company, any items lost or destroyed. It is also the easiest way to establish their replacement value.

Backstamps

Ink Stamps

Most of the ink stamps used are black, although some Wade Heath and Wade marks are red, grey, green, brown or orange. The earliest ink stamps found in this book, which were used in the early 1930s, have a lion included in the stamp, along with "Wade England" or "Wadeheath England."

From the mid 1930s, the lion was omitted from the backstamp and often the design name - such as Flaxman Ware or Orcadia Ware - was included. Toward the end of the 1930s, the name *Wadeheath* was split in two to make *Wade Heath*; by the end of World War II, the *Heath* was dropped, leaving a Wade backstamp.

Beginning in the mid 1950s, Wade Ireland also used ink stamps to mark its models.

Transfer Prints

Transfer-printed backstamps were introduced in 1953, and from that date onwards, they were used by both the English Wade potteries. Wade Ireland did use transfer prints, but they are not as common as ink stamps or their impressed and embossed backstamps.

Impressed and Embossed Backstamps

Impressed and embossed backstamps are incorporated into the mould. It is very difficult to identify the dates of items marked with these backstamps, because when these models were reissued, sometimes as long as 20 years later, the same backstamp appeared. It is often impossible to tell which items were issued first, unless different colours were used on the reissue. This is often the case with Wade Ireland, which issued and reissued some of their popular lines two or three times, all of which carry the identical impressed or embossed backstamp.

ASHTRAYS AND LIGHTER
c.1935-1993

Wade did not produce many ashtrays for the giftware market; most of its ashtrays were for advertising purposes. The majority of the ashtrays in this section were made by Wade Ireland from the mid 1950s to the late 1980s. The ashtrays decorated with transfer prints were produced from the late 1950s to the early 1960s and again in 1993. Except for lighter cases made for advertising ware, only one lighter has been reported.

The items in this section are listed in alphabetical order.

BACKSTAMPS

Ink Stamps

The first type of backstamp used by Wade on its ashtrays was the black ink stamp that appeared on the primrose ashtray, produced from the mid 1930s to 1939.

Transfer Prints

Beginning in 1953 transfer prints were the predominant backstamp used by Wade.

Embossed Backstamps

All the ashtrays with embossed backstamps were produced by Wade Ireland from the mid 1950s to the late 1970s.

Impressed Backstamps

All the ashtrays with impressed backstamps were produced by Wade Ireland in the 1950s. The lighter, produced from the late 1950s to the early 1970s, also has an impressed mark.

BARREL ASHTRAYS, c.1958

The original price of version AL-1a was 9/6d. The print on version AL-1b is of a Bugatti car.

Backstamp: Red transfer print "Wade England"

No.	Description	Colourways	Size	U.S.$	Can.$	U.K.£
AL-1a	Half barrel	Amber; two silver lustre bands	153	30.00	40.00	15.00
AL-1b	Half barrel	Amber; silver lustre band; multi-coloured print	150	30.00	40.00	15.00

CUBE ASHTRAYS, 1959-c.1963

A transfer print of a different animal's head is found on each side of these cube ashtrays. The same prints were also used on the Countrymen tankards.

Backstamp: Transfer print "Wade England"

No.	Description	Colourways	Size	U.S.$	Can.$	U.K.£
AL-2a	Poodle/terrier/ scottie/spaniel	White; black poodle; brown/white terrier/grey scottie; black spaniel	67	15.00	20.00	8.00
AL-2b	Poodle/terrier/ scottie/spaniel	White; grey poodle; brown/white terrier/grey scottie; brown spaniel	67	15.00	20.00	8.00
AL-2c	Horses	White; multi-coloured print (1 horse's head, 2 horses' heads)	67	10.00	15.00	3.00

EXECUTIVE DESK SET ASHTRAY, 1993

This ashtray was part of an executive desk set produced by Wade for companies to present to their business clients. It was produced in an all-over black glaze with gold edging and a gold stylized lily transfer print in the centre.

For an illustration of this ashtray
see page 198

Backstamp: Unknown

No.	Description	Colourways	Size	U.S.$	Can.$	U.K.£
AL-3	Ashtray	Black; gold edges, emblem	Unknown	Unknown		

IRISH WADE ASHTRAYS AND LIGHTER, c.1955–c.1987

A large range of Wade Ireland ashtrays was introduced and reissued throughout its 33 years of production. Only approximate dates can be given as very often the original moulds, which included impressed and embossed marks, were reissued with those same marks. With the exception of the shamrock range, all the ashtrays are in the easily recognizable Irish Wade mottled blues and brownish green glazes. Almost all the Wade Ireland ashtrays have a shape number (*I.P.* stands for Irish porcelain; *S.R.* for Shamrock Range).

Candle-holder Ashtray, c.1965

This unusual ashtray has a round candle holder fitted in the centre.

Photograph not available
at press time

Backstamp: Embossed "Irish Porcelain Made in Ireland" inside an Irish-knot wreath

No.	Description	Colourways	Size	U.S.$	Can.$	U.K.£
AL-4	Candle-holder ashtray	Blue/grey	205	20.00	30.00	10.00

Crinkled Ashtrays, c.1958–c.1975

This round ashtray has crinkled edges and a print in the centre.

For an illustration of these ashtrays
see page 38

Backstamp: A. Embossed circular "Irish Porcelain Made in Ireland" around a centre shamrock with a letter underneath
B. Embossed circular "Made in Ireland Irish Porcelain" around a crown and shamrock design with "Wade Eire tir a dheanta" underneath
Shape No.: I.P.607—style AL-5
I.P.622—style AL-6

No.	Description	Colourways	Shape No./Size	U.S.$	Can.$	U.K.£
AL-5a	Fisherman walking	Olive green/grey; multi-coloured print	I.P.607/120	20.00	30.00	10.00
AL-5b	Fisherman with salmon	Olive green/grey; multi-coloured print	I.P.607/120	20.00	30.00	10.00
AL-5c	Irish colleen carrying peat	Olive green/grey; multi-coloured print	I.P.607/120	20.00	30.00	10.00
AL-6a	Irish colleen carrying peat	Olive green/grey; multi-coloured print	I.P.622/146	25.00	35.00	12.00
AL-6b	Irish colleen carrying peat	Olive green/grey; multi-coloured print; black lettering "Ireland"	I.P.622/146	25.00	35.00	12.00
AL-6c	Flying pheasants	Olive green/grey; multi-coloured print	I.P.622/146	25.00	35.00	12.00
AL-6d	Fox hunter on horse	Olive green/grey; multi-coloured print	I.P.622/146	25.00	35.00	12.00
AL-6e	Paddy McGredy roses	Olive green/grey; multi-coloured print	I.P.622/146	25.00	35.00	12.00

Hexagonal Ashtrays, c.1955

The transfer print is in the centre.

For an illustration of these ashtrays
see page 38

Backstamp: Impressed "Irish Porcelain" over a large shamrock, with "Made in Ireland by Wade of Co. Armagh"
printed underneath
Shape No.: I.P.634

No.	Description	Colourways	Size	U.S.$	Can.$	U.K.£
AL-7a	Irish colleen carrying peat	Olive/brown/pale blue; multi-coloured print	146	20.00	30.00	8.00
AL-7b	Irish jaunting car	Olive/brown/pale blue; multi-coloured print	146	20.00	30.00	8.00

Pipe Ashtray, c.1955

This round ashtray has a knurled pattern running around the body. There is a pear-shaped hollow on one side for a pipe to rest in and a raised plinth in the centre with a fitted piece of cork for knocking out the tobacco from the pipe.

Photograph not available
at press time

Backstamp: Impressed "Irish Porcelain" over a large shamrock, with "Made in Ireland by Wade of Co. Armagh"
printed underneath
Shape No.: I.P.623

No.	Description	Colourways	Size	U.S.$	Can.$	U.K.£
AL-8	Pipe ashtray	Blue/green	153	20.00	30.00	8.00

Raindrop Design Ashtray, c.1965

This round ashtray has a ribbed design of raindrops around the rim.

Photograph not available
at press time

Backstamp: Embossed "Calibria made in U.K."

No.	Description	Colourways	Size	U.S.$	Can.$	U.K.£
AL-9	Raindrop ashtray	Blue/grey/green	55	20.00	30.00	8.00

Rose Design Ashtrays, c.1972-c.1975

This unusual-shaped ashtray is half round and half square, with an embossed design of roses around the top edge and a transfer print in the centre.

For an illustration of these ashtrays
see page 38

Backstamp: Embossed circular "Made in Ireland Irish Porcelain Wade Eire tir a dheanta" around a crown and shamrock
Shape No.: I.P.627

No.	Description	Colourways	Size	U.S.$	Can.$	U.K.£
AL-10a	Fox hunter on horse	Olive green/brown; multi-coloured print	146	20.00	30.00	10.00
AL-10b	Fox hunter on galloping horse	Olive green/brown; multi-coloured print	146	20.00	30.00	10.00
AL-10c	Two fisherman/river	Olive green/brown; multi-coloured print	146	20.00	30.00	10.00
AL-10d	Two fisherman/river	Olive green/brown; multi-coloured print	146	20.00	30.00	10.00

Shamrock Design Ashtrays, c.1955

This square ashtray has an embossed design of shamrocks around the top edge and a transfer print in the centre.

For an illustration of these ashtrays
see page 38

Backstamp: Impressed "Irish Porcelain" over a small shamrock with "Made In Ireland by Wade of Co. Armagh" underneath
Shape No.: I.P.626

No.	Description	Colourways	Size	U.S.$	Can.$	U.K.£
AL-11a	Finn MacCaul	Blue/grey; multi-coloured print	153	25.00	35.00	12.00
AL-11b	Fisherman in river	Blue/grey; multi-coloured print	153	25.00	35.00	12.00
AL-11c	Fox hunter on horse	Blue/grey; multi-coloured print	153	25.00	35.00	12.00
AL-11d	Foxhunter on galloping horse	Blue/grey; multi-coloured print	153	25.00	35.00	12.00
AL-11e	Irish kitchen	Blue/grey; multi-coloured print	153	25.00	35.00	12.00

Shamrock Range Ashtrays, c.1987

The transfer prints on these ashtrays are of shamrocks.

For an illustration of these ashtrays
see page 94

Backstamp: Circular transfer print "Made in Ireland Porcelain Wade Eire tir a dheanta" around a shamrock and crown
Shape No.: S.R.17—style AL-12
S.R.18—style AL-13

No.	Description	Colourways	Shape No./Size	U.S.$	Can.$	U.K.£
AL-12	Shamrock ashtray	White; gold rim; green print	S.R.17/177	20.00	30.00	10.00
AL-13	Shamrock ashtray	White; green print	S.R.18/153	20.00	30.00	10.00

Shamrocks and Irish-knot Design Ashtrays, c.1955-c.1958, c.1972-c.1975

The top edges of these ashtrays are embossed with a design of shamrocks and Irish knots. There is a transfer print in the centre. The style AL-14 ashtrays are square; style AL-15 is triangular.

For an illustration of these ashtrays
see page 38

Backstamp: A. Embossed circular "Irish Porcelain Made in Ireland" around a shamrock with a letter underneath
B. Embossed circular "Made in Ireland Irish Porcelain" around a crown and shamrock design with "Wade Eire tir a dheanta" underneath
Shape No.: I.P.611—style AL-14
I.P.612—style AL-15

No.	Description	Colourways	Shape No./Size	U.S.$	Can.$	U.K.£
AL-14a	Irish jaunting car	Grey/blue; multi-coloured print	I.P.611/100	25.00	35.00	12.00
AL-14b	Irish kitchen	Grey/blue; multi-coloured print	I.P.611/100	25.00	35.00	12.00
AL-14c	Irish passenger coach	Olive/grey; multi-coloured print	I.P.611/100	25.00	35.00	12.00
AL-15a	Finn MacCaul	Blue/grey/green; multi-coloured print	I.P.612/95	20.00	30.00	10.00
AL-15b	Irish cottage	Blue/grey/green; multi-coloured print	I.P.612/95	20.00	30.00	10.00
AL-15c	Irish jaunting car	Blue/grey/green; multi-coloured print	I.P.612/95	20.00	30.00	10.00
AL-15d	Irish passenger coach	Blue/grey/green; multi-coloured print	I.P.612/95	20.00	30.00	10.00
AL-15e	Stag's head	Blue/grey/green; multi-coloured print	I.P.612/95	20.00	30.00	10.00

Table Lighter, c.1958–c.1973

This table lighter is set in the top of an urn-shaped holder, which is very similar to the Killarney urn posy bowls. There is a band of shamrocks around the middle of the lighter.

Backstamp: Impressed "Irish Porcelain Made in Ireland" curved over a shamrock
Shape No.: I.P.95

No.	Description	Colourways	Size	U.S.$	Can.$	U.K.£
AL-16	Table lighter	Grey/blue	100	35.00	45.00	8.00

Thistle Ashtrays, c.1972–c.1977

These round ashtrays have an embossed design of thistles around the top edge and a transfer print in the centre.

For an illustration of these ashtrays
see page 38

Backstamp: Embossed circular "Made in Ireland Irish Porcelain Wade Eire tir a dheanta" around a shamrock and crown
Shape No.: I.P.628

No.	Description	Colourways	Size	U.S.$	Can.$	U.K.£
AL-17a	Flying pheasants	Blue/grey; multi-coloured print	153	20.00	30.00	10.00
AL-17b	Fox hunter on horse	Blue/grey; multi-coloured print	153	20.00	30.00	10.00
AL-17c	Hunter firing rifle	Blue/grey; multi-coloured print	153	20.00	30.00	10.00
AL-17d	Stag's head	Blue/grey; multi-coloured print	153	20.00	30.00	10.00
AL-17d	Trotting horse	Blue/grey; multi-coloured print	153	20.00	30.00	10.00

PRIMROSE ASHTRAY, c.1935-1939

This ashtray was produced as part of the second series of flowers (see section entitled Flowers).

Backstamp: Black ink stamp "Wade Made in England"

No.	Description	Colourways	Size	U.S.$	Can.$	U.K.£
AL-18	Primroses	Pink; yellow flowers	20	20.00	25.00	10.00

SOUVENIR ASHTRAY, c.1953

This square ashtray has a transfer print of Niagara Falls in the centre.

Photograph not available
at press time

Backstamp: Circular transfer print "Royal Victoria Pottery Wade England"

No.	Description	Colourways	Shape/Size	U.S.$	Can.$	U.K.£
AL-19	Niagara Falls	Cream/green; black print	Square/127	15.00	20.00	8.00

BASKETS
c.1930-c.1952

Most Wade baskets were produced in all-over colours, many with embossed designs. A few were decorated with hand-painted flowers. The baskets are listed in shape-number order.

BACKSTAMPS

Ink Stamps

The first backstamps used on Wade's baskets were Flaxman ink stamps, from 1937 to 1939. Harvest Ware and Wade Heath stamps also appear on the baskets. In most cases the shape number is impressed on the base.

SHAPE 161
Gothic Ware Basket, 1937-1939

This basket is embossed with a design of swirling leaves and tulips and has a matt finish.

Backstamp: Ink stamp "Flaxman Wade Heath England"

No.	Description	Colourways	Size	U.S.$	Can.$	U.K.£
BA-1	Gothic	Mottled green/orange	175	90.00	125.00	45.00

SHAPE 246
Flaxman Ware Baskets, 1937-1939

These baskets are decorated with an embossed design of swirling leaves.

Backstamp: **A.** Black ink stamp "Flaxman Wade Heath England"
B. Black ink stamp "Gothic Wade England"

No.	Description	Colourways	Size	U.S.$	Can.$	U.K.£
BA-2a	Flaxman 246	Mottled pale yellow/brown	125	65.00	85.00	30.00
BA-2b	Flaxman 246	Mottled pale orange/green	125	65.00	85.00	30.00
BA-2c	Flaxman 246	Mottled blue/green/brown	125	65.00	85.00	30.00
BA-2d	Flaxman 246	Cream; gold rim; mottled green leaves	125	65.00	85.00	30.00
BA-2E	Gothic 246	Cream; gold rim; pink/lilac flowers; green/yellow leaves	125	70.00	95.00	35.00

SHAPE 247
Baskets, c.1938

These baskets are embossed with a brick design.

Backstamp: Black ink stamp "Wade England Flaxman"

No.	Description	Colourways	Size	U.S.$	Can.$	U.K.£
BA-3a	Flaxman 247	Mottled pale yellow/green	130	65.00	85.00	30.00
BA-3b	Flaxman 247	Mottled green/dark yellow	130	65.00	85.00	30.00
BA-3c	Flaxman 247	Pale yellow	130	65.00	85.00	30.00

SHAPE 248
Baskets, 1937-1939, 1953

The flaxman ware baskets were issued between 1937 and 1939. They have ribs running down the body. Version BA-4a is decorated with hand-painted flowers and leaves. The Peony Series baskets were in production between c.1948 and c.1952.

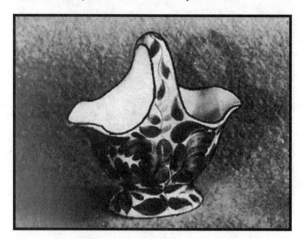

Backstamp: A. Black ink stamp "Flaxman Wade Heath England"
B. Black ink stamp "Harvest Ware Wade England" with impressed "248"

No.	Description	Colourways	Size	U.S.$	Can.$	U.K.£
BA-4a	Flaxman 248	Cream; large purple flowers; green leaves	130	70.00	95.00	35.00
BA-4b	Flaxman 248	Mottled blue/brown	130	65.00	85.00	30.00
BA-4c	Flaxman 248	Mottled green/pale yellow	130	65.00	85.00	30.00
BA-4d	Flaxman 248	Mottled orange/green	130	65.00	85.00	30.00
BA-4e	Flaxman 248	Mottled yellow/green	130	65.00	85.00	30.00
BA-5	Peony 248	Cream; purple/mauve/dark red peonies	155	65.00	85.00	30.00

SHAPE 250
Basket, 1937-1939

This basket has an embossed basket-weave design on it, with embossed flowers on the front.

Backstamp: **A.** Black ink stamp "Flaxman Wade Heath England"
B. Black ink stamp "Wade Heath England"
C. Impressed "250"

No.	Description	Colourways	Size	U.S.$	Can.$	U.K.£
BA-6	Shape 250	Cream; pink/mauve/yellow flowers	130	65.00	85.00	30.00

WOVEN BASKET WITH ROSES, c.1930-c.1935

This earthenware basket was part of the first series of flowers made by Wade (see Flowers section).

Backstamp: **A.** Raised "British Made" and black handwritten "Wade England"
B. Raised "British Made"
C. Black handwritten "Wade England"

No.	Description	Colourways	Size	U.S.$	Can.$	U.K.£
BA-7	Basket with roses	Four pink flowers on rim; pale blue basket	25 x 80	20.00	25.00	10.00

BOWLS
c.1930-1992

Many bowls produced by Wade — such as Black Frost, Gothic Ware, Harmony Ware, Orcadia Ware and the Peony Series — were part of a set that could include dishes, jugs and vases. The bowls in this section are listed in alphabetical order.

BACKSTAMPS

Handwritten Backstamp

The first backstamp Wade used on its bowls was handwritten and appeared from circa 1930 to circa 1935.

Ink Stamps

Ink stamps were used on bowls from 1933 to the early 1950s, after which time transfer prints were generally used.

Transfer Prints

Transfer prints were commonly used as backstamps beginning in 1953. They appear on many of Wade's bowls from 1953 to 1992.

Impressed Backstamps

The only impressed mark on the bowls appears on some of the Harmony Ware, from 1957 to the mid 1960s.

Embossed Backstamps

The only embossed backstamp used on Wade's bowls appears on the Celtic Porcelain bowl, produced in 1965.

BEACON BOWLS, 1958-1959

This set of four round bowls came boxed together. They were designed as nut or candy bowls for bridge parties. The prices below are for single bowls.

Backstamp: Red transfer print "Wade England"

No.	Description	Colourways	Size	U.S.$	Can.$	U.K.£
BO-1a	Beacon	White rim; black centre	100	15.00	22.00	8.00
BO-1b	Beacon	White rim; green centre	100	15.00	22.00	8.00
BO-1c	Beacon	White rim; red centre	100	15.00	22.00	8.00
BO-1d	Beacon	White rim; yellow centre	100	15.00	22.00	8.00

BLACK FROST SERIES NUT BOWLS, 1957-c.1960

In 1957 a series of ten black pottery items was produced with frosted white transfer prints of British wild flowers on the front and back.

Backstamp: **A.** Red print "Wade England"
B. White print "Wade England"

No.	Description	Colourways	Size	U.S.$	Can.$	U.K.£
BO-2	Black Frost	Black; white flowers; gold rim	100	8.00	10.00	3.00

BOWL FOR FLOWER CENTRES, c.1930-c.1935

This earthenware bowl was made to hold the flower centres produced by Wade (see Flowers section). It was part of the first series of flowers.

Photograph not available
at press time

Backstamp: Raised "British Made" with an impressed code letter and sometimes a black handwritten "Wade England" or "Made in England"

No.	Description	Colourways	Size	U.S.$	Can.$	U.K.£
BO-3	Bowl	Black	Small/25 x 45	10.00	15.00	3.00

CELTIC PORCELAIN BOWL, 1965

The design of writhing snakes found on this bowl was copied from illustrations made by medieval monks in an Irish manuscript entitled, *The Book of Kells*. The snakes represent those banished from Ireland by Saint Patrick. Only a small quantity of bowls was issued.

Photograph not available
at press time

Backstamp: Embossed "Celtic Porcelain by Wade Ireland" in an Irish knot wreath
Shape No.: CK6

No.	Description	Colourways	Size	U.S.$	Can.$	U.K.£
BO-4	Celtic Porcelain	Mottled blue-green	50	80.00	110.00	40.00

CHELSEA SERIES BOWLS, 1962

This series of bowls is very similar to those of the Empress Series.

Chelsea bowl, ribbed foot (BO-5)	Chelsea bowl, handles at base (BO-8b)

Backstamp: Red transfer print "Wade England"

No.	Description	Colourways	Size	U.S.$	Can.$	U.K.£
BO-5	Ribbed foot	Black	92	40.00	55.00	20.00
BO-6	Small foot	Black	57	30.00	40.00	15.00
BO-7	Plain foot/sloping rim	Black	133	51.00	70.00	25.00
BO-8a	Ribbed foot/ handles at base	White	108	40.00	55.00	20.00
BO-8b	Ribbed foot/ handles at base	White; gold	108	50.00	70.00	25.00
BO-9	Plain foot/ handles at base	White	108	40.00	55.00	20.00
BO-10	Plain foot	Black	108	40.00	55.00	20.00

COPPER-LUSTRE POWDER BOWLS, c.1948

These copper-lustre powder bowls were all hand decorated; therefore, each decoration is slightly different. The original price was 2/9d.

Photograph not available
at press time

Backstamp: Green ink stamp "Harvest Ware Wade England" and impressed "Made in England"

No.	Description	Colourways	Size	U.S.$	Can.$	U.K.£
BO-11a	Harvest Ware	Copper bowl; cream lid with copper rim; mauve/ yellow flower; green leaves; brown streaks	45 x 105	30.00	40.00	15.00
BO-11b	Harvest Ware	Copper bowl, lid; pink/yellow flower; pale green leaves	45 x 105	30.00	40.00	15.00
BO-11c	Harvest Ware	All-over copper lustre	45 x 105	30.00	40.00	15.00

EARTHENWARE POWDER BOWL, c.1930-c.1935

This item was part of the first series of flowers produced by Wade (see section entitled Flowers).

Photograph not available
at press time

Backstamp: Black handwritten "Wade England" with "126"
Shape No.: 126

No.	Description	Colourways	Size	U.S.$	Can.$	U.K.£
BO-12	Earthenware	Mottled cream/green; pink roses	60 x 100	80.00	110.00	40.00

EMPRESS SERIES FRUIT BOWLS, c.1948-c.1950

The fruit bowls have swirling handles on the sides of the base. Style BO-13a was issued in the late 1940s, style BO-13b circa 1950.

Backstamp: **A.** Circular ink stamp "Royal Victoria Pottery Wade England"
B. Black ink stamp "Wade England" with impressed "408"
C. Black ink stamp "Wade England"
Shape No.: 408

No.	Description	Colourways	Size	U.S.$	Can.$	U.K.£
BO-13a	Empress 408	Mottled green	177	300.00	400.00	150.00
BO-13b	Empress 408	White	177	90.00	120.00	45.00

GOTHIC WARE BOWLS, 1938-1939

These shallow bowls were embossed with a design of swirling leaves and tulips and had a matt finish.

Backstamp: Black ink stamp "Gothic Wade Heath England"

No.	Description	Colourways	Size	U.S.$	Can.$	U.K.£
BO-14a	Gothic	Cream; pink flowers; pale green leaves	55 x 235	60.00	80.00	30.00
BO-14b	Gothic	Cream	55 x 235	60.00	80.00	30.00
BO-14c	Gothic	Pale green	55 x 235	60.00	80.00	30.00

GREAT BRITAIN NUT BOWLS, 1959

These bowls came from the same moulds as the 1958 Beacon bowls.

Eros, Piccadilly Circus (BO-15a)

Backstamp: Green transfer print "Wade England"

No.	Description	Colourways	Size	U.S.$	Can.$	U.K.£
BO-15a	Eros, Piccadilly Circus	Black; gold rim; white print	100	12.00	16.00	6.00
BO-15b	London, coat of arms	White; red band; multi-coloured print	100	12.00	16.00	6.00
BO-15c	London, coat of arms	White; black band; multi-coloured print	100	12.00	16.00	6.00

HARMONY WARE BOWLS, 1957-c.1962

Between 1957 and the early 1960s, Wade produced 13 assorted shaped bowls, jugs and vases that were called Harmony Ware. They were decorated with transfer prints in four different designs. For a short time, they were also produced in solid and two-tone colours.

Shape No. 439

Carnival (BO-16a)

Backstamp: A. Red transfer "Wade England" with impressed "England" and shape number
B. Red transfer "Wade England Fern" with impressed "England" and shape number
C. Black transfer "Wade England Parasol" with impressed "England" and shape number
D. Black transfer "Wade England" with impressed England and shape number
E. Black transfer "Wade England" and green shooting stars with impressed "England" and shape number
F. Impressed "Wade England" and shape number
Shape No.: 439

No.	Description	Colourways	Size	U.S.$	Can.$	U.K.£
BO-16a	Carnival	White; yellow/red/green flowers	140 x 280	90.00	120.00	45.00
BO-16b	Fern	White; black/red/fern	140 x 280	90.00	120.00	45.00
BO-16c	Parasols	White; multi-coloured parasols	140 x 280	90.00	120.00	45.00
BO-16d	Shooting stars	White; multi-coloured stars	140 x 280	90.00	120.00	45.00
BO-16e	Solid colour	Black	140 x 280	90.00	120.00	45.00
BO-16f	Solid colour	White	140 x 280	90.00	120.00	45.00
BO-16g	Solid colour	Green	140 x 280	90.00	120.00	45.00
BO-16h	Solid colour	Yellow	140 x 280	90.00	120.00	45.00
BO-16i	Two-tone	Grey/pink	140 x 280	90.00	120.00	45.00
BO-16j	Two-tone	Green/peach	140 x 280	90.00	120.00	45.00

Shape No. 440

Parasols (BO-17c)

Backstamp: **A.** Red transfer "Wade England" with impressed "England" and "440"
B. Red transfer "Wade England Fern" with impressed "England" and "440"
C. Black transfer "Wade England Parasol" with impressed "England" and "440"
D. Black transfer "Wade England" with impressed England and "440"
E. Black transfer "Wade England" and green shooting stars with impressed "England" and "440"
F. Impressed "Wade England" and "440"

Shape No.: 440

No.	Description	Colourways	Size	U.S.$	Can.$	U.K.£
BO-17a	Carnival	White; yellow/red/green flowers	125 x 222	90.00	120.00	45.00
BO-17b	Fern	White; black/red fern	125 x 222	90.00	120.00	45.00
BO-17c	Parasols	White; multi-coloured parasols	125 x 222	90.00	120.00	45.00
BO-17d	Shooting stars	White; multi-coloured stars	125 x 222	90.00	120.00	45.00
BO-17e	Solid colour	Black	125 x 222	90.00	120.00	45.00
BO-17f	Solid colour	White	125 x 222	90.00	120.00	45.00
BO-17g	Solid colour	Green	125 x 222	90.00	120.00	45.00
BO-17h	Solid colour	Yellow	125 x 222	90.00	120.00	45.00
BO-17i	Two-tone	Grey/pink	125 x 222	90.00	120.00	45.00
BO-17j	Two-tone	Green/peach	125 x 222	90.00	120.00	45.00

Shape No. 449

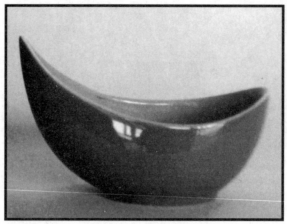

Two-tone (BO-18e)

Backstamp: **A.** Red transfer "Wade England" with impressed "England" and "449"
B. Red transfer "Wade England Fern" with impressed "England" and "449"
C. Black transfer "Wade England Parasol" with impressed "England" and "449"
D. Black transfer "Wade England" with impressed England and "449"
E. Black transfer "Wade England" and green shooting stars with impressed "England" and "449"
F. Impressed "Wade England" and "449"

Shape No.: 449

No.	Description	Colourways	Size	U.S.$	Can.$	U.K.£
BO-18a	Carnival	White; yellow/red/green flowers	62 x 105	10.00	15.00	5.00
BO-18b	Fern	White; black/red fern	62 x 105	10.00	15.00	5.00
BO-18c	Parasols	White; multi-coloured parasols	62 x 105	10.00	15.00	5.00
BO-18d	Shooting stars	White; multi-coloured stars	62 x 105	10.00	15.00	5.00
BO-18e	Two-tone	Grey/pink	62 x 105	8.00	10.00	4.00
BO-18f	Two-tone	Green/peach	62 x 105	8.00	10.00	4.00

Shape No. 450

Shooting stars (BO-19d)

Backstamp: **A.** Red transfer "Wade England" with impressed "England" and "450"
B. Red transfer "Wade England Fern" with impressed "England" and "450"
C. Black transfer "Wade England Parasol" with impressed "England" and"450"
D. Black transfer "Wade England" with impressed England and "450"
E. Black transfer "Wade England" and green shooting stars with impressed "England" and "450"
F. Impressed "Wade England" and "450"

Shape No.: 450

No.	Description	Colourways	Size	U.S.$	Can.$	U.K.£
BO-19a	Carnival	White; yellow/red/green flowers	62 x 130	8.00	10.00	3.00
BO-19b	Fern	White; black/red fern	62 x 130	8.00	10.00	3.00
BO-19c	Parasols	White; multi-coloured parasols	62 x 130	8.00	10.00	3.00
BO-19d	Shooting stars	White; multi-coloured stars	62 x 130	8.00	10.00	3.00
BO-19e	Two-tone	Grey/pink	62 x 130	8.00	10.00	3.00
BO-19f	Two-tone	Green/peach	62 x 130	8.00	10.00	3.00

Five-Sided Bowl, c.1965

In the mid 1960s, a shallow bowl with a hole on each side and five odd-shaped sides, resembling a spinning Catherine wheel, was added to the Harmony range. It is a larger version of a four-sided bowl produced by Wadeheath in its early-1950s Bramble tableware series.

Photograph not available
at press time

Backstamp: Unknown

No.	Description	Colourways	Size	U.S.$	Can.$	U.K.£
BO-20	Parasols	White; multi-coloured parasols	45 x 175	25.00	35.00	12.00

IMPERIAL SERIES BOWL, 1955

Part of the Imperial Series, this bowl was produced in early 1955.

Photograph not available
at press time

Backstamp: Circular print "Wade Made in England Hand Painted"

No.	Description	Colourways	Size	U.S.$	Can.$	U.K.£
BO-21	Imperial	Burgundy; white seed; gold highlights	140	60.00	80.00	30.00

JACOBEAN AND KAWA POWDER BOWLS, 1990-1992

The Jacobean design is of red and black enamelled exotic flowers. Kawa is a Japanese design of pastel pink peonies and bamboo stems with gold highlighting.

Photograph not available
at press time

Backstamp: **A.** Red transfer print "Wade England" with two red lines and "Jacobean"
B. Gold transfer print "Wade England" with two gold lines and "Kawa"

No.	Description	Colourways	Size	U.S.$	Can.$	U.K.£
BO-22a	Jacobean	White; red/black enamelled print	70	30.00	40.00	15.00
BO-22b	Kawa	White; pastel pink/green print; gold highlights	70	30.00	40.00	15.00

NUT BOWLS, 1953-c.1968

Produced as nut bowls for card parties, these bowls have different transfer prints in the centre. They are the same shape as the Beacon Bowls and were sold in boxed sets of two. The prices below are for a single bowl.

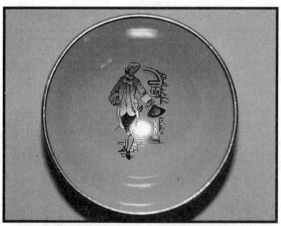

Georgian man (BO-23a)

Backstamp: **A.** Red transfer print "Wade England"
B. Green transfer print "Wade England"

No.	Description	Colourways	Size	U.S.$	Can.$	U.K.£
BO-23a	Georgian lady	Pink; gold rim; gold/pink print	100	10.00	15.00	5.00
BO-23b	Georgian man	Turquoise; gold rim; gold/black print	100	10.00	15.00	5.00
BO-23c	Flower	White; grey/pale blue flower	100	10.00	15.00	5.00
BO-23d	Plain	Pale yellow	100	10.00	15.00	5.00

ORCADIA WARE FRUIT BOWL, 1933-1935

Orcadia Ware was produced in vivid glazes with streaks that occurred when the glaze ran over the rims..

Backstamp: Black ink stamp "Wadeheath Orcadia Ware British Made"

No.	Description	Colourways	Size	U.S.$	Can.$	U.K.£
BO-24	Orcadia	Orange/green streaks; yellow inside, base	95 x 205	120.00	160.00	60.00

PEONY SERIES BOWL, c.1948-c.1952

The Peony Series had free-hand underglaze decorations of large purple, mauve and dark red peonies.

Backstamp: Black ink stamp "Harvest Ware Wade England" with "369" impressed on the base
Shape No.: 369

No.	Description	Colourways	Size	U.S.$	Can.$	U.K.£
BO-25	Harvest Ware	Cream; multi-coloured flowers	85 x 220	60.00	80.00	30.00

REGENCY SERIES BOWLS, 1959-1961

The miniature Regency Series bowl is a scaled-down version of the Empress fruit bowl.

Backstamp: A. Red transfer print "Wade England"
B. Black transfer print "Wade England"

No.	Description	Colourways	Size	U.S.$	Can.$	U.K.£
BO-26	Regency	White; gold highlights	52 x 112	30.00	40.00	15.00

ROSES POWDER BOWL, c.1938-c.1943

This powder bowl has earthenware roses on the top of the lid.

Photograph not available
at press time

Backstamp: Ink stamp "Wade England"

No.	Description	Colourways	Size	U.S.$	Can.$	U.K.£
BO-27	Roses powder bowl	Mottled green; red/yellow roses	70 x 101	50.00	70.00	25.00

BOXES
1936-1993

Most of these boxes were decorated with transfer prints and were produced by Wade England. Wade Heath made hand-painted and copper-lustre boxes from 1936 to the mid 1940s, and Wade Ireland issued boxes in the mid 1950s and again in 1976. The boxes are listed in alphabetical order.

BACKSTAMPS

Ink Stamps

Ink stamps were used on boxes from 1936 to 1953.

Impressed Backstamp

An impressed backstamp was used by Wade Ireland on its Irish Wade boxes in the 1950s.

Transfer Prints

Various transfer prints were used on boxes from 1957 to the mid 1960s.

Embossed Backstamps

In 1960 and 1961, then again from 1983 to 1985, some Wade England boxes were marked with embossed backstamps. Wade Ireland used an embossed backstamp in 1976.

ABSTRACT DESIGN CIGARETTE BOX, c.1965

This box is from the same mould as the veteran cars boxes. It has an abstract design of rectangles and squares printed on the lid.

Backstamp: Transfer print "Wade England"

No.	Description	Colourways	Size	U.S.$	Can.$	U.K.£
BX-1	Cigarette box	White; multi-coloured print	127 x 95	50.00	70.00	25.00

BUTTERFLY AND FLOWERS TRINKET BOX, 1936–c.1945

This hand-decorated, rectangular trinket box could also be used for ladies' handkerchiefs.

Photograph not available
at press time

Backstamp: Ink stamp "WadeHeath England"

No.	Description	Colourways	Size	U.S.$	Can.$	U.K.£
BX-2	Trinket box	Cream; yellow/brown butterfly; pink/blue/yellow flowers	242 x 108	70.00	90.00	35.00

CAPT. KIDD CIGARETTE BOX, c.1958

This cigarette box is shaped like a pirate's treasure chest and has "Capt. Kidd 1698" impressed on the lid. The original price was 9/6d.

Backstamp: Red transfer print "Wade England"

No.	Description	Colourways	Size	U.S.$	Can.$	U.K.£
BX-3	Captain Kidd	Amber; copper lustre hinges, lock	80 x 105	40.00	55.00	20.00

COPPER-LUSTRE CANDY BOXES, c.1945

These boxes stand on four small feet. Because they were hand decorated, no two designs are identical. The original price was 5/-.

Photograph not available
at press time

Backstamp: A. Green ink stamp "Wade Heath England" with impressed "241"
B. Black ink stamp "Wade England"
Shape No.: 241

No.	Description	Colourways	Size	U.S.$	Can.$	U.K.£
BX-4a	Shape 241	Copper box; copper/cream lid; maroon/ yellow flower; green leaves; brown streaks	177 x 127	20.00	28.00	10.00
BX-4b	Shape 241	Copper box, lid; yellow/green/pink clover leaves, flowers	177 x 127	20.00	28.00	10.00

COPPER-LUSTRE CIGARETTE BOXES, c.1945

Some of these rectangular cigarette boxes were sold gift boxed with a matching tray. The original price was 3/6d.

Copper-lustre cigarette box (BX-5f)

Backstamp: A. Ink stamp "Wade England"
B. Green ink stamp "Harvest Ware Wade England"
Shape No.: 242

No.	Description	Colourways	Size	U.S.$	Can.$	U.K.£
BX-5a	Shape 242	Cream box, lid; copper band, leaves, flowers	127 x 88	40.00	55.00	20.00
BX-5b	Shape 242	Copper box; cream lid with copper band; purple/yellow flower; green leaves; brown streaks	127 x 88	40.00	55.00	20.00
BX-5c	Shape 242	Copper box, lid; pale blue stylized flowers; grey leaves	127 x 88	40.00	55.00	20.00
BX-5d	Shape 242	White box, lid; pale blue stylized flowers; grey leaves	127 x 88	40.00	55.00	20.00
BX-5e	Harvest 242	Copper/cream box, lid; two purple/yellow flowers; green leaves	127 x 88	40.00	55.00	20.00
BX-5f	Harvest 242	Copper box, lid; pale pink/yellow/green clover flowers, leaves	127 x 88	40.00	55.00	20.00

COPPER-LUSTRE TRINKET BOX, c.1945

As this box was hand decorated, the design will vary slightly among pieces. The original price was 3/6d

Photograph not available at press time

Backstamp: Unknown

No.	Description	Colourways	Shape/Size	U.S.$	Can.$	U.K.£
BX-6	Trinket box	Copper box; cream lid; copper band; mauve/green flower	Square/76	40.00	55.00	20.00

COTTAGE AND GARDEN TRINKET BOX

The edges of this box are curved, and it is decorated with a print of a cottage and garden.

Photograph not available at press time

Backstamp: Unknown

No.	Description	Colourways	Size	U.S.$	Can.$	U.K.£
BX-7	Trinket box	White; gold bands; multi-coloured print	88 x 63	40.00	55.00	20.00

EXECUTIVE TRINKET BOX, 1993

This round box was part of an eight-piece executive desk set that Wade sold to companies as presentation sets. It has a stylized lily transfer print in the centre.

For an illustration of this box
see page 198

Backstamp: Unknown

No.	Description	Colourways	Size	U.S.$	Can.$	U.K.£
BX-8	Trinket box	Black; gold edge, emblem	Round/63	30.00	40.00	15.00

GOTHIC SERIES TRINKET BOX, c.1948-c.1952

This large basket-shaped trinket box has a flat lid and is decorated with embossed leaves and tulips and edged with gold lustre.

Photograph not available
at press time

Backstamp: Ink stamp "Wade England"

No.	Description	Colourways	Size	U.S.$	Can.$	U.K.£
BX-9	Gothic	Cream; pale pink tulips; pale green/yellow leaves; gold lustre	153 x 101	60.00	80.00	30.00

IRISH WADE BOXES, c.1955

These boxes have been sold both as cigarette boxes and as candy boxes. One gift pack comprised a cigarette box, tankard and ashtray and another included a cigarette box and ashtray. When they were sold as candy boxes, they were sold separately. All had embossed shamrocks around the box and on the lid with a transfer print in the centre.

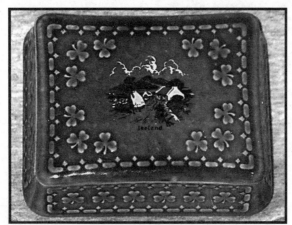

Irish colleen carrying peat (BX-10d)

Backstamp: Impressed "Irish Porcelain" over a small shamrock with "Made in Ireland by Wade of Co. Armagh" underneath
Shape No.: I.P.92

No.	Description	Colourways	Size	U.S.$	Can.$	U.K.£
BX-10a	Fox hunter, hat on head	Grey/blue/green; multi-coloured print	127 x 101	60.00	80.00	30.00
BX-10b	Fox hunter, hat in hand	Grey/blue/green; multi-coloured print	127 x 101	60.00	80.00	30.00
BX-10c	Hunter firing rifle	Grey/blue/green; multi-coloured print	127 x 101	60.00	80.00	30.00
BX-10d	Irish colleen carrying peat	Grey/blue/green; multi-coloured print	127 x 101	60.00	80.00	30.00
BX-10e	Irish kitchen	Grey/blue/green; multi-coloured print	127 x 101	60.00	80.00	30.00
BX-10f	Paddy McGredy rose	Grey/blue/green; multi-coloured print	127 x 101	60.00	80.00	30.00

MOURNE SERIES CANDY BOX, 1976

This rectangular candy box was produced with the Mourne Series of porcelain vases and is completely different in colour and style from previously produced Wade Ireland products.

Photograph not available at press time

Backstamp: Embossed circular "Made in Ireland Irish Porcelain Wade eire tir a dheanta" around a small shamrock and crown

No.	Description	Colourways	Size	U.S.$	Can.$	U.K.£
BX-11	Mourne	Green-brown; orange flower	50 x 127	80.00	110.00	40.00

ROMANCE SERIES TRINKET BOXES, 1983-1985

The original price was £1.99 each.

Egg-shaped trinket box (BX-12)

Rectangular-shaped trinket box (BX-13)

Backstamp: Raised "Wade Made in England"

No.	Description	Colourways	Shape/Size	U.S.$	Can.$	U.K.£
BX-12a	Romance	Fawn; grey/yellow/white design	Egg/40	20.00	30.00	10.00
BX-12b	Romance	Cream; blue/grey/fawn design	Egg/40	20.00	30.00	10.00
BX-13a	Romance	Fawn; grey/yellow/white design	Rectangular/46	20.00	30.00	10.00
BX-13b	Romance	Cream; blue/grey/fawn design	Rectangular/46	20.00	30.00	10.00

TEENAGE HEART-SHAPED CASKETS, 1960

The original price of these caskets was 7/6d

Heart-shaped casket, Tommy Steele (BX-14b)

Backstamp: Embossed "Wade Porcelain Made in England"

No.	Name	Colourways	Size	U.S.$	Can.$	U.K.£
BX-14a	Cliff Richard	Pink; multi-coloured print	40 x 85	150.00	200.00	75.00
BX-14b	Tommy Steele	Pink; multi-coloured print	40 x 85	150.00	200.00	75.00
BX-14c	Marty Wilde	Pink; multi-coloured print	40 x 85	150.00	200.00	75.00
BX-14d	Frankie Vaughan	Pink; multi-coloured print	40 x 85	150.00	200.00	75.00

TREASURE CHEST TRINKET BOX, 1961

The original price was 4/11d.

Backstamp: Embossed "Wade Porcelain Made in England"

No.	Description	Colourways	Size	U.S.$	Can.$	U.K.£
BX-15	Trinket box	Honey-brown; red-brown straps, hinges	40 x 90	60.00	80.00	30.00

VETERAN CARS AND HORSE-DRAWN BUS BOXES, 1957, 1958-1962

These boxes have been advertised as both candy and cigarette boxes and could be purchased in gift-box packs. Style BX-16 was issued in 1957; style BX-17 from 1958 to 1962.

Photograph not available
at press time

Backstamp: **A.** Black print "A Moko Product by Wade England"
B. Transfer print "Wade England"

No.	Description	Colourways	Size	U.S.$	Can.$	U.K.£
BX-16a	Benz	Black box, print; white lid	55 x 140	40.00	55.00	20.00
BX-16b	Darracq	Black box, print; white lid	55 x 140	40.00	55.00	20.00
BX-16c	Ford	Black box, print; white lid	55 x 140	40.00	55.00	20.00
BX-17a	Baby Peugeot, 1902	Black box, print; white lid	50 x 127	40.00	55.00	20.00
BX-17b	Benz, 1899	Black box, print; white lid	50 x 127	40.00	55.00	20.00
BX-17c	Bugatti, 1927	Black box; multi-coloured print; white lid	50 x 127	40.00	55.00	20.00
BX-17d	Cadillac, 1903	Black box, print; white lid	50 x 127	40.00	55.00	20.00
BX-17e	Darracq, 1904	Black box, print; white lid	50 x 127	40.00	55.00	20.00
BX-17f	De Dion Bouton, 1904	Black box, print; white lid	50 x 127	40.00	55.00	20.00
BX-17g	Ford, 1912	Black box, print; white lid	50 x 127	40.00	55.00	20.00
BX-17h	Horse-drawn bus	Black box; multi-coloured print; white lid	50 x 127	50.00	65.00	22.00
BX-17i	Itala, 1908	Black box; multi-coloured print; white lid	50 x 127	40.00	55.00	20.00
BX-17j	Lanchester, 1903	Black box, print; white lid	50 x 127	40.00	55.00	20.00
BX-17k	Oldsmobile, 1904	Black box, print; white lid	50 x 127	40.00	55.00	20.00
BX-17l	Rolls-Royce, 1907	Black box, print; white lid	50 x 127	40.00	55.00	20.00
BX-17m	Spyker, 1905	Black box, print; white lid	50 x 127	40.00	55.00	20.00
BX-17n	Sunbeam, 1904	Black box, print; white lid	50 x 127	40.00	55.00	20.00
BX-17o	Sunbeam, 1914	Black box; multi-coloured print; white lid	50 x 127	40.00	55.00	20.00
BX-17p	White Steam Car, 1903	Black box, print; white lid	50 x 127	40.00	55.00	20.00

VICTORIAN LADIES CAMEO PORTRAIT TRINKET POTS, c.1988-1991

These small trinket pots with cameos of Victorian ladies on the lid were produced by Wade Ireland. It is believed they were produced at the same time as Wade Ireland's Gray Fine Art plaques.

Backstamp: Unmarked

No.	Description	Colourways	Shape/Size	U.S.$	Can.$	U.K.£
BX-18	Victorian ladies	Light grey; off-white lid	Round/35 x 65	70.00	95.00	35.00
BX-19a	Victorian ladies	Dark green; blue-grey lid	Oblong/35 x 80	70.00	95.00	35.00
BX-19b	Victorian ladies	Light grey; blue-grey lid	Oblong/35 x 80	70.00	95.00	35.00

WADE
Irish Porcelain

Portadown, Co. Armagh, Northern Ireland

Telephone: Portadown 32288

Telex: 747128

Ashtrays

SHEET 6

1. *IP.611*   Square Ashtray
2. *IP.612*   Triangular Ashtray
3. *IP.609P*   Shamrock Ashtray with Leprechaun

4. *IP.609*   Shamrock Ashtray
5. *IP.634*   Hexagonal Ashtray
6. *IP.619*   Pin Tray
7. *IP.619L*   Leprechaun Pin Tray
8. *IP.622*   Large Crinkled Ashtray

9. *IP.607*   Small Crinkled Ashtray
10. *IP.627*   Rose Ashtray
11. *IP.626*   Large Square Ashtray
12. *IP.628*   Thistle Ashtray

CANDLES AND CANDLE HOLDERS
1937-c.1988

Wade Heath produced a candle holder in the late 1930s, Wade England made candles and holders in the 1950s, and Wade Ireland issued its candle holders in the late 1980s. The items in this section are listed in alphabetical order.

BACKSTAMPS

Ink Stamp

The earliest candle holder produced by Wade, from 1937 to 1938, was marked with a Wade Heath ink stamp.

Transfer Prints

Wade began using transfer prints for its backstamps in 1953. From 1953 to 1954 they were used to mark the everlasting candles. In the late 1980s, Wade Ireland used a transfer print.

Embossed Backstamp

From 1957 to 1959, Wade used an embossed backstamp to mark its candle holders.

EVERLASTING CANDLES, 1953-1954

This pair of porcelain candles is decorated with flowers. They are hollow with a rubber bung in the base and sit in a candle holder, which consists of six modelled petals. The candles were filled with pink paraffin. The original price was 30/- per boxed pair.

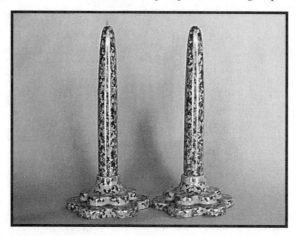

Backstamp: Black transfer print "Wade England"

No.	Description	Colourways	Size	U.S.$	Can.$	U.K.£
CH-1a	Everlasting candle	White; gold flowers	225	80.00	110.00	40.00
CH-1b	Everlasting candle	White; yellow flowers	225	100.00	135.00	50.00
CH-1c	Everlasting candle	White; multi-coloured flowers	225	100.00	135.00	50.00
CH-1d	Everlasting candle	Yellow; orange/blue flowers	225	100.00	135.00	50.00
CH-1e	Everlasting candle	Pale blue; multi-coloured flowers	225	100.00	135.00	50.00
CH-1f	Everlasting candle	Pale green; gold flowers	225	100.00	135.00	50.00

HOLLY LEAF CANDLE HOLDER, 1961

This pair of low candle holders, modelled in the shape of holly leaves, was sold with two red candy-twist candles in a presentation box marked "Wade Porcelain Candlesticks." They were also found in a presentation box marked "Wade Two Christmas Candle Holders with Candles." The original price was 3/6d.

Backstamp: Unmarked

No.	Description	Colourways	Size	U.S.$	Can.$	U.K.£
CH-2	Candle holder	Dark green leaf; red berries	98	30.00	40.00	15.00

HORSE'S HEAD CANDLE HOLDER, c.1988

A limited number of candle holders with a portrait of a horse's head in the centre was produced by Wade Ireland. There are indentations for four candles, one in each corner. The corners are decorated with shamrock leaves.

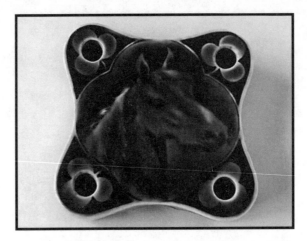

Backstamp: Unmarked

No.	Description	Colourways	Size	U.S.$	Can.$	U.K.£
CH-3	Candle holder	Chestnut brown/beige/grey	23 x 95	40.00	55.00	20.00

OAK LEAF DISH CANDLE HOLDERS, 1957-1959

The leaf dishes were adapted to form a candle holder with the addition of a brass foot, a handle and a candle cup. This adaptation may have been done by the Peerage Brass Company.

Photograph not available
at press time

Backstamp: Embossed "Wade Porcelain Made in England"

No.	Description	Colourways	Size	U.S.$	Can.$	U.K.£
CH-4a	Candle holder	Beige	45 x 100	25.00	35.00	12.00
CH-4b	Candle holder	Green	45 x 100	25.00	35.00	12.00

RABBIT NIGHT LIGHT, 1937-1938

This model is in two parts. On the bottom a night-light candle sits in the hollow centre of the tray base. The upper part is moulded in the shape of a rabbit sitting in front of a burrow, which has flowers on it and irregular holes around the sides and in the top.

Backstamp: Black ink stamp "Wadeheath Ware England"

No.	Description	Colourways	Size	U.S.$	Can.$	U.K.£
CH-5	Night light	Orange rabbit; green burrow, tray; yellow/ orange flowers	115 x 140	250.00	335.00	125.00

SHAMROCK RANGE CANDLE HOLDER, c.1987

This Wade Ireland candle holder has a print of shamrocks on it.

For an illustration of this candle holder
see page 94

Backstamp: Circular transfer print "Made in Ireland Porcelain Wade eire tire a dheanta" around a shamrock and crown
Shape No.: SR12

No.	Description	Colourways	Size	U.S.$	Can.$	U.K.£
CH-6	Shamrock Range	White; gold rim; green prints	101	20.00	30.00	10.00

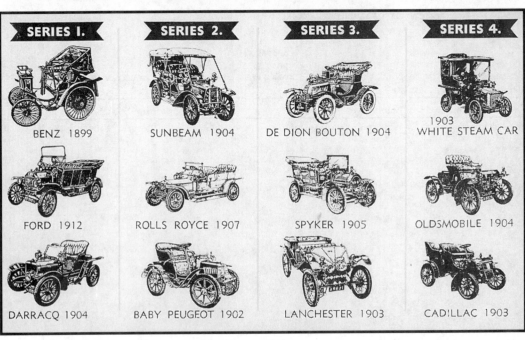

DISHES
c.1930-1992

The dishes included in this section are considered decorative rather than utilitarian. Some were produced in novelty shapes—such as the aqua dishes, hedgehog tray, pet face dishes and starfish pin tray—and some include a model of a figure attached to the dish—for example, the doggie dishes, the man in a rowboat tray, the swallow dishes and T.T. trays. There is also a wide selection of souvenir dishes.

The dishes are listed in alphabetical order.

BACKSTAMPS

Ink Stamps

Ink stamps were used to mark dishes from the late 1930s to the mid 1950s and from 1963 to 1964.

Transfer Prints

Beginning in 1953 until 1992, most of the dishes produced by Wade were marked with a transfer-print backstamp.

Embossed Backstamps

Like transfer prints, embossed backstamps were commonly used on dishes. They were in use from 1953 to 1984.

Impressed Backstamps

From 1956 to 1986 impressed backstamps were used by Wade on its dishes.

"A" DISH, c.1955

This dish has a gold *A* in the centre. There is no information as to why this dish bears the initial.

Backstamp: Red transfer print "Wade England"

No.	Description	Colourways	Size	U.S.$	Can.$	U.K.£
D-1	"A" dish	White; gold rim, letter	114	6.00	8.00	3.00

ANIMAL DISHES, 1955-1959

Although Wade called these items butter dishes, they are much more ornamental than utilitarian. The squirrel and rabbit dishes were produced from 1955 to 1959; the koala dish was issued in 1959 only.

Koala animal dish

Squirrel animal dish

Backstamp: Embossed "Wade England"

No.	Description	Colourways	Size	U.S.$	Can.$	U.K.£
D-2a	Koala	Green; beige/white koala	80	25.00	35.00	12.00
D-2b	Koala	Brown; beige/white koala	80	25.00	35.00	12.00
D-3a	Rabbit	Beige	80	25.00	35.00	12.00
D-3b	Rabbit	Green	80	25.00	35.00	12.00
D-4a	Squirrel	Beige	80	25.00	35.00	12.00
D-4b	Squirrel	Green	80	25.00	35.00	12.00

AQUA DISHES, 1958-1961, 1973

These bloater- and goldfish-shaped dishes were produced in Wade's high-gloss Scintillite finish with an embossed scale design. Packaged as a boxed pair, the original price was 3/11d per box. The goldfish dish was first issued in January 1958 and withdrawn in January 1960. It was reissued by Wade Ireland in 1973 in lighter colours and priced at 4/6d per boxed pair. The bloater dish was first issued in January 1960.

Bloater dishes

Goldfish dishes

Backstamp: A. Embossed "Wade Porcelain Made In England"
B. Embossed "Wade Porcelain Made In Ireland"

No.	Description	Colourways	Size	U.S.$	Can.$	U.K.£
D-5	Bloater	Brown/dark blue	65 x 98	10.00	15.00	5.00
D-6a	Goldfish	Brown/dark blue	100 x 80	10.00	15.00	5.00
D-6b	Goldfish	Beige/light blue	100 x 80	10.00	15.00	5.00

BALLET SERIES DISHES, 1957-1958

The Ballet Series comprises dishes and vases in white with black silhouette transfer prints of ballerinas in dance poses. The dishes were originally sold either individually boxed, as a set of four dishes or one dish with two miniature vases.

Backstamp: Black and red transfer print "Ballet Wade of England"

No.	Description	Colourways	Size	U.S.$	Can.$	U.K.£
D-7a	Ballerina, hands forward	White; red/yellow/black print	112	10.00	15.00	5.00
D-7b	Ballerina, head turned back	White; red/yellow/black print	112	10.00	15.00	5.00
D-7c	Ballerina on one toe	White; red/yellow/black print	112	10.00	15.00	5.00
D-7d	Ballerina on points	White; red/yellow/black print	112	10.00	15.00	5.00

B.O.A.C. AIRCRAFT DISHES, 1960

This set comprises four square dishes with transfer prints of Boeing airplanes in the centre.

Boeing 707 (D-8c)

Backstamp: **A.** Black transfer print "Boeing 707 Engines: Rolls Royce Conway Pure Jet. Length: 152 ft 11 ins.
Span: 142 ft 5 ins. All up Weight: 295,000 lbs. Average Cruising Speed: 530 m.p.h.
Maximum Range: 6,650 miles. Reproduction by Wade of England in collaboration with B.O.A.C."
B. Black transfer print "Bristol Britania 312 Engine: Bristol Proteus 755 Turbo Prop Length: 124 ft 3 ins.
Span: 142 ft 3 ins. All up Weight: 180,000 lbs. Average Cruising Speed: 360 m.p.h. Maximum Range: 4,400 miles.
Reproduction by Wade of England in collaboration with B.O.A.C."

No.	Description	Colourways	Size	U.S.$	Can.$	U.K.£
D-8a	Boeing	White; blue/black/silver print	107	20.00	30.00	10.00
D-8b	Boeing Bristol Britannia 312	White; blue/black/silver print	107	20.00	30.00	10.00
D-8c	Boeing 707	White; blue/black/silver print	107	20.00	30.00	10.00
D-8d	4 D.H. Comet 4	White; blue/black/silver print	107	20.00	30.00	10.00

BRITISH FORD DISHES, 1959-1960

This set of square dishes depicts modern British Ford cars of the time. A different well-known London scene is in the background of each dish.

Ford Consul (D-9a)   Ford Zodiac (D-9c)

Backstamp: **A.** Black transfer print "Ford Consul Saloon. 4-Cyl Reproduced by Wade England"
B. Black transfer print "Ford Zodiac Saloon. G Cyl 2553 C.C. Reproduced by Wade England"

No.	Description	Colourways	Size	U.S.$	Can.$	U.K.£
D-9a	Ford Consul saloon car	White; red car; black Tower Bridge	110	10.00	15.00	5.00
D-9b	Ford Zephyr saloon car	White; yellow car; black Big Ben	110	10.00	15.00	5.00
D-9c	Ford Zodiac	White; blue car; black St. Paul's Cathedral	110	10.00	15.00	5.00

CAMEO DISHES, 1965

This series of oval, round-cornered and round dishes has an embossed design of an animal or roses in the centre. The original price was 5/11d each.

Fawn Cameo dish

Backstamp: Embossed "Wade England"

No.	Description	Colourways	Shape/Size	U.S.$	Can.$	U.K.£
D-10a	Fawn	Brown/dark blue rim	Oval/110	10.00	15.00	5.00
D-10b	Fawn	Green/dark green rim	Oval/110	10.00	15.00	5.00
D-11a	Kitten	Brown/dark blue rim	Oval/110	10.00	15.00	5.00
D-11b	Kitten	Green/dark green rim	Oval/110	10.00	15.00	5.00
D-12a	Cairn	Brown/dark blue rim	Round corners/110	10.00	15.00	5.00
D-12b	Cairn	Green/dark green rim	Round corners/110	10.00	15.00	5.00
D-13a	Horse	Brown/dark blue rim	Round corners/110	10.00	15.00	5.00
D-13b	Horse	Green/dark green rim	Round corners/110	10.00	15.00	5.00
D-14a	Chicks	Brown/dark blue rim	Round/100	10.00	15.00	5.00
D-14b	Chicks	Green/dark green rim	Round/100	10.00	15.00	5.00
D-15a	Roses	Brown/dark blue rim	Round/100	10.00	15.00	5.00
D-15b	Roses	Green/dark green rim	Round/100	10.00	15.00	5.00

Reissued as Pet Dishes, 1979-1982

The cameo dishes were reissued in 1979 in an all-over, one-colour glaze and renamed pet dishes.

Backstamp: Embossed "Wade England"

No.	Description	Colourways	Shape/Size	U.S.$	Can.$	U.K.£
D-16a	Fawn	Brown	Oval/110	8.00	10.00	4.00
D-16b	Fawn	Green	Oval/110	8.00	10.00	4.00
D-17a	Kitten	Brown	Oval/110	8.00	10.00	4.00
D-17b	Kitten	Green	Oval/110	8.00	10.00	4.00
D-18a	Cairn	Brown	Round corners/110	8.00	10.00	4.00
D-18b	Cairn	Green	Round corners/110	8.00	10.00	4.00
D-19a	Horse	Brown	Round corners/110	8.00	10.00	4.00
D-19b	Horse	Green	Round corners/110	8.00	10.00	4.00
D-20a	Chicks	Brown	Round/100	8.00	10.00	4.00
D-20b	Chicks	Green	Round/100	8.00	10.00	4.00
D-21a	Roses	Brown	Round/100	8.00	10.00	4.00
D-21b	Roses	Green	Round/100	8.00	10.00	4.00

CANDY DISH, 1953

This candy dish is from the same mould as the 1953 coronation dish, but with all the animals and inscriptions removed. The original selling price was 2/11d.

Photograph not available
at press time

Backstamp: Embossed "Wade England"

No.	Description	Colourways	Size	U.S.$	Can.$	U.K.£
D-22	Candy dish	Pale ming green	120	10.00	15.00	5.00

CELTIC PORCELAIN DISH, 1965

The embossed design of writhing snakes was copied from illustrations made by medieval monks in an Irish manuscript entitled, *The Book of Kells*. The snakes represent those banished from Ireland by Saint Patrick.

Photograph not available
at press time

Backstamp: Embossed "Celtic Porcelain by Wade Ireland" in an Irish knot wreath
Shape No.: CK2

No.	Description	Colourways	Size	U.S.$	Can.$	U.K.£
D-23	Celtic	Mottled blue-green	114	40.00	55.00	20.00

CHARLES DICKENS DISHES, 1959-1960

The transfer prints on this set of octagonal dishes portray characters from Dickens's novels.

Backstamp: Red transfer print "Wade England" and a black print of Dickens's portrait

No.	Description	Colourways	Size	U.S.$	Can.$	U.K.£
D-24a	Little Nell	White; silver band; multi-coloured print	110	10.00	15.00	5.00
D-24b	Miss Nipper	White; silver band; multi-coloured print	110	10.00	15.00	5.00
D-24c	Mr. Micawber	White; silver band; multi-coloured print	110	10.00	15.00	5.00
D-24d	Mr. Pickwick	White; silver band; multi-coloured print	110	10.00	15.00	5.00
D-24e	Mrs. Gamp	White; silver band; multi-coloured print	110	10.00	15.00	5.00
D-24f	Uriah Heep	White; silver band; multi-coloured print	110	10.00	15.00	5.00

DISH FOR FLOWER CENTRES, c.1930-c.1935

This earthenware dish was made to hold the flower centres produced by Wade (see Flowers section). It was part of the first series of flowers.

Photograph not available
at press time

Backstamp: Raised "British Made" with an impressed code letter and sometimes a black handwritten "Wade England" or "Made in England"

No.	Description	Colourways	Size	U.S.$	Can.$	U.K.£
D-25	Dish	Black	Large/25 x 60	10.00	15.00	5.00

DOG AND HORSE HEAD DISHES, 1959-c.1962

These round dishes have a wide brown band around the rim and a transfer print of an animal head or heads in the centre. The same prints were used on the Countrymen pint traditional tankards and on the cube ashtrays.

Photograph not available
at press time

Backstamp: Red transfer print "Wade England"

No.	Description	Colourways	Size	U.S.$	Can.$	U.K.£
D-26a	Horse	White; brown band; multi-coloured print	108	10.00	15.00	5.00
D-26b	Two horses	White; brown band; multi-coloured print	108	10.00	15.00	5.00
D-26c	Black poodle	White; brown band; multi-coloured print	108	10.00	15.00	5.00
D-26d	Grey poodle	White; brown band; multi-coloured print	108	10.00	15.00	5.00
D-26e	Black spaniel	White; brown band; multi-coloured print	108	10.00	15.00	5.00
D-26f	Brown spaniel	White; brown band; multi-coloured print	108	10.00	15.00	5.00

DOGGIE DISHES, 1956-1958

These kidney-shaped dishes have a model of a fox terrier or a spaniel on the back rim. The dish with the fox terrier was issued in January 1956 and was withdrawn in January 1958. The spaniel dish was introduced in February 1957 and was discontinued in January 1958. Their original price was 3/11d. This dish shape was reused for the Lesney gift trays in 1961 (see *The Charlton Standard Catalogue of Wade, Volume One*).

Fox terrier doggie dish (D-27a)

Backstamp: Impressed "Wade Made In England"

No.	Description	Colourways	Size	U.S.$	Can.$	U.K.£
D-27a	Fox terrier	Beige; white/brown dog	100	50.00	70.00	25.00
D-27b	Fox terrier	Green; white/brown dog	100	50.00	70.00	25.00
D-27c	Fox terrier	Light grey; white/brown dog	100	50.00	70.00	25.00
D-27d	Fox terrier	Dark grey; white/brown dog	100	50.00	70.00	25.00
D-28a	Spaniel	Beige; white/brown dog	100	50.00	70.00	25.00
D-28b	Spaniel	Green; white/brown dog	100	50.00	70.00	25.00
D-28c	Spaniel	Light grey; white/brown dog	100	50.00	70.00	25.00
D-28d	Spaniel	Dark grey; white/brown dog	100	50.00	70.00	25.00

EMETTS DISHES, c.1958

These dishes are decorated in the centre with a cartoon by British cartoonist Rowland Emetts. They were sold individually and in a boxed set of four dishes.

Top D-29d, D-29c; bottom D-29b, D-29a

Backstamp: **A.** Black transfer print "Emetts by Wade of England Town Carriage for a Ninth Earl"
B. Black transfer print "Emetts by Wade of England Pastoral Interlude"
C. Black transfer print "Emetts by Wade of England Dog and Dogstar"
D. Black transfer print "Emetts by Wade of England Chivalry"

No.	Description	Colourways	Size	U.S.$	Can.$	U.K.£
29a	Chivalry	White; yellow/blue/pink print	106	10.00	15.00	5.00
29b	Dog and dogstar	White; yellow/blue/pink print	106	10.00	15.00	5.00
29c	Pastoral interlude	White; yellow/blue/pink print	106	10.00	15.00	5.00
29d	Town carriage for a Ninth Earl	White; yellow/blue/pink print	106	10.00	15.00	5.00

ENGLISH COACHING INNS DISHES, 1959-c1962

Bristol, left; Stratford, right

Backstamp: Red transfer print "Wade England"

No.	Description		Colourways	Size	U.S.$	Can.$	U.K.£
D-30a	Old Coach House, Bristol		White; multi-coloured print	110	10.00	15.00	5.00
D-30b	Old Coach House, Stratford		White; multi-coloured print	110	10.00	15.00	5.00
D-30c	Old Coach House, York		White; multi-coloured print	110	10.00	15.00	5.00

FAMOUS SHIPS DISHES, 1958

This set of three white tyre dishes is decorated with transfer prints of famous sailing ships in the centre. The same prints were originally used on the 1956 Snippets sailing ships set.

Photograph not available
at press time

Backstamp: Red transfer print "Wade England"

No.	Description	Colourways	Size	U.S.$	Can.$	U.K.£
D-31a	Mayflower	White; multi-coloured print	105	10.00	15.00	5.00
D-31b	Santa Maria	White; multi-coloured print	105	10.00	15.00	5.00
D-31c	The Revenge	White; multi-coloured print	105	10.00	15.00	5.00

FANTASIA SERIES DISHES, 1961

The transfer prints used on this set of decorative ware were based on a scene from the 1940 Walt Disney film, *Fantasia*. These dishes are flat and stand on three feet. They were first used in the 1957 Harmony Series.

Backstamp: Black transfer print "Fantasia by Wade of England—copyright Walt Disney Productions," impressed "England 455"
Shape No.: 455

No.	Description	Colourways	Size	U.S.$	Can.$	U.K.£
D-32a	Fantasia 455	Grey outside/pink inside; black/white/pink print	55	80.00	110.00	40.00
D-32b	Fantasia 455	Pink outside/grey inside; black/white/pink print	55	80.00	110.00	40.00

FAWN TRAY, 1961

This tray or butter dish was produced in the shape of a sliced log with a model of a fawn lying on the back rim. It was first issued in September 1961.

Backstamp: Embossed "Wade Porcelain Made in England"

No.	Description	Colourways	Size	U.S.$	Can.$	U.K.£
D-33	Fawn	Honey/dark brown; beige/orange-brown fawn	95	50.00	70.00	25.00

GIRAFFE DISH, c.1962

This round dish has a transfer print of a pair of giraffes in the centre.

Photograph not available
at press time

Backstamp: Black transfer print "Wade England"

No.	Description	Colourways	Size	U.S.$	Can.$	U.K.£
D-34	Giraffe	White; yellow print; gold rim	112	10.00	15.00	5.00

HARLEQUIN DISHES, 1957-1958

This set of four curved-edge, nesting dishes has a starburst design in the centre. They were issued in February 1957 and withdrawn in January 1958. The original price for a boxed set was 6/11d.

Backstamp: Embossed "Wade Porcelain Made in England"

No.	Description	Colourways	Size	U.S.$	Can.$	U.K.£
D-35a	Harlequin	Dark grey	70	10.00	15.00	5.00
D-35b	Harlequin	Yellow	70	10.00	15.00	5.00
D-35c	Harlequin	Blue	70	10.00	15.00	5.00
D-35d	Harlequin	Pink	70	10.00	15.00	5.00

HARMONY WARE DISHES, 1957-c.1962

Wade produced 13 assorted shapes of bowls, jugs and vases called Harmony Ware, which was decorated in four different patterns.

Shape No. 438

This dish is kidney-shaped and has three feet.

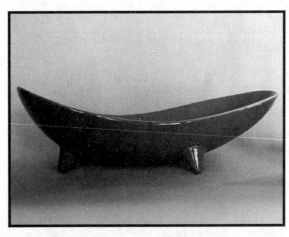

Backstamp: **A.** Red transfer print "Wade England" with impressed "England" and shape number
B. Red transfer print "Wade England Fern" with impressed "England" and shape number
C. Black transfer print "Wade England Parasol" with impressed "England" and shape number
D. Black "Wade England" and green shooting stars with impressed England and shape number
E. Impressed "Wade England" and the shape number
Shape No.: 438

No.	Description	Colourways	Size	U.S.$	Can.$	U.K.£
D-36a	Carnival	White; yellow/red/green flowers	98 x 300	50.00	70.00	25.00
D-36b	Fern	White; black/red fern	98 x 300	50.00	70.00	25.00
D-36c	Parasols	White; multi-coloured parasols	98 x 300	50.00	70.00	25.00
D-36d	Shooting Stars	White; multi-coloured stars	98 x 300	50.00	70.00	25.00
D-36e	Solid colour	Black	98 x 300	40.00	55.00	20.00
D-36f	Solid colour	White	98 x 300	40.00	55.00	20.00
D-36g	Solid colour	Green	98 x 300	40.00	55.00	20.00
D-36h	Solid colour	Yellow	98 x 300	40.00	55.00	20.00
D-36i	Two-tone	Grey/pink	98 x 300	40.00	55.00	20.00
D-36j	Two-tone	Green/peach	98 x 300	40.00	55.00	20.00

Shape No. 455

This flat dish stands on three feet.

Photograph not available
at press time

Backstamp: A. Red transfer print "Wade England" with impressed "England" and shape number
B. Red transfer print "Wade England Fern" with impressed "England" and shape number
C. Black transfer print "Wade England Parasol" with impressed "England" and shape number
D. Black "Wade England" and green shooting Stars' with impressed England and shape number
E. Impressed "Wade England" and the shape number

Shape No.: 455

No.	Description	Colourways	Size	U.S.$	Can.$	U.K.£
D-37a	Carnival	White; yellow/red/green flowers	50 x 275	40.00	55.00	20.00
D-37b	Fern	White; black/red fern	50 x 275	40.00	55.00	20.00
D-37c	Parasols	White; multi-coloured parasols	50 x 275	40.00	55.00	20.00
D-37d	Shooting stars	White; multi-coloured stars	50 x 275	40.00	55.00	20.00
D-37e	Solid colour	Black	50 x 275	30.00	40.00	15.00
D-37f	Solid colour	White	50 x 275	30.00	40.00	15.00
D-37g	Solid colour	Green	50 x 275	30.00	40.00	15.00
D-37h	Solid colour	Yellow	50 x 275	30.00	40.00	15.00
D-37i	Two-tone	Grey/pink	50 x 275	30.00	40.00	15.00
D-37j	Two-tone	Green/peach	50 x 275	30.00	40.00	15.00

HEDGEHOG TRAY, 1961

Modelled in the shape of a hedgehog, the spiney back of the animal forms a detachable blue-grey lid. The original price was 6/6d.

Backstamp: Embossed "Wade Porcelain Made in England"

No.	Description	Colourways	Size	U.S.$	Can.$	U.K.£
D-38	Hedgehog	Honey/red-brown; blue-grey design, lid	100	80.00	110.00	40.00

INDIAN CHIEF DISH, 1954

Issued in January 1954, the Indian chief dish portrays the embossed head of a Indian chief wearing a feather bonnet. The original price was 11d.

Backstamp: Embossed "Wade England"
Shape No.: S.25/37

No.	Description	Colourways	Size	U.S.$	Can.$	U.K.£
D-39	Indian chief	Honey brown	85 x 90	101.00	145.00	55.00

JACOBEAN AND KAWA PEDESTAL DISHES, 1990-1992

The Jacobean design is of red and black enamelled exotic flowers. Kawa is a Japanese design of peonies and bamboo stems.

Backstamp: **A.** Red print "Wade England" with two red lines and "Jacobean"
B. Gold print "Wade England" with two gold lines and "Kawa"

No.	Description	Colourways	Size	U.S.$	Can.$	U.K.£
D-40a	Jacobean	White; red/black print	Unknown	30.00	40.00	15.00
D-40b	Kawa	White; pastel pink/green print; gold highlights	Unknown	30.00	40.00	15.00

LADIES' TRAYS, c.1985

Backstamp: Green transfer print "Wade England"

No.	Description	Colourways	Size	U.S.$	Can.$	U.K.£
D-41a	Man's head	White; gold rim, silhouette; turquoise band, centre	125	15.00	20.00	8.00
D-41b	Regency couple	White; gold rim, decorations; multi-coloured print	125	15.00	20.00	8.00

LADY AND THE TRAMP SWEET TRAY, 1955

Backstamp: Blue transfer print "Scenes from Walt Disney's 'Lady & the Tramp' Sweet Tray by Wade England" in a scroll and "Copyright Walt Disney Productions. Made in England"

No.	Description	Colourways	Size	U.S.$	Can.$	U.K.£
D-42	Lady and the Tramp	White; yellow rim; multi-coloured print	112	20.00	30.00	10.00

LEAF DISHES, 1957-1959

Three types of leaf-shaped dishes were produced between 1957 and 1959. The oak leaf dishes were issued from January 1957 to January 1958, the horse chestnut leaf dishes were issued from August 1957 to January 1958, and the ash-leaf dishes were issued from August 1958 to January 1959. They were originally sold in a boxed set of two for 3/6d.

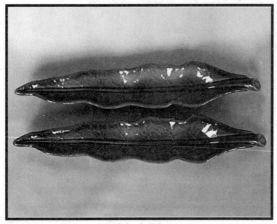

Ash leaf dishes

Horse chestnut leaf dishes

Backstamp: Embossed "Wade Porcelain Made in England"

No.	Description	Colourways	Size	U.S.$	Can.$	U.K.£
D-43a	Ash	Green	190	40.00	55.00	20.00
D-43b	Ash	Beige	190	40.00	55.00	20.00
D-44a	Horse chestnut	Beige	80	8.00	10.00	4.00
D-44b	Horse chestnut	Green	80	8.00	10.00	4.00
D-45a	Oak	Beige	100	8.00	10.00	4.00
D-45b	Oak	Green	100	8.00	10.00	4.00

Reissued Horse Chestnut Leaf Dishes, 1980-1986

These dishes were reissued by Wade Ireland in the same colours as the originals.

Photograph not available
at press time

Backstamp: Impressed "Made in Ireland—Irish Porcelain—Eire tir a dheanta" with a crown and shamrock leaf

No.	Description	Colourways	Size	U.S.$	Can.$	U.K.£
D-46a	Horse chestnut	Beige	80	8.00	10.00	4.00
D-46b	Horse chestnut	Green	80	8.00	10.00	4.00

MAN IN A ROWBOAT TRAY, 1978-1984

The original tool for the 1961 seagull and boat tray was used for this model. A sleeping, bearded fisherman was added to the boat and the seagull was omitted, however the plinth on which it stood still appeared on some early models. The later style of boat does not have the plinth, and the width of the boat has been altered slightly.

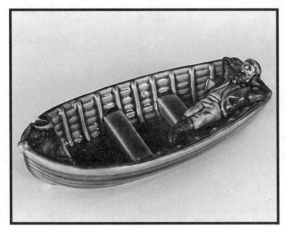

With plinth (D-47)

Without plinth (D-48)

Backstamp: Embossed "Wade Porcelain Made in England"

No.	Description	Colourways	Size	U.S.$	Can.$	U.K.£
D-47	With plinth	Honey-brown boat; blue/green/brown man	50 x 155	80.00	110.00	40.00
D-48	Without plinth	Honey-brown boat; blue/green/brown man	45 x 155	80.00	110.00	40.00

MISCELLANEOUS DISHES, 1959–c.1962

A number of dishes was produced by Wade with different multi-coloured transfer prints on them. The name of the set or the theme is unknown.

Horse-drawn passenger coach (D-50e)

Backstamp: Red transfer print "Wade England"

No.	Description	Colourways	Shape/Size	U.S.$	Can.$	U.K.£
D-49a	Baby Pan	White; pale blue/yellow/green print	Square/106	20.00	30.00	10.00
D-49b	Baby Pegasus	White; pale blue/yellow/green print	Square/106	20.00	30.00	10.00
D-50a	Crinoline girl dancing	White; gold line; blue dress	Octagonal/110	10.00	15.00	5.00
D-50b	Crinoline girl dancing	White; gold line; green dress	Octagonal/110	10.00	15.00	5.00
D-50c	Crinoline girl dancing	White; gold line; grey dress	Octagonal/110	10.00	15.00	5.00
D-50d	Deer and rabbits in snow	White; gold line; black/blue print	Octagonal/110	10.00	15.00	5.00
D-50e	Horse-drawn passenger coach	White; gold line; multi-coloured print	Octagonal/110	10.00	15.00	5.00
D-50f	Kitten in hat	Blue; brown hat; white kitten	Octagonal/110	10.00	15.00	5.00
D-50g	Lady with parasol	White; gold line; blue dress	Octagonal/110	10.00	15.00	5.00
D-50h	Mountain and lake	White; brown mountain; blue lake	Octagonal/110	10.00	15.00	5.00
D-50i	Public house	White; gold line	Octagonal/110	10.00	15.00	5.00
D-50j	Shepherd and Star of Bethlehem	White; gold line; black/blue print	Octagonal/110	10.00	15.00	5.00
D-50k	Trees and cottage in snow	White; gold line; black/blue print	Octagonal/110	10.00	15.00	5.00
D-50l	Trees and cottage in snow	White; gold line; red cottage	Octagonal/110	10.00	15.00	5.00
D-51a	Prince Festiniog Railway	White; green train	Round/112	15.00	20.00	8.00
D-51b	Roses	White; gold rim; blue roses	Round/108	10.00	15.00	5.00

MOURNE DISHES, 1976

These three dishes are completely different in colour and style from previously produced Irish Wade. The background colours are mottled.

Shape no. C349

Shape no. C354

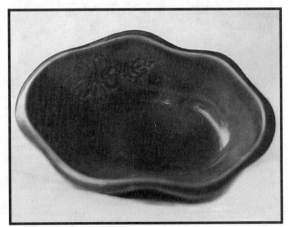

Shape no. C360

Backstamp: **A.** Black print "Made in Ireland Porcelain Wade eire tira dheanta"
B. Black print "Made in Ireland Porcelain Wade eire tira dheanta" and red transfer print "Wade"
Shape No.: C349 — Footed, rectangular
C354 — Square
C360 — Oval

No.	Description	Colourways	Shape/Size	U.S.$	Can.$	U.K.£
D-52	Mourne C349	Browny green; orange flowers	Footed, rectangular/185	50.00	70.00	25.00
D-53	Mourne C354	Grey/green; red rose	Square/135	50.00	70.00	25.00
D-54	Mourne C360	Grey/green; orange rose	Oval/130	50.00	70.00	25.00

MY FAIR LADY DISHES, 1958

This set of four square dishes is decorated with transfer prints of characters from George Bernard Shaw's play, *Pygmalion*, which was produced in 1956 as the musical, *My Fair Lady*.

Photograph not available
at press time

Backstamp: Red transfer print "Wade England"

No.	Description	Colourways	Size	U.S.$	Can.$	U.K.£
D-55a	Eliza Dolittle, flower girl	White; blue/black print	112	8.00	10.00	4.00
D-55b	Eliza Dolittle at Ascot	White; blue/black print	112	8.00	10.00	4.00
D-55c	Professor Henry Higgins	White; blue/black print	112	8.00	10.00	4.00
D-55d	Eliza Dolittle and Professor Higgins	White; blue/black print	112	8.00	10.00	4.00

NEST-O-TRAYS, 1960-1961

First issued in August 1960, this set of four nesting trays has impressed buttercups in the centre of each. The original price was 7/11d for a set of four.

Backstamp: Embossed "Wade Porcelain Made in England"

No.	Description	Colourways	Size	U.S.$	Can.$	U.K.£
D-56a	Nest-o-trays	Beige/grey	96	8.00	10.00	4.00
D-56b	Nest-o-trays	Black	96	8.00	10.00	4.00
D-56c	Nest-o-trays	Grey-blue	96	8.00	10.00	4.00
D-56d	Nest-o-trays	Honey	96	8.00	10.00	4.00
D-56e	Nest-o-trays	Rose	96	8.00	10.00	4.00
D-56f	Nest-o-trays	Straw yellow	96	8.00	10.00	4.00
D-56g	Nest-o-trays	White	96	8.00	10.00	4.00

NEW ZEALAND DISHES, EARLY 1960s

Wade produced a boxed set of four round dishes with a coloured transfer print in the centre. The kiwi is the national bird of New Zealand, and Tiki is a Maori god of good luck.

Backstamp: Red transfer print "Wade England"

No.	Description	Colourways	Size	U.S.$	Can.$	U.K.£
D-57a	Kiwi	White; multi-coloured print	112	10.00	15.00	5.00
D-57b	Tiki	White; multi-coloured print	112	10.00	15.00	5.00
D-57c	Maori house	White; multi-coloured print	112	10.00	15.00	5.00
D-57d	Maori chief	White; multi-coloured print	112	10.00	15.00	5.00

NUT TRAYS, c.1938

Cob nuts and flowers

Backstamp: Green ink stamp "Wade Heath England"

No.	Description	Colourways	Size	U.S.$	Can.$	U.K.£
D-58	Hollyhock and lupins	Cream; multi-coloured flowers	173	40.00	55.00	20.00
D-59	Cob nuts and flowers	Cream; yellow cob nuts; mauve/maroon flowers	180	40.00	55.00	20.00

ORCHARD FRUITS AND BERRIES DISHES, 1960

Apples and grapes (D-60a)

Backstamp: Red transfer print "Wade England"

No.	Description	Colourways	Size	U.S.$	Can.$	U.K.£
D-60a	Apples and grapes	White; multi-coloured print	105	10.00	15.00	5.00
D-60b	Apples and strawberries	White; multi-coloured print	105	10.00	15.00	5.00
D-60c	Pears and grapes	White; multi-coloured print	105	10.00	15.00	5.00
D-60d	Plums and grapes	White; multi-coloured print	105	10.00	15.00	5.00

PEARLSTONE GEODE DISH, 1963-1964

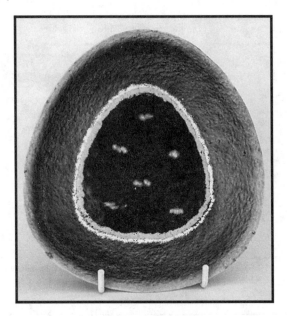

Backstamp: Black ink stamp "Made in Ireland by Wade County Armagh"

No.	Description	Colourways	Size	U.S.$	Can.$	U.K.£
D-61	Pearlstone	Stone rim; white/yellow bands; shiny brown centre; white crystals	150	35.00	45.00	18.00

PET FACES DISHES, 1959-1960

Pekinese pet-face dishes (D-62)

Siamese pet-face dishes (D-63)

Backstamp: Impressed "Wade Porcelain Made in England"

No.	Description	Colourways	Size	U.S.$	Can.$	U.K.£
D-62	Pekinese	Beige; blue markings	75	25.00	35.00	12.00
	Boxed pair			50.00	70.00	25.00
D-63	Siamese cat	Beige; blue markings	80	25.00	35.00	12.00
	Boxed pair			50.00	70.00	25.00

RECTANGULAR TRAYS, c.1945

Some of these trays were sold packaged with a matching box, which could be used for cigarettes or candy. Because they were all hand decorated, the decoration varies somewhat from piece to piece. The original price was 1/6d each.

Rectangular tray (D-64a)   Rectangular tray (D-64h)

Backstamp: **A.** Green ink stamp "Harvest Ware Wade England"
B. Black ink stamp "Wade England," 1940s-early 1950s

No.	Description	Colourways	Shape/Size	U.S.$	Can.$	U.K.£
D-64a	Tray	Copper outside; cream inside; mauve/ yellow flower; green leaves; brown lines	Rectangular/105	25.00	35.00	12.00
D-64b	Tray	Copper outside; cream inside; copper/ purple lustre clover leaves	Rectangular/105	25.00	35.00	12.00
D-64c	Tray	Copper outside; white inside; red berries; brown streaks; green leaves	Rectangular/105	25.00	35.00	12.00
D-64d	Tray	Cream; pink/yellow flower; green leaves; brown streaks	Rectangular/105	25.00	35.00	12.00
D-64e	Tray	Cream; purple daisy; green/brown leaves	Rectangular/105	25.00	35.00	12.00
D-64f	Tray	Cream; large purple/brown flower; green leaves; brown streaks	Rectangular/105	25.00	35.00	12.00
D-64g	Tray	White; pale blue stylized flower; grey leaves	Rectangular/105	25.00	35.00	12.00
D-64h	Tray	White/maroon; copper lustre; maroon leaves; black berries	Rectangular/105	25.00	35.00	12.00

SCALLOPED DISHES, 1954

These dishes were soon discontinued and new all-over, one-colour pastel glazes were used. These dishes were sold individually boxed for an original price of 1/6d each.

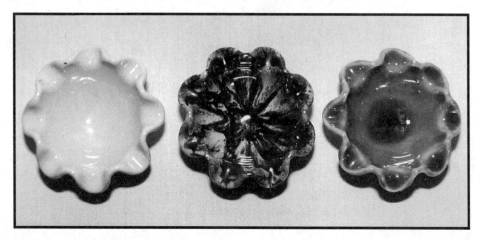

Backstamp: Embossed "Wade England" in the hollow of the base

No.	Description	Colourways	Size	U.S.$	Can.$	U.K.£
D-65a	Scalloped	Dark green	85	13.00	18.00	5.00
D-65b	Scalloped	Beige	85	13.00	18.00	5.00
D-65c	Scalloped	Ming green	85	13.00	18.00	5.00
D-65d	Scalloped	Light grey	85	13.00	18.00	5.00
D-65e	Scalloped	Pale blue	85	13.00	18.00	5.00
D-65f	Scalloped	Pale yellow	85	13.00	18.00	5.00
D-65g	Scalloped	Turquoise	85	13.00	18.00	5.00

Reissued as Crackle Ashtrays, 1962

Reissued in 1962 andcalled crackle ashtrays. They were coloured in marbled glazes and were sold in a boxed set of four for 7/11.

Backstamp: Embossed "Wade England"

No.	Description	Colourways	Size	U.S.$	Can.$	U.K.£
D-66a	Crackle	Maroon/cream	85	13.00	18.00	5.00
D-66b	Crackle	Dark brown/grey	85	13.00	18.00	5.00
D-66c	Crackle	Dark blue/light blue	85	13.00	18.00	5.00
D-66d	Crackle	Dark blue/light green	85	13.00	18.00	5.00
D-66e	Crackle	Dark red/light red	85	13.00	18.00	5.00
D-66f	Crackle	Yellow/brown	85	13.00	18.00	5.00
D-66g	Crackle	Purple/blue	85	13.00	18.00	5.00
D-66h	Crackle	Turquoise/green	85	13.00	18.00	5.00

Reissued as Crackle Dishes, 1971

Now named crackle dishes, they were glazed in darker colours than the original 1950s dishes. They were individually boxed.

Backstamp: Embossed "Wade England"

No.	Description	Colourways	Size	U.S.$	Can.$	U.K.£
D-67a	Crackle	Dark blue	85	13.00	18.00	5.00
D-67b	Crackle	Honey brown	85	13.00	18.00	5.00
D-67c	Crackle	Dark grey	85	13.00	18.00	5.00
D-67d	Crackle	Dark green	85	13.00	18.00	5.00
D-67e	Crackle	Maroon	85	13.00	18.00	5.00

SCOTSMEN DISHES, 1959-c.1962

These dishes are decorated with prints of Scotsmen.

Backstamp: Red transfer print "Wade England"

No.	Description	Colourways	Shape/Size	U.S.$	Can.$	U.K.£
D-68a	Scots piper/busby	White; silver bands; red/yellow/ blue tartan	Round/108	10.00	15.00	5.00
D-68b	Scots piper/glengarry	White; silver bands; blue/red tartan	Round/108	10.00	15.00	5.00
D-68c	Scots dancer	White; silver bands; red/yellow tartan	Round/108	10.00	15.00	5.00
D-69a	Scots piper/busby	White; red/yellow/blue tartan	Octagonal /110	10.00	15.00	5.00
D-69b	Scots piper/glengarry	White; blue/red tartan	Octagonal /110	10.00	15.00	5.00
D-69c	Scots dancer	White; red/yellow tartan	Octagonal /110	10.00	15.00	5.00

SEAGULL AND BOAT TRAY, 1961

This tray comprises a rowboat with an open-winged seagull perched on a small plinth in the prow. First issued in January 1961, it sold for 6/11d.

Backstamp: Embossed "Wade Porcelain Made in England"

No.	Description	Colourways	Size	U.S.$	Can.$	U.K.£
D-70	Seagull and boat tray	Honey-brown boat; white seagull; black wing tips	155	80.00	110.00	40.00

SHAMROCK DISH, c.1955-c.1958

This unusual three-section dish has a raised shamrock inside each section.

...ck leaf that has "Wade" in the centre and "Co. Armagh" underneath

	Size	U.S.$	Can.$	U.K.£
	120	25.00	35.00	12.00

...e of this dish. It was reissued with the addition of a pixie and tree stump ...gue of Wade Whimsical Collectables).

...in Ireland" with a shamrock in the centre

	Size	U.S.$	Can.$	U.K.£
	90	8.00	10.00	4.00

SHELL DISHES, 1953-1956

The base of the shell on style D-73 is plain; style D-74 is decorated with a curling rib on each side of the base.

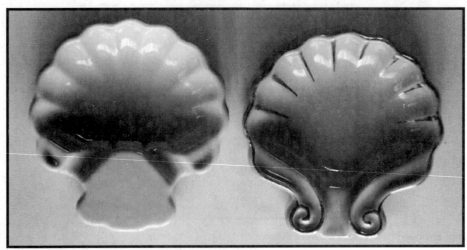

Shell dish, plain (left)   Shell dish, curl (right)

Backstamp: **A.** Gold transfer print "Wade England A" with embossed "BCM/OWL"
B. Embossed "BCM/OWL"

No.	Description	Colourways	Size	U.S.$	Can.$	U.K.£
D-73a	Shell/plain	Beige	85	20.00	30.00	10.00
D-73b	Shell/plain	Pale green	85	20.00	30.00	10.00
D-73c	Shell/plain	Pale blue	85	20.00	30.00	10.00
D-73d	Shell/plain	Pink	85	20.00	30.00	10.00
D-73e	Shell/plain	Yellow	85	20.00	30.00	10.00
D-74a	Shell/curl	Pale blue; gold edging	85	20.00	30.00	10.00
D-74b	Shell/curl	Pink; gold edging	85	20.00	30.00	10.00
D-74c	Shell/curl	Yellow; gold edging	85	20.00	30.00	10.00

SHORE CRAB DISH, 1960-1961

This crab-shaped dish has an embossed lift-off lid. First issued in January 1960, the original price was 4/6.

Photograph not available
at press time

Backstamp: Embossed "Wade Porcelain Made in England"

No.	Description	Colourways	Size	U.S.$	Can.$	U.K.£
D-75	Shore crab	Brown; blue/grey design	75	50.00	70.00	25.00

SILHOUETTE SERIES TRAYS, 1961-1962

These trays were modelled in the shape of a parallelogram with animals embossed on them. The giraffe and zebra trays were first issued in September 1961, their original price was 3/11d. In the spring of 1962 a Viking ship tray, with an original price of 4/6d, was added to the series. During the summer of 1962, a lion tray was also added to the series.

Backstamp: Embossed "Wade Porcelain made in England"

No.	Description	Colourways	Size	U.S.$	Can.$	U.K.£
D-76a	Giraffe	Pale blue/black; white giraffe	130	25.00	35.00	12.00
D-76b	Giraffe	Pale blue/black; blue giraffe	130	25.00	35.00	12.00
D-77a	Lion	Pale blue/black; white lion	120	25.00	35.00	12.00
D-77b	Lion	Pale blue/black; blue lion	120	25.00	35.00	12.00
D-78a	Viking ship	Pale blue/black; yellow/lilac ship	135	25.00	35.00	12.00
D-78b	Viking ship	Pale blue/black; white ship	135	25.00	35.00	12.00
D-78c	Viking ship	Pale blue/black; blue ship	135	25.00	35.00	12.00
D-79a	Zebra	Pale blue/black; white zebra	130	25.00	35.00	12.00
D-79b	Zebra	Pale blue/black; blue zebra	130	25.00	35.00	12.00
D-79c	Zebra	Blue	130	25.00	35.00	12.00

SOLDIERS OF THE QUEEN DISHES, 1959

These transfer prints were also used on tankards.

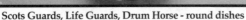

Scots Guards, Life Guards, Drum Horse - round dishes   Trumpeter - square dish

Backstamp: **A.** Black transfer print "Drum Horse - drums were formerly used for giving orders to a regiment. Their combined weight is 116lbs. Pompey is probably the most illustrious Drum Horse of recent years. He was on duty at the Coronation of Queen Elizabeth II. By Wade of England"

B. Black transfer print "The Life Guards - Formed in 1660 from a body of gentlemen who went into exile with Charles Stuart. The scarlet cloak was worn by the regiment in the eighteenth century. Sleeves were added in 1796. By Wade of England"

C. Black transfer print "The Scots Guards - Formed in 1642 by the 8th Earl of Argyll. Officers wear 'Orders of the Thistle' as Badges of rank. The Guards fought at the battle of Dettengen in 1764 under George II. The last British Sovereign to lead his army in the field. By Wade of England"

D. Black transfer print "Trumpeters - Were originally chosen as having an acceptable manner to act as special orderlies to Generals, & to parley with the enemy. Their swords had broken off blades, to symbolise these non-combatant roles. By Wade of England"

E. Black transfer print "The Royal Horse Guards - the only old regiment which has always worn blue. At the battle of Warburg 1760 their commander. The Marquess of Granby lost his wig while leading a charge. giving rise to the expression 'going for it baldheaded', by Wade of England"

No.	Description	Colourways	Shape/Size	U.S.$	Can.$	U.K.£
D-80a	Drum horse	White; gold rim; multi-coloured print	Round/105-110	10.00	15.00	5.00
D-80b	Life Guards	White; gold rim; multi-coloured print	Round/105-110	10.00	15.00	5.00
D-80c	Life Guards trooper	White; gold rim; multi-coloured print	Round/105-110	10.00	15.00	5.00
D-80d	The Royal Horse Guards	White; gold rim; multi-coloured print	Round/105-110	10.00	15.00	5.00
D-80e	Scots Guards	White; gold rim; multi-coloured print	Round/105-110	10.00	15.00	5.00
D-80f	Trumpeter	White; gold rim; multi-coloured print	Round/105-110	10.00	15.00	5.00
D-81a	Drum horse	White; multi-coloured print	Square/110	10.00	15.00	5.00
D-81b	Life Guards	White; multi-coloured print	Square/110	10.00	15.00	5.00
D-81c	Life Guards trooper	White; multi-coloured print	Square/110	10.00	15.00	5.00
D-81d	The Royal Horse Guards	White; multi-coloured print	Square/110	10.00	15.00	5.00
D-81e	Scots Guards	White; multi-coloured print	Square/110	10.00	15.00	5.00
D-81f	Trumpeter	White; multi-coloured print	Square/110	10.00	15.00	5.00

SOUTH AFRICA DISHES, c.1962

These four dishes, decorated with coloured transfer prints of African animals, were sold as a boxed set.

Backstamp: Red transfer print "Wade England"

No.	Description	Colourways	Size	U.S.$	Can.$	U.K.£
D-82a	Giraffe	White; multi-coloured print	112	10.00	15.00	5.00
D-82b	Lion	White; multi-coloured print	112	10.00	15.00	5.00
D-82c	Rhino	White; multi-coloured print	112	10.00	15.00	5.00
D-82d	Zebra	White; multi-coloured print	112	10.00	15.00	5.00

SOUVENIR DISHES

Bahamas Dishes, c.1952-c.1962

These dishes have a transfer print of various Bahamian scenes in the centre. The tyre dish is from the same mould as the Veteran Car tyre dishes.

Nassau, horse and landau (D-83b)

Backstamp: Red transfer print "Wade England"

No.	Description	Colourways	Shape/Size	U.S.$	Can.$	U.K.£
D-83a	Bahamian constable	White; red band; multi-coloured print	Round/110	10.00	14.00	3.00
D-83b	Nassau, horse and landau	White; red band; multi-coloured print	Round/110	10.00	14.00	3.00
D-84	Paradise Beach, Nassau	White; multi-coloured print	Square/130	13.00	18.00	5.00
D-85	Nassau, horse and landau	White; grey rim; multi-coloured print	Tyre/105	13.00	18.00	3.00

British Columbia, c.1952-c.1962

Backstamp: Black transfer print "British Columbia Canada's evergreen playground on the Pacific Coast has for its official emblem the flower of the Dogwood tree - by Wade of England"

No.	Description	Colourways	Shape/Size	U.S.$	Can.$	U.K.£
D-86	Victoria, dogwood	White; multi-coloured print	Round/110	10.00	14.00	3.00

British Dishes, 1957-c.1962

These dishes have a coloured transfer print in the centre showing a British scene.

Forth Bridge, Firth of Forth, Scotland   **Bexhill-on-Sea**   **Great Britain**

Backstamp: Red transfer print "Wade England"

No.	Description	Colourways	Shape/Size	U.S.$	Can.$	U.K.£
D-87	Forth Bridge, Firth of Forth, Scotland	White; gold band; black/blue print	Octagonal/110	10.00	15.00	5.00
D-88a	Bexhill-on-Sea, pixie and mushrooms	White; yellow band; red/green pixie	Round/110	10.00	15.00	5.00
D-88b	Stockport, gypsy caravan	White; yellow band; multi-coloured print	Round/110	10.00	15.00	5.00
D-88c	Warkworth Castle	White; yellow band; multi-coloured print	Round/110	10.00	15.00	5.00
D-89a	Great Britain	White; multi-coloured flags	Square/108	10.00	15.00	5.00
D-89b	Guernsey, cow	White; multi-coloured print	Square/108	10.00	15.00	5.00
D-89c	Woolcombe, pixie on mushroom	White; red/green pixie	Square/108	10.00	15.00	5.00

British Seaside Tyre Dishes, c.1955-c.1962

Backstamp: Red transfer print "Wade England"

No.	Description	Colourways	Size	U.S.$	Can.$	U.K.£
D-90a	Brightlingsea	White; red line, sail	105	10.00	15.00	5.00
D-90b	Isle of Wight	White; red line, sail	105	10.00	15.00	5.00
D-90c	Oulton Broad	White; red line, sail	105	10.00	15.00	5.00

Canadian Themes, c.1952-c.1962

The Royal Canadian Mounted Police (D-91e)

Backstamp: Red transfer print "Wade England"

No.	Description	Colourways	Shape/Size	U.S.$	Can.$	U.K.£
D-91a	Lobster and miniature trap	White; pale blue band; multi-colouredprint	Round/110	10.00	15.00	8.00
D-91b	Lobster and miniature trap	White; red band; multi-coloured print	Round/110	10.00	15.00	8.00
D-91c	Lobster and miniature trap	White; yellow band; multi-coloured print	Round/110	10.00	15.00	8.00
D-91d	Lobster, Canada's East Coast	White; red band; multi-coloured print	Round/110	10.00	15.00	8.00
D-91e	Royal Canadian Mounted Police	White; black band; multi-coloured print	Round/110	10.00	15.00	8.00

London Souvenir Dishes, c.1955–c.1962

The style D-92 round dishes were issued in 1957 only. Sold in gift boxes of four, each dish in the box had a different coloured rim. The style D-93 dishes were produced from the mid 1950s to the early 1960s. They are square with ribbed edges.

Eros, Piccadilly Circus (D-92)

St. Paul's Cathedral (D-93d)

Backstamp: **A.** Red transfer print "Wade England"
B. Small transfer print of a lamppost and wrought-iron fence

No.	Description	Colourways	Shape/Size	U.S.$	Can.$	U.K.£
D-92a	Big Ben	White; blue band; black/blue print	Round/110	10.00	15.00	5.00
D-92b	Big Ben	White; green band; black/blue print	Round/110	10.00	15.00	5.00
D-92c	Big Ben	White; red band; black/blue print	Round/110	10.00	15.00	5.00
D-92d	Big Ben	White; yellow band; black/blue print	Round/110	10.00	15.00	5.00
D-92e	City of London arms	White; gold line; multi-coloured print	Round/110	10.00	15.00	5.00
D-92f	Eros, Piccadilly Circus	White; blue band; black/blue print	Round/110	10.00	15.00	5.00
D-92g	Eros, Piccadilly Circus	White; green band; black/blue print	Round/110	10.00	15.00	5.00
D-92h	Eros, Piccadilly Circus	White; red band; black/blue print	Round/110	10.00	15.00	5.00
D-92i	Eros, Piccadilly Circus	White; yellow band; black/blue print	Round/110	10.00	15.00	5.00
D-92j	Tower Bridge	White; blue band; black/blue print	Round/110	10.00	15.00	5.00
D-92k	Tower Bridge	White; green band; black/blue print	Round/110	10.00	15.00	5.00
D-92l	Tower Bridge	White; red band; black/blue print	Round/110	10.00	15.00	5.00
D-92m	Tower Bridge	White; yellow band; black/blue print	Round/110	10.00	15.00	5.00
D-92n	Tower Bridge	Black; gold line; white print	Round/110	10.00	15.00	5.00
D-92o	Trafalgar Square	White; blue band; black/blue print	Round/110	10.00	15.00	5.00
D-92p	Trafalgar Square	White; green band; black/blue print	Round/110	10.00	15.00	5.00
D-92q	Trafalgar Square	White; red band; black/blue print	Round/110	10.00	15.00	5.00
D-92r	Trafalgar Square	White; yellow band; black/blue print	Round/110	10.00	15.00	5.00
D-93a	Buckingham Palace	White; gold rim; multi-coloured print	Square/108	10.00	15.00	5.00
D-93b	Houses of Parliament	White; gold rim; multi-coloured print	Square/108	10.00	15.00	5.00
D-93c	Houses of Parliament	White; multi-coloured print	Square/108	10.00	15.00	5.00
D-93d	Piccadilly Circus	White; multi-coloured print	Square/108	10.00	15.00	5.00
D-93e	Piccadilly Circus and Big Ben	White; gold rim; multi-coloured print	Square/108	10.00	15.00	5.00
D-93f	St. Paul's Cathedral	White; gold rim; multi-coloured print	Square/108	10.00	15.00	5.00
D-93g	Tower Bridge	White; gold rim; multi-coloured print	Square/108	10.00	15.00	5.00
D-93h	Tower Bridge	White; multi-coloured print	Square/108	10.00	15.00	5.00
D-93i	Trafalgar Square	White; gold rim; multi-coloured print	Square/108	10.00	15.00	5.00

New Brunswick, c.1952-c.1962

Photograph not available at press time

Backstamp: Red transfer print "Wade England"

No.	Description	Colourways	Shape/Size	U.S.$	Can.$	U.K.£
D-94a	Covered bridge	White; red band; multi-coloured print	Round/110	10.00	15.00	8.00
D-94b	Map	White; red band; multi-coloured print	Round/110	10.00	15.00	8.00
D-94c	Reversing Falls	White; red band; multi-coloured print	Round/110	10.00	15.00	8.00
D-94d	Reversing Falls	White; yellow band; multi-coloured print	Round/108	10.00	15.00	8.00
D-95a	Map and emblems	White; multi-coloured print	Square/108	10.00	15.00	8.00
D-95b	Alexander Graham Bell Museum	White; multi-coloured print	Square/108	10.00	15.00	8.00

Nova Scotia, c.1952-c.1962

Nova Scotia, "The Gateway to Canada" (D-96c)

Backstamp: Red transfer print "Wade England"

No.	Description	Colourways	Shape/Size	U.S.$	Can.$	U.K.£
D-96a	Canso Causeway	White; red band; multi-coloured print	Round/110	10.00	15.00	8.00
D-96b	Cape Breton Island	White; green band; multi coloured print	Round/110	10.00	15.00	8.00
D-96c	Nova Scotia, "The Gateway to Canada"	White; red band; multi-coloured print	Round/110	10.00	15.00	8.00
D-96d	Scotsman with bagpipes	White; yellow band; multi-coloured print	Round/110	10.00	15.00	8.00
D-96e	Scotsman with bagpipes	White; black band; multi-coloured print	Round/110	10.00	15.00	8.00
D-97a	Map and emblems	White; multi-coloured print	Square/108	10.00	15.00	8.00
D-97b	Nova Scotia, "The Gateway to Canada"	White; multi-coloured print	Square/108	10.00	15.00	8.00

Prince Edward Island, c.1952-c.1962

Photograph not available at press time

Backstamp: Red transfer print "Wade England"

No.	Description	Colourways	Shape/Size	U.S.$	Can.$	U.K.£
D-98a	Anne of Green Gables' home	White; yellow band; multi-coloured print	Round/110	10.00	15.00	8.00
D-98b	Anne of Green Gables' home	White; pale blue band; multi-coloured print	Round/110	10.00	15.00	8.00
D-98c	Map	White; pale blue band; multi-coloured print	Round/110	10.00	15.00	8.00

Remember Dishes, 1957-c.1960

These dishes all have the same multi-coloured print of a very tired baggage porter in the centre, but with different names of tourist attractions.

Remember? Broadway (D-99b)

Backstamp: **A.** Red transfer print "Wade England"
B. Black transfer print "Wade England"

No.	Description	Colourways	Shape/Size	U.S.$	Can.$	U.K.£
D-99a	Remember? Aberdovey	White; red band; multi-coloured print	Round/110	10.00	15.00	5.00
D-99b	Remember? Broadway	White; yellow band; multi-coloured print	Round/110	10.00	15.00	5.00
D-99c	Remember? London	White; blue band; multi-coloured print	Round/110	10.00	15.00	5.00
D-99d	Remember? London	White; red band; multi-coloured print	Round/110	10.00	15.00	5.00
D-100	Remember? Broadway	White; multi-coloured print	Square/108	10.00	15.00	5.00

STARFISH PIN TRAY, 1959-1961, 1973

First issued in December 1959, this embossed dish was intended to be used as a pin tray or as an ashtray. The original price was 3/6d. The 1973 reissue of the starfish pin tray was produced by Wade Ireland and also sold for 3/6d.

Backstamp: A. Impressed "Wade Made in England"
B. Impressed "Made in Ireland-Irish Porcelain-Eire tir a dheanta" with a crown and shamrock leaf

No.	Description	Colourways	Size	U.S.$	Can.$	U.K.£
D-101a	Starfish	Brown; dark blue design	115	25.00	35.00	12.00
D-101b	Starfish	Beige; light blue design	115	25.00	35.00	12.00

SWALLOW DISHES, 1958-1961

First issued in August 1958, these oval-shaped dishes have an open-winged bird on the rear edge of the dish. The original price was 3/3d. This dish shape was reused for the Lesney gift trays in 1961 (see *The Charlton Standard Catalogue of Wade, Volume One*).

Backstamp: Embossed "Wade Porcelain Made in England"

No.	Description	Colourways	Size	U.S.$	Can.$	U.K.£
D-102a	Swallow	Beige; beige/blue bird	145	30.00	40.00	15.00
D-102b	Swallow	Lime green; grey/green bird	145	40.00	55.00	20.00

TYRE DISHES, c.1962

1914 Guy (D-103a)

Backstamp: A. Black transfer print "By Wade of England 30 CWT. Guy Lorry, Built in 1914. The first product of Guy Motors Ltd. Incorporated an overdrive gear & independent 3 point engine mounting"
B. Black transfer print "1909 The Little Britain - 2Cyl 4 x 4.5 - 10. H.P. Wade England"

No.	Description	Colourways	Size	U.S.$	Can.$	U.K.£
D-103a	Guy Lorry, 1914	White; grey rim; black print	125	30.00	40.00	15.00
D-103b	The Little Britain, 1909	White; grey rim; black print	125	30.00	40.00	15.00

TOPLINE DISHES, 1963

These round dishes are from a short series produced in 1963. Two designs of these dishes have been found. Versions D-104a and D-104b are decorated with green, pink and yellow transfer prints of early 19th-century transport with drivers and passengers. Style D-104c has a stylized medallion of a leaf and of a feather in the centre of the dish, with gold and black bands round it. The dishes were sold as a pair in black presentation boxes.

Governess cart - 1900 (D-104b)

Leaf and feather medallion (D-104c)

Backstamp: Red transfer print "Wade England"
Style No.: 102 — 1a, 1b; 104 — 1c

No.	Description	Colourways	Size	U.S.$	Can.$	U.K.£
D-104a	Benz - 1898	White; gold band; multi-coloured print	111	15.00	20.00	8.00
D-104b	Governess cart - 1900	White; gold band; multi-coloured print	111	15.00	20.00	8.00
D-104c	Leaf and feather medallion	Off white; gold/black bands; black/ silver-grey medallion	111	25.00	35.00	12.00

TROPICAL FRUIT GATHERERS DISHES, 1961

| Pineapple gatherer (D-105d) | Prickly pear gatherer (D-105e) | Sugar cane cutter (D-105f) |

Backstamp: Red transfer print "Wade England"

No.	Description	Colourways	Size	U.S.$	Can.$	U.K.£
D-105a	Banana gatherer	White; multi-coloured print	105	10.00	15.00	5.00
D-105b	Coconut gatherer	White; multi-coloured print	105	10.00	15.00	5.00
D-105c	Date gatherer	White; multi-coloured print	105	10.00	15.00	5.00
D-105d	Pineapple gatherer	White; multi-coloured print	105	10.00	15.00	5.00
D-105e	Prickly pear gatherer	White; multi-coloured print	105	10.00	15.00	5.00
D-105f	Sugar cane cutter	White; multi-coloured print	105	10.00	15.00	5.00

TRUMPS DISHES, 1961

Designed as nut dishes for card parties, these dishes have a cartoon transfer print of a king, queen or knave in the centre. They were sold in a boxed set of four.

Backstamp: Red transfer print "Wade England"

No.	Description	Colourways	Size	U.S.$	Can.$	U.K.£
D-106a	King of Diamonds	White; black rim; multi-coloured print	112	15.00	20.00	8.00
D-106b	Knave of Spades	White; red rim; multi-coloured print	112	15.00	20.00	8.00
D-106c	Queen of Clubs	White; red rim; multi-coloured print	112	15.00	20.00	8.00
D-106d	Queen Of Hearts	White; black rim; multi-coloured print	112	15.00	20.00	8.00

T.T. TRAYS, 1959-1960

These rarely seen trays have a sloping ramp at the back edge, on top of which is a motorcycle (number 7) with a rider. They were produced as a souvenir of the Tourist Trophy Motorcycle Races held on the Isle of Man. They were sold in a boxes decorated with a chequered flag design. The original price was 5/6d.

Backstamp: Black transfer print "Wade England"

No.	Description	Colourways	Size	U.S.$	Can.$	U.K.£
D-107a	T.T. tray	Grey tray, rider; white/dark red bike; blue helmet	74 x 90	180.00	240.00	90.00
D-107b	T.T. tray	Grey; beige rider; white/dark red bike; grey helmet	74 x 90	180.00	240.00	90.00
D-107c	T.T. tray	Grey; white rider; white/dark red bike; blue helmet	74 x 90	180.00	240.00	90.00
D-107d	T.T. tray	Grey; beige rider; white/dark red bike; white helmet	74 x 90	180.00	240.00	90.00

VETERAN CAR DISHES

Version D-108a has a transfer print of a veteran car in the centre with the information on the vehicle and its series number on the base. The other dishes in the series also have a veteran car transfer print in the centre, but do not have information or a series number on the back.

Benz, 1899 (D-108a)

Backstamp: **A.** Gold transfer print "A Moko Product by Wade England Design authenticated by the Vintage Sports Car Club of Great Britain"
B. Red transfer print "Wade England"

No.	Description	Colourways	Size	U.S.$	Can.$	U.K.£
D-108a	Benz, 1899	Black; gold rim, white print	110	10.00	15.00	5.00
D-108b	Bugatti, 1913	White; gold rim; multi-coloured print	110	10.00	15.00	5.00
D-108c	Itala, 1908	White; gold rim; multi-coloured print	110	10.00	15.00	5.00
D-108d	Vauxhall, 1913	White; gold rim; multi-coloured print	110	10.00	15.00	5.00

VETERAN CAR PEANUT DISHES, c1958

These dishes vary slightly from the Veteran Car tyre dishes in that they are deeper and have a smooth rim instead of a ribbed design. They were issued in a box as a pair.

Photograph not available
at press time

Backstamp: "A Moko Product by Wade England"

No.	Description	Colourways	Size	U.S.$	Can.$	U.K.£
D-109a	Bugatti	White; grey rim; black/grey/yellow print	105	10.00	15.00	5.00
D-109b	Itala	White; grey rim; red/black/yellow print	105	10.00	15.00	5.00

VETERAN CAR TYRE DISHES, 1956-c.1965

Backstamp: **A.** "A Moko Product by Wade England"
B. "A Moko Line by Wade England"
C. "An RK Product by Wade of England"

Set 1 — Black Transfer Print

No.	Description	Colourways	Size	U.S.$	Can.$	U.K.£
D-110a	Benz	White; grey rim; black print	125	10.00	15.00	5.00
D-110b	Darracq	White; grey rim; black print	125	10.00	15.00	5.00
D-110c	Ford	White; grey rim; black print	125	10.00	15.00	5.00

Set 2 — Black Transfer Print

No.	Description	Colourways	Size	U.S.$	Can.$	U.K.£
D-111a	Baby Peugeot	White; grey rim; black print	125	10.00	15.00	5.00
D-111b	Rolls-Royce	White; grey rim; black print	125	10.00	15.00	5.00
D-111c	Sunbeam	White; grey rim; black print	125	10.00	15.00	5.00

Set 3 — Black Transfer Print

No.	Description	Colourways	Size	U.S.$	Can.$	U.K.£
D-112a	De Dion Bouton	White; grey rim; black print	125	10.00	15.00	5.00
D-112b	Lanchester	White; grey rim; black print	125	10.00	15.00	5.00
D-112c	Spyker	White; grey rim; black print	125	10.00	15.00	5.00

Set 4 — Black Transfer Print

No.	Description	Colourways	Size	U.S.$	Can.$	U.K.£
D-113a	Cadillac	White; grey rim; black print	125	10.00	15.00	5.00
D-113b	Oldsmobile	White; grey rim; black print	125	10.00	15.00	5.00
D-113c	White Steam Car	White; grey rim; black print	125	10.00	15.00	5.00

Set 5 — Multi-coloured Transfer Print

No.	Description	Colourways	Size	U.S.$	Can.$	U.K.£
D-114b	Bugatti, 1913	White; grey rim; black/grey/yellow print	125	10.00	15.00	5.00
D-114a	Itala, 1908	White; grey rim; red/black/yellow print	125	10.00	15.00	5.00
D-114c	Sunbeam	White; grey rim; green/black/brown print	125	10.00	15.00	5.00

WAGON TRAIN DISHES, 1960-1961

First issued in August 1960, the original price for each dish was 6/6d.

Flint McCullough (D-115)   Major Seth Adams (D-116)

Backstamp: Impressed "Wade Porcelain made in England © 1960 by Revue Studios"

No.	Description	Colourways	Size	U.S.$	Can.$	U.K.£
D-115	Flint McCullogh	Brown/honey	140	70.00	95.00	35.00
D-116	Major Seth Adams	Brown/honey	140	70.00	95.00	35.00

WINDSOR CASTLE PIN TRAY, c.1952-c.1955

Backstamp: Gold transfer print "Royal Victoria Pottery - Wade England"

No.	Description	Colourways	Size	U.S.$	Can.$	U.K.£
D-117	Windsor Castle	Off white; gold rim; multi-coloured print	105	20.00	30.00	10.00

ZAMBA DISHES, 1957
Shape No. 462

Backstamp: Red transfer print "Wade England"
  Shape No.: 462

No.	Description	Colourways	Shape/Size	U.S.$	Can.$	U.K.£
D-118	Two dancers	White; black prints	Oblong/125	40.00	55.00	20.00

Shape No. 474

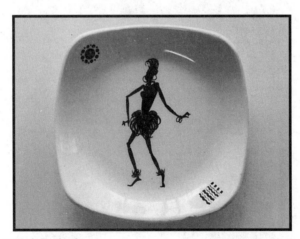

Backstamp: Red transfer print "Wade England"
  Shape No.: 474

No.	Description	Colourways	Shape/Size	U.S.$	Can.$	U.K.£
D-119a	Dancer, both hands raised	White; black print	Square/107	10.00	15.00	5.00
D-119b	Dancer, leaning forward, hands out	White; black print	Square/107	10.00	15.00	5.00
D-119c	Dancer, left hand on skirt, right hand out	White; black print	Square/107	10.00	15.00	5.00
D-119d	Dancer, right hand and leg raised	White; black print	Square/107	10.00	15.00	5.00
D-119e	Dancer, right hand on skirt, left hand out	White; black print	Square/107	10.00	15.00	5.00
D-119f	Two dancers	White; black print	Square/107	10.00	15.00	5.00

WADE (IRELAND) LTD

ONE OF THE WADE GROUP

Registered Office:

WATSON STREET
PORTADOWN
CO. ARMAGH BT 63 5AH
NORTHERN IRELAND

TELEPHONE:
(0762) 332288
TELEX: 747128

SHAMROCK RANGE
1. SR01 Half Pint Tankard
2. SR02 One Pint Tankard

3. SR17 Large Ashtray with Gold Rim
4. SR18 Small Ashtray without Gold Rim

SHEET S6

5. SR12 Candlestick

FLOWERS
c.1930-1939

At the same time they were producing the lady figures (see volume one), the George Wade and Wade Heath potteries issued a long series of hand-made earthenware and china flowers in bowls, pots, vases, baskets, miniature jugs and other containers. Included in this range are flowers that were produced without containers. Over a hundred variations of flowers, pots and bowls are known to exist.

EARTHENWARE FLOWERS, c.1930-c.1935

The first series of flowers was made of earthenware. Ninety percent of the bowls, baskets, vases and pots, etc., that contain the flowers are black, but a few examples were also produced in mottled greens and yellows and in plain yellow. The earthenware flower colours can be easily recognised, as they were all hand painted in dark blue, dark red, dark pink, maroon, purple, mauve and deep yellow with bright green leaves.

CHINA FLOWERS, c.1935-1939

The second series was produced in china and includes a variety of spring flowers. These flowers were produced in natural pastel shades of pale blues, pinks, mauves and yellows.

Unfortunately these flowers are rarely found undamaged. With so many edges to chip and snap off, it is the fortunate collector who finds a perfect example. The price guide is for flowers in mint or near-mint condition; damaged models are worth 50 to 75 percent less. In 1939 the original price for the china flowers ranged from 1/- to 25/-.

When an item is described as miniature, small, medium, large or extra large, that refers to the container only, not the size of the flowers. Because all the flowers are hand made, their sizes vary.

This section is divided into two parts—flower centres and holders with flowers—and the items are listed alphabetically within each part.

BACKSTAMPS

Handwritten Backstamps

Handwritten marks can be found on both series of flowers. They all say "Wade England."

Ink Stamps

Flaxman Ware ink stamps, as well as "Wade Made in England" and "Wade England," can be found on series one and series two flowers.

Embossed Backstamps

Almost all the embossed backstamps found on series one and two flowers include the words, "British Made."

Some flowers have two handwritten numbers and a handwritten letter on them. One of the numbers corresponds to the Wade catalogue number, the other number is the code for the variety of flower. A letter refers to the size and type of container.

FLOWER CODE NUMBERS

1. Primula	13. Unknown
2. Poppy	14. Stock elsa
3. Tulip	15. Unknown
4. Primrose	16. Violet
5. Narcissus	17. Wild rose
6. Forget-me-not	18. Carnation
7. Unknown	19. Unknown
8. Anemone or daffodil	20. Unknown
9. Rose	21. Unknown
10. Pansy	22. Unknown
11. Rosebud	23. Unknown
12. Oleander	

Some of the flowers are hard to distinguish from one another because of their similarity and the colours used. For example, it is difficult to tell a tulip and rosebud apart, but on close inspection you will see that the central petals of the tulip come to a point, while the rosebud petals have a swirl with a small central hole. The difference between the anemone and the wild rose is that the anemone has long black stamens.

To date 23 flower types are known, but the code numbers for the buttercup, campanula, daisy, delphinium, hibiscus, shamrock and water lily have not yet been identified. We would welcome any further information on this. Both the anemone and daffodil have been found with the number 8 on the base.

CONTAINER CODE LETTERS

D. Medium	J. Large
E. Small	K. Extra large
G. Miniature	SB. Small basket
H. Flower centre, long stem, no container	

EARTHENWARE FLOWERS

Two types of flower centres were produced:

1. Flowers on long stems with no container

Miniature—three flowers
Small—four flowers
Medium—six flowers
Large—eight or more flowers, approximately 130 x 100 mm
Extra large—eight or more flowers, approximately 175 x 150 mm

2. Flowers on short stems with no container

Large—eight or more flowers, approximately 110 x 110mm
Extra large—12 or more flowers, approximately 135 x 155 mm

Wade produced two types of containers for the flower centres, low bowls and dishes in small, medium and large sizes, which could be purchased separately from the flowers. Apparently there were 79 models in the earthenware set, although information is not available for numbers 66 to 79.

FLOWER CENTRES

FLOWER CENTRES (EARTHENWARE), c.1930-c.1935

Anemones (FL-3)

Roses/wild roses, short stemmed (FL-6)

Tulips, long stemmed (FL-7)

Wild roses, long stemmed (FL-8)

Backstamp: **A.** Raised "British Made"
B. Raised "British Made" and black handwritten "Wade England"
C. Raised "British Made" and black handwritten "Made in England"
D. Black handwritten "Wade England"

No.	Description	Colourways	Size	U.S.$	Can.$	U.K.£
FL-1	Tulips/long stem	Blue/dark pink/yellow flowers	Miniature/60 x 50	40.00	55.00	20.00
FL-2	Rose bud/long stem	Yellow/blue/dark pink flowers	Medium/95 x 50	30.00	40.00	15.00
FL-3	Anemones/long stem	Maroon/mauve/yellow/pink flowers	Large/146 x 170	70.00	95.00	35.00
FL-4	Pansies/ long stem	Blue/maroon/yellow flowers	Large/145 x 120	30.00	40.00	15.00
FL-5	Poppies/long stem	Blue/maroon/yellow flowers	Large/140 x 120	30.00	40.00	15.00
FL-6	Roses/wild roses/ short stem	Pink/yellow/blue flowers;	Large/105 x 120	70.00	95.00	35.00
FL-7	Tulips/long stem	Yellow/blue/dark pink flowers	Large/146 x 78	40.00	55.00	20.00
FL-8	Wild roses/ long stem	Purple/pink/yellow/blue flowers	Small/70 x 60	40.00	55.00	20.00

FLOWER CENTRES (CHINA), c.1935-1939

Tulips (FL-9)   Unknown flower (FL-12)

Backstamp: **A.** Handwritten "Wade England"
              B. Black ink stamp "Wade Made in England"

No.	Description	Colourways	Size	U.S.$	Can.$	U.K.£
FL-9	Tulips	Pale blue/pale pink/pale yellow flowers	Miniature/60 x 50	40.00	55.00	20.00
FL-10	Anemones	Mauve/white flowers	Small/60 x 60	70.00	95.00	35.00
FL-11	Daffodils	Pale yellow/orange flowers	Small/60 x 50	40.00	55.00	20.00
FL-12	Unknown flower	White/mauve/dark pink flowers	Small/60 x 60	70.00	95.00	35.00

HOLDERS WITH FLOWERS

ARCHES (EARTHENWARE), c.1930-c.1935

Roses (FL-15)

Backstamp: **A.** Black handwritten "Wade England"
             B. Black ink stamp "Wade England"

No.	Name	Colourways	Size	U.S.$	Can.$	U.K.£
FL-13	Assorted flowers	Red/blue/yellow flowers; dark green arch	Small/Unknown	Unknown		
FL-14a	Anemones	Blue/maroon/red/pink/yellow flowers; cream/pale green arch	Large/130x 142	80.00	110.00	40.00
FL-14b	Anemones	Blue/maroon/red, pink/yellow flowers; yellow arch	Large/130 x 142	80.00	110.00	40.00
FL-15	Roses	Pink/yellow flowers; pale green arch	Large/130 x 142	80.00	110.00	40.00

BASKETS

BASKETS WITH HANDLES (EARTHENWARE), c.1930-c.1935

Wild roses (FL-17b)

Backstamp: Black ink stamp "Wade England"

No.	Description	Colourways	Size	U.S.$	Can.$	U.K.£
FL-16	Pansies	Yellow/pink flowers; yellow basket	75 x 86	40.00	55.00	20.00
FL-17a	Wild roses	Blue/yellow/pink/maroon flowers; black basket	75 x 86	40.00	55.00	20.00
FL-17b	Wild roses	Blue/yellow/pink/maroon flowers; yellow basket	75 x 86	40.00	55.00	20.00

LARGE OVAL BASKETS, WITHOUT HANDLES (EARTHENWARE), c.1930-c.1935

Photograph not available
at press time

Backstamp: Black handwritten "Wade England"

No.	Description	Colourways	Size	U.S.$	Can.$	U.K.£
FL-18a	Pansies	Yellow/blue/maroon flowers; black basket	70 x 105	30.00	40.00	15.00
FL-18b	Pansies	Yellow/blue/dark pink flowers; yellow basket	70 x 105	30.00	40.00	15.00
FL-19	Tulips	Yellow/blue/maroon flowers; black basket	70 x 105	30.00	40.00	15.00
FL-20	Wild roses	Yellow/pink/maroon/blue flowers; black basket	65 x 105	30.00	40.00	15.00

ROUND BASKETS WITHOUT HANDLES (EARTHENWARE), c.1930-c.1935

Assorted flowers (FL-21)

Backstamp: **A.** Raised "British Made" and black handwritten "Wade England"
B. Raised "British Made"
C. Black handwritten "Wade England"
D. Raised "Made in England" and model number

No.	Description	Colourways	Size	U.S.$	Can.$	U.K.£
FL-21	Assorted flowers	Yellow/blue/pink/maroon flowers; black basket	66 x 50	25.00	35.00	12.00
FL-22	Roses	Yellow/blue/red/pink flowers; black basket	66 x 50	25.00	35.00	12.00
FL-23	Tulips	Yellow/pink/maroon flowers; black basket	66 x 50	25.00	35.00	12.00
FL-24	Wild roses	Blue/yellow/pink/maroon flowers; black basket	66 x 50	25.00	35.00	12.00

SMALL OVAL BASKETS, WITHOUT HANDLES (CHINA), c.1935-1939

Primrose, pansy, rose (FL-25)

Backstamp: Black handwritten "Wade England"

No.	Description	Colourways	Size	U.S.$	Can.$	U.K.£
FL-25	Primrose/pansy/rose	Pale yellow/pink/mauve flowers; black basket	37 x 70	20.00	30.00	10.00
FL-26	Primroses	Pale yellow flowers; black basket	37 x 70	20.00	30.00	10.00

BOWLS AND POTS

AJAX BOWL (EARTHENWARE), c.1930-c.1935

Backstamp: Black handwritten "Wade England"

No.	Description	Colourways	Size	U.S.$	Can.$	U.K.£
FL-27	Tulips	Purple/pink/yellow/blue tulips; black bowl	130 x 110	40.00	55.00	20.00

BASKET-WEAVE BOWL (EARTHENWARE), c.1930-c.1935

Wild roses (FL-29)

Backstamp: Black ink stamp "Wade England GAY"

No.	Description	Colourways	Size	U.S.$	Can.$	U.K.£
FL-28	Anemones	Blue/red/maroon/yellow flowers; black bowl	116 x 60	40.00	55.00	20.00
FL-29	Wild roses	Blue/red/maroon/yellow flowers; black bowl	116 x 60	40.00	55.00	20.00

BINNIE POTS (EARTHENWARE), c.1930-c.1935

Wild roses (FL-31)

Backstamp: Black ink stamp "Wade England"

No.	Description	Colourways	Size	U.S.$	Can.$	U.K.£
FL-30	Pansies	Purple/blue/yellow flowers; black pot	145 x 77	40.00	55.00	20.00
FL-31	Wild roses	Purple/blue /yellow flowers; yellow pot	145 x 77	40.00	55.00	20.00

MEDIUM BOWLS (EARTHENWARE), c.1930-c.1935

Photograph not available
at press time

Backstamp: **A.** Black handwritten "Wade England"
B. Raised "British Made"
C. Raised "British Made" and black handwritten "Wade England"
D. Raised "British Made," black handwritten "Wade England" and " Made in England"

No.	Description	Colourways	Size	U.S.$	Can.$	U.K.£
FL-32	Assorted flowers	Blue/yellow/pink/maroon flowers; black bowl	65 x 57	30.00	40.00	15.00
FL-33	Tulips	Pink/yellow/blue flowers; blackbowlt	58 x 45	30.00	40.00	15.00
FL-34	Wild rose	Blue/yellow/pink/maroon flowers; black bowl	65 x 57	30.00	40.00	15.00

OCTAGONAL BOWLS

Earthenware Bowls, c.1930-c.1935

Backstamp: A. Raised "British Made" and "Wade England Made in England"
B. Raised "British Made" and black handwritten "Wade England"
C. Raised "British Made"
D. Black handwritten "Wade England"
E. Black ink stamp "Wade England"

No.	Description	Colourways	Size	U.S.$	Can.$	U.K.£
FL-35	Poppies	Yellow/mauve/purple flowers; yellow bowl	70 x 60	60.00	80.00	30.00

China Bowls, c.1935-1939

Forget-me-nots (FL-36)

Narcissus (FL-37)

No.	Description	Colourways	Size	U.S.$	Can.$	U.K.£
FL-36	Forget-me-nots	Pale blue /pink flowers; black bowl	Miniature/60 x 60	60.00	80.00	30.00
FL-37	Narcissus	White/yellow flowers; black bowl	Large/60 x 75	40.00	55.00	20.00
FL-38	Primula	Blue/yellow/pink flowers; black bowl	Extra large/75 x 90	50.00	70.00	25.00

POTS (CHINA), c.1935-1939

Backstamp: Raised "British Made"

No.	Description	Colourways	Size	U.S.$	Can.$	U.K.£
FL-39	Oleanders	Yellow/maroon/mauve flowers; black pot	66 x 50	26.00	36.00	12.00

SHALLOW BOWLS

| Anemone and rose buds (FL-40) | Tulips (FL-45) | Wild roses (FL-46) |

Backstamp: **A.** Raised "British Made" with an impressed code letter (sometimes includes a black handwritten "Wade England" or "Made in England"
B. Raised "British Made" and "Wade England"
C. Raised "British Made" and "Made in England"
D. Handwritten "Wade England"

Earthenware Bowls, c.1930-c.1935

No.	Description	Colourways	Size	U.S.$	Can.$	U.K.£
FL-40	Anemone/rose buds	Mauve/pale yellow/pale pink flowers	Miniature/32 x 35	19.00	26.00	8.00
FL-41	Assorted flowers	Pink/maroon/yellow/blue flowers	Miniature/30 x 35	19.00	26.00	8.00
FL-42	Rosebuds	Pink/maroon/yellow/blue flowers	Miniature/35 x 35	19.00	26.00	8.00
FL-43	Roses	Pink/maroon/yellow/blue flowers	Miniature/35 x 35	19.00	26.00	8.00
FL-44	Roses/rose buds	Mauve/pale yellow/pink flowers	Miniature/32 x 35	19.00	26.00	8.00
FL-45	Tulips	Yellow/pink/maroon/blue flowers	Miniature/35 x 35	19.00	26.00	8.00
FL-46	Wild roses	Yellow/pink/maroon/blue flowers	Miniature/32 x 35	19.00	26.00	8.00
FL-47	Assorted flowers	Blue; yellow; maroon flowers	Small/42 x 45	26.00	36.00	12.00
FL-48	Roses	Pink/maroon/yellow/blue flowers	Small/40 x 45	26.00	36.00	12.00
FL-49	Tulips	Pink/maroon/yellow/blue flowers	Small/40 x 35	26.00	36.00	12.00
FL-50a	Wild roses	Purple/yellow/pink/blue flowers	Small/45 x 57	26.00	36.00	12.00
FL-50b	Wild roses	Yellow/blue/pink flowers	Small/42 x 45	26.00	36.00	12.00
FL-51	Rosebuds	Pink/yellow/blue flowers	Medium/58 x 45	36.00	50.00	15.00

China Bowls, c.1935-1939

No.	Description	Colourways	Size	U.S.$	Can.$	U.K.£
FL-52	Roses/rose buds	Pale yellow/pale pink flowers	Small/45 x 60	19.00	26.00	8.00

SPHERICAL BOWL (EARTHENWARE), c.1930-c.1935

Backstamp: Black handwritten "Wade England"

No.	Description	Colourways	Size	U.S.$	Can.$	U.K.£
FL-53	Stock elsa	Bright yellow/pink/blue/maroon flowers; black bowl	Miniature/190 x 70	40.00	55.00	20.00

VULCAN POTS (EARTHENWARE), c.1930-c.1935

Wild roses (FL-57)

Backstamp: Black handwritten "Wade England"

No.	Name	Description	Size	U.S.$	Can.$	U.K.£
FL-54	Pansies	Purple/blue/yellow flowers; black pot	110 x 75	40.00	55.00	20.00
FL-55	Poppies	Red/purple/yellow flowers; black pot	110 x 75	40.00	55.00	20.00
FL-56	Tulips	Red/blue/yellow flowers; black pot	110 x 75	40.00	55.00	20.00
FL-57	Wild roses	Purple/blue/yellow flowers; yellow pot	110 x 75	40.00	55.00	20.00

MENU HOLDERS (EARTHENWARE), c.1930-c.1935

Photograph not available
at press time

Backstamp: Black handwritten "Wade England"

No.	Description	Colourways	Size	U.S.$	Can.$	U.K.£
FL-58	Roses	Pink/maroon/yellow/blue flowers; green leaves	Small/30 x 45	15.00	20.00	8.00
FL-59	Water lilies	Pink flower; green leaves	Small/Unknown	15.00	20.00	8.00
FL-60	Roses	Pink/maroon/yellow/blue flowers; green leaves	Large/45 x 45	25.00	35.00	12.00
FL-61	Water lilies	Pink flower; green leaves	Large/Unknown	25.00	35.00	12.00

MISCELLANEOUS SHAPES

BRICK (EARTHENWARE), c.1930-c.1935

Photograph not available
at press time

Backstamp: "Black handwritten "Wade England"

No.	Description	Colourways	Size	U.S.$	Can.$	U.K.£
FL-62	Assorted flowers	Yellow/blue/maroon flowers; light green brick	150 x 175	80.00	110.00	40.00

GLOBE (CHINA), 1936-1937

This globe is from the Wadeheath Flaxman range of ornamental ware.

Photograph not available
at press time

Backstamp: Black ink stamp "Flaxman Ware Hand Made Pottery By Wadeheath England"

No.	Description	Colourways	Size	U.S.$	Can.$	U.K.£
FL-63	Assorted flowers	Maroon/blue/red/yellow flowers; mottled green/brown globe	Large/225 x 175	150.00	200.00	75.00

HORSESHOES (EARTHENWARE), c.1930-c.1935

"May Window Box" is handwritten on the bottom of the style FL-64 horseshoe.

Roses (FL-64)

Rose/wild roses (FL-65)

Backstamp: Black handwritten "Wade England"

No.	Description	Colourways	Size	U.S.$	Can.$	U.K.£
FL-64	Roses	Pink/yellow flowers; green/maroon container	55 x 130	70.00	95.00	35.00
FL-65	Roses/wild roses	Yellow/pink/blue flowers; green window box	95 x 140	80.00	110.00	40.00

RINGS (EARTHENWARE), c.1930-c.1935

Wild roses/pansies (FL-67)

Backstamp: A. Raised "British Made," "Wade England" and "Made in England"
B. Black handwritten "Wade England"

No.	Description	Colourways	Size	U.S.$	Can.$	U.K.£
FL-66	Pansies	Yellow/maroon/blue flowers; black holder(centre empty)	60 x 130	80.00	110.00	40.00
FL-67	Wild roses/pansies	Yellow/maroon/blue/pink/mauve flowers; black holder (centre filled)	60 x 130	80.00	110.00	40.00

ROCK GARDENS WITH GNOME (EARTHENWARE), c.1930-c.1935

Photograph not available at press time

Backstamp: Unknown

No.	Description	Colourways	Size	U.S.$	Can.$	U.K.£
FL-68	Garden/gnome	Red hat, jacket, shoes; pink trousers; green garden	Small/45 x 65	60.00	80.00	30.00
FL-69	Garden/gnome	Red hat, jacket, shoes; pink trousers; green garden	Large/70 x 100	90.00	120.00	45.00

SQUARE (EARTHENWARE), c.1930-c.1935

Photograph not available at press time

Backstamp: Unknown

No.	Description	Colourways	Size	U.S.$	Can.$	U.K.£
FL-70	Assorted flowers	Multi-coloured; black square	Unknown	60.00	80.00	30.00

TRIANGLE (EARTHENWARE), c.1930-c.1935

Photograph not available at press time

Backstamp: Black ink stamp "Wade England"

No.	Description	Colourways	Size	U.S.$	Can.$	U.K.£
FL-71	Pansies	Yellow/maroon/blue flowers; black triangle	Unknown	60.00	80.00	30.00

JUGS (EARTHENWARE), c.1930-c.1935

LARGE-SPOUT MINIATURE JUGS

Poppies (FL-72)

Roses (FL-74)

Backstamp: Black handwritten "Wade England"

No.	Description	Colourways	Size	U.S.$	Can.$	U.K.£
FL-72	Poppies	Maroon/yellow flowers; yellow jug; green handle	66 x 68	15.00	20.00	8.00
FL-73	Rose buds	Pink/yellow flowers; black jug; yellow handle	60 x 68	15.00	20.00	8.00
FL-74	Roses	Pink/yellow flowers; black jug	66 x 68	15.00	20.00	8.00

LONG-NECK MINIATURE JUGS

Photograph not available
at press time

Backstamp: Unknown

No.	Description	Colourways	Size	U.S.$	Can.$	U.K.£
FL-75	Wild roses	Dark pink/yellow/blue flowers; black jug	110 X 40	15.00	20.00	8.00

SHORT-NECKED MINIATURE JUG

Photograph not available
at press time

Backstamp: Unknown

No.	Description	Colourways	Size	U.S.$	Can.$	U.K.£
FL-76	Tulips	Dark pink/yellow flowers; black jug	60 X 35	15.00	20.00	8.00

SLOPING-NECK MINIATURE JUGS

Pansies (FL-77)

Backstamp: Black handwriten "Wade England"

No.	Description	Colourways	Size	U.S.$	Can.$	U.K.£
FL-77	Pansies	Blue/yellow/maroon flowers; black jug; pale yellow handle	65 x 21	15.00	20.00	8.00
FL-78	Wild roses	Blue/yellow/maroon flowers; black jug; pale yellow handle	80 x 22	15.00	20.00	8.00

STRAIGHT-BACKED JUGS

Roses (FL-79a)

Backstamp: Black handwritten "Wade England"

No.	Description	Colourways	Size	U.S.$	Can.$	U.K.£
FL-79a	Roses	Pink/yellow flowers; yellow jug; pale green handle	85 x 25	15.00	20.00	8.00
FL-79b	Roses	Pink/yellow flowers; yellow jug; black handle	85 x 25	15.00	20.00	8.00

WIDE-MOUTH JUG

Backstamp: Raised "British Made" and black handwritten "Wade England"

No.	Description	Colourways	Size	U.S.$	Can.$	U.K.£
FL-80	Wild roses	Pink/yellow flowers; black jug; yellow handle	75 x 50	15.00	20.00	8.00

VASES

ART DECO VASE (EARTHENWARE), c.1930-c.1935

Backstamp: Black handwritten "Wade England"

No.	Description	Colourways	Size	U.S.$	Can.$	U.K.£
FL-81	Assorted flowers	Red/pink/blue/yellow flowers; light grey/blue vase	305 x 250	150.00	200.00	75.00

MINIATURE VASE WITH HANDLES (EARTHENWARE), c.1930-c.1935

Backstamp: Black handwritten "Wade England"

No.	Description	Colourways	Size	U.S.$	Can.$	U.K.£
FL-82	Roses/pansies	Purple/yellow/blue flowers; black vase; green handles	80 x 50	15.00	20.00	8.00

MINIATURE VASE WITH HANDLES (CHINA), c.1935-1939

Photograph not available
at press time

Backstamp: Black handwritten "Wade England"

No.	Description	Colourways	Size	U.S.$	Can.$	U.K.£
FL-83	Primula	Purple/yellow/blue flowers; yellow vase; black handles	80 x 50	15.00	20.00	8.00

SATURN VASES (EARTHENWARE), c.1930-c.1935

Photograph not available
at press time

Backstamp: **A.** Black handwritten "Wade England" and model name
B. Black handwritten "Wade England"
C. Black ink stamp "Wade England"

No.	Name	Description	Size	U.S.$	Can.$	U.K.£
FL-84	Primroses	Yellow flowers; pale green ring	Small/125 x 55	65.00	80.00	30.00
FL-85	Rose	Yellow/pink/blue flowers; cream/green speckled ring	Small/125 x 55	65.00	80.00	30.00
FL-86	Wild roses	Yellow/maroon/pink/blue flowers; bright yellow ring	Small/125 x 55	65.00	80.00	30.00
FL-87	Roses	Yellow/maroon/pink/blue flowers; cream/green ring	Medium/140 x 70	70.00	90.00	35.00
FL-88	Roses	Green ring; yellow/maroon/blue flowers	Large/Unknown	80.00	110.00	40.00

SMALL-WAISTED VASES (CHINA), c.1935-1939

Oleanders (FL-93b)

Backstamp: A. Black handwritten "Wade England"
B. Black ink stamp "Wade Made in England"

No.	Description	Colourways	Size	U.S.$	Can.$	U.K.£
FL-89	Campanula/ primroses/roses	Blue/yellow/pink flowers; white vase; green base; gold band	80 x 40	50.00	70.00	25.00
FL-90a	Carnations/tulips	Pink/yellow/red flowers; black vase	80 x 40	50.00	70.00	25.00
FL-90b	Carnations/tulips	Pink/yellow/red flowers; white vase; gold band	80 x 40	50.00	70.00	25.00
FL-91	Daisies/violets/ tulips	White/violet/red flowers; black vase	80 x 40	50.00	70.00	25.00
FL-92	Hibiscus	White/yellow flowers; black vase	95 x 80	40.00	55.00	20.00
FL-93a	Oleanders	Dark pink/yellow flowers; black vase	95 x 80	50.00	70.00	25.00
FL-93b	Oleanders	Dark pink/yellow flowers; light green vase	95 x 80	50.00	70.00	25.00
FL-94	Pansies	Yellow/mauve/dark pink flowers; white/green vase; gold band	85 x 80	40.00	55.00	20.00
FL-95	Roses/primroses	Yellow/pink/maroon flowers; black vase	80 x 40	50.00	70.00	25.00

TEMPLE VASE (EARTHENWARE), c.1930-c.1935

Photograph not available
at press time

Backstamp: Unknown

No.	Description	Colourways	Size	U.S.$	Can.$	U.K.£
FL-96	Wild rose	Red/yellow/blue flowers; black vase	145 x 100	40.00	55.00	20.00

TRIANGULAR VASE, STEPPED BASE (EARTHENWARE), c.1930-c.1935

Photograph not available
at press time

Backstamp: Black handwritten "Wade England"

No.	Description	Colourways	Size	U.S.$	Can.$	U.K.£
FL-97	Assorted flowers	Red/blue/yellow flowers; green vase	130 x 85	80.00	100.00	55.00

JARS
1963-1992

All the jars are part of series that contain matching vases, dishes or bowls. They are listed in alphabetical order.

BACKSTAMPS

Transfer Prints

From 1963 through to 1992, Wade used transfer prints on its jars. Wade Ireland used a transfer print on its Celtic Porcelain jars in 1965.

Embossed Backstamp

Wade Ireland used an embossed backstamp on its Celtic Porcelain jars in 1965.

CELTIC PORCELAIN JARS, 1965

The designs of writhing snakes and men with long beards were copied from illustrations made by medieval monks in an Irish manuscript called, *The Book of Kells*. The snakes represent those banished from Ireland by Saint Patrick. The beard-pullers jar has an embossed design of old men with entwined arms, legs, hair and long beards. These men are said to represent the merchants and money changers who were cast out of the temple by Jesus.

Serpent jar, shape CK1

Backstamp: **A.** Embossed "Celtic Porcelain by Wade Ireland" in an Irish knot wreath
B. Black transfer print "Celtic Porcelain made in Ireland by Wade Co. Armagh"
Shape No.: CK1 —Serpent jar
CK4 — Beard-pullers jar

No.	Description	Colourways	Size	U.S.$	Can.$	U.K.£
JA-1	Shape CK1/serpents	Mottled blue-green	114	80.00	110.00	40.00
JA-2	Shape CK4/beard pullers	Blue/green	114	91.00	125.00	45.00

JACOBEAN AND KAWA GINGER JARS, 1990-1992

The Jacobean design consists of enamelled exotic flowers, and Kawa is a Japanese design of peonies and bamboo stems.

Jacobean ginger jar (JA-3a)

Backstamp: **A.** Red print "Wade England" with two red lines and "Jacobean"
B. Gold print "Wade England" with two gold lines and "Kawa"

No.	Name	Colourways	Size	U.S.$	Can.$	U.K.£
JA-3a	Jacobean	White; red/black print	Small/Unknown	30.00	40.00	15.00
JA-3b	Kawa	White; pastel pink/green print; gold highlights	Small/Unknown	30.00	40.00	15.00
JA-4a	Jacobean	White; red/black print	Medium/Unknown	40.00	55.00	20.00
JA-4b	Kawa	White; pastel pink/green print; gold highlights	Medium/Unknown	40.00	55.00	20.00

TOPLINE JARS, 1963

Topline is a series of contemporary shapes and decoration by freelance designer Michael Caddy and produced for only a short time in 1963. The jars are cylindrical and all have lids.

Backstamp: Red print "Wade England"

No.	Description	Colourways	Size	U.S.$	Can.$	U.K.£
JA-5a	Jar/lid	White; purple abstract panels; black/white lid	76	70.00	95.00	35.00
JA-5b	Jar/lid	White; purple/gold abstract panels; black/white lid	76	70.00	95.00	35.00
JA-5c	Jar/lid	White; gold abstract panels; black/white lid	76	70.00	95.00	35.00
JA-6	Jar/lid	White; multi-coloured print; black/white lid	97	60.00	80.00	30.00
JA-7	Jar/domed, pointed lid	Black; gold bands, feather medallion	140	60.00	80.00	30.00
JA-8	Jar/lid, pointed finial	White; gold abstract panels, finial	114	60.00	80.00	30.00
JA-9	Jar/lid, pointed finial	White; black bands; gold abstract panels, finial	148	70.00	95.00	35.00

JUGS
c.1928-1995

The jugs in this section are more decorative than utilitarian. They come in a large range of shapes with embossed or impressed designs, with hand-painted decorations, transfer prints or in plain or mottled colours, sometimes with several of these components combined on one item.

Flaxman Ware jugs are usually produced with a mottled glaze, although this is not always the case. Transfer prints began to be used as decoration on jugs in the 1950s.

The jugs are listed first in shape-number order, then those without shape numbers follow in alphabetical order.

BACKSTAMPS

Impressed Backstamp

The first jug produced by Wade, shape 98/2, which was issued in the late 1920s, has an impressed backstamp. Except for this jug, Wade used impressed backstamps from 1957 to the early 1960s, and they appeared on some of its Harmony Ware jugs.

Hand-painted Backstamp

Only one jug has a hand-painted backstamp, the Big Bad Wolf jug, produced from 1937 to 1939.

Ink Stamps

From 1933 to the 1940s, Wade Heath marked its jugs with ink stamps in a variety of colours —black, red, grey, green, brown and orange. Many of these backstamps included a lion and either an impressed or embossed shape number.

For Gothic Ware jugs, produced from 1937 to 1939, black and gold ink stamps were used. Black ink stamps can be found on Harvest Ware jugs from the late 1940s to the early 1950s.

Standard Wade England ink stamps were used on jugs from 1934 to 1961, in either black, red or grey. They often included either an impressed or embossed shape number.

Transfer Prints

Beginning with a Gothic Ware jug of 1953, Wade used a variety of transfer-printed backstamps on its jugs until 1995. They can be found in gold, red, black, white and in black and orange.

SHAPE 13
Jugs, 1933-c.1945

These waisted jugs are decorated with swirling tree branches around the bowl. A woodpecker forms the handle.

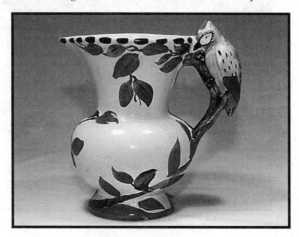

Backstamp: **A.** Red ink stamp "Wadeheath England" with a lion
B. Black ink stamp "Wadeheath England" with a lion
C. Black ink stamp "Wade Heath England
D. Black ink stamp "Wadeheath Orcadia Ware British Made"

No.	Description	Colourways	Size	U.S.$	Can.$	U.K.£
JU-1a	Shape 13	Yellow/brown/orange; green/yellow/orange/ blue bird	Small/180	150.00	200.00	75.00
JU-1b	Shape 13	Yellow/brown; yellow/orange/brown bird	Small/180	150.00	200.00	75.00
JU-2a	Orcadia 13	Orange/black; orange/blue/green/yellow bird	Medium/190	150.00	200.00	75.00
JU-2b	Shape 13	Yellow/orange/black; blue/orange bird	Medium/190	150.00	200.00	75.00
JU-2c	Shape 13	Yellow/orange/brown; green/orange bird	Medium/190	150.00	200.00	75.00
JU-2d	Shape 13	Amber/brown jug, bird	Medium/190	150.00	200.00	75.00

SHAPE 14
Jugs, 1934-1935

Backstamp: Black ink stamp "Wadeheath England" with a lion

No.	Description	Colourways	Size	U.S.$	Can.$	U.K.£
JU-3	Shape 14	Yellow; brown handle; green/orange birds	Small/165	180.00	240.00	90.00
JU-4	Shape 14	Yellow; brown handle; green/orange birds	Large/ 193	180.00	240.00	90.00

SHAPE 15
Flaxman Ware Jugs, 1937-1939

These miniature jugs in one-colour glazes were moulded in the shape of a crouching squirrel. The spout is formed by its ears, and the tail curling upwards forms the handle.

Backstamp: Black ink stamp "Flaxman Wade Heath England" with impressed "15"

No.	Description	Colourways	Size	U.S.$	Can.$	U.K.£
JU-5a	Flaxman 15	Blue	100	80.00	110.00	40.00
JU-5b	Flaxman 15	Beige	100	80.00	110.00	40.00
JU-5c	Flaxman 15	Cream	100	70.00	95.00	35.00
JU-5d	Flaxman 15	Yellow	100	80.00	110.00	40.00
JU-5e	Flaxman 15	White	100	70.00	95.00	35.00

SHAPE 16
Castile Jugs, 1934-1935

The top of these jugs are castellated, and they have a long triangular handle.

Photograph not available
at press time

Backstamp: Black ink stamp "Wadeheath England" with a lion and impressed "Castile 16"

No.	Description	Colourways	Size	U.S.$	Can.$	U.K.£
JU-6a	Castile 16	Off white; green handle, leaves; pink flowers; yellow butterfly	220	170.00	225.00	85.00
JU-6b	Castile 16	Off white; brown handle, leaves; orange flowers; brown bird	220	170.00	225.00	85.00

SHAPE 88
Jugs, 1934-1937

These jugs are hand painted jugs and have a spout that is moulded in a V shape.

Backstamp: **A.** Black ink stamp "WadeHeath England" with a lion and impressed shape number
B. Black ink stamp "Flaxman Ware Hand Made Pottery by Wadeheath, England" with impressed shape number
C. Black ink stamp "Wadeheath Ware England" with impressed shape number

Shape No.: 88M — Miniature
88MS — Medium
88 — Large

No.	Description	Colourways	Size	U.S.$	Can.$	U.K.£
JU-7a	Flaxman 88M	Mottled brown; mottled light brown neck	Miniature/140	70.00	95.00	35.00
JU-7b	Flaxman 88M	Cream; pink/mauve flowers	Miniature/140	70.00	95.00	35.00
JU-7c	Flaxman 88M	Cream; blue handle; pink flowers	Miniature/140	70.00	95.00	35.00
JU-7d	Flaxman 88M	Cream; dark brown/light brown streaks	Miniature/140	60.00	80.00	30.00
JU-7e	Flaxman 88M	Cream; green spatters	Miniature/140	60.00	80.00	30.00
JU-7f	Flaxman 88M	Green	Miniature/140	60.00	80.00	30.00
JU-7g	Shape 88M	Cream; pink/blue flowers; green leaves	Miniature/140	70.00	95.00	35.00
JU-7h	Shape 88M	Cream; orange/yellow/brown streaks	Miniature/140	60.00	80.00	30.00
JU-7i	Shape 88M	Cream; yellow/orange flowers; grey cross stripes	Miniature/140	70.00	90.00	35.00
JU-7j	Shape 88M	Cream; yellow/red flowers	Miniature/140	70.00	90.00	35.00
JU-7k	Shape 88M	Yellow; large orange flower	Miniature/140	60.00	80.00	30.00
JU-7l	Shape 88M	Yellow/brown speckles	Miniature/140	60.00	80.00	30.00
JU-8a	Shape 88MS	Off white; red/yellow windmill; green trees	Medium/185	80.00	110.00	40.00
JU-8b	Shape 88MS	Streaked orange/yellow/brown; orange handle, bowl; brown base	Medium/185	80.00	110.00	40.00
JU-8c	Shape 88MS	Cream; blue/yellow flowers	Medium/185	80.00	110.00	40.00
JU-9a	Shape 88	Cream; blue spout, handle; grey base; red/blue flowers; green leaves	Large/210	90.00	120.00	45.00
JU-9b	Shape 88	Green/yellow; blue/yellow flowers; brown bird	Large/210	90.00	120.00	45.00

SHAPE 89
Jugs, 1934-1935

This jug has a long pointed spout and an impressed and embossed triangle design around the neck.

Photograph not available
at press time

Backstamp: A. Black ink stamp "WadeHeath England" with a lion and impressed "89"
B. Orange ink stamp "Wadeheath Orcadia Ware"

No.	Description	Colourways	Size	U.S.$	Can.$	U.K.£
JU-10a	Shape 89	Cream; blue/yellow/ orange flowers; green leaves	160	130.00	175.00	65.00
JU-10b	Orcadia 89	Orange/brown	155	120.00	160.00	60.00

SHAPE 90
Jugs, 1934-1935

These jugs are similar to shape 89, but the spout extends down to the waist of the jug and the triangle design is around the waist.

Backstamp: A. Black ink stamp "WadeHeath England" with a lion and embossed "90," 1934-1935
B. Black ink stamp "Flaxman Ware Hand Made Pottery by Wadeheath England," 1935-1937

No.	Description	Colourways	Size	U.S.$	Can.$	U.K.£
JU-11a	Shape 90	Cream; blue/yellow flowers; brown trees, bird	215	150.00	200.00	75.00
JU-11b	Shape 90	Cream; yellow/blue flowers; green leaves	215	130.00	185.00	65.00
JU-11c	Shape 90	Orange/brown/yellow streaks; orange band	215	90.00	120.00	45.00
JU-11d	Shape 90	Cream/green; blue/brown,/yellow flowers	215	130.00	185.00	65.00
JU-11e	Shape 90	Green; brown flowers, green leaves (top); blue/brown flowers; black outlined butterflies	215	150.00	200.00	75.00
JU-11f	Shape 90	Green; brown flowers (top); blue flowers; brown tree outline, hummingbirds	215	150.00	200.00	75.00
JU-12	Shape 90	Green; blue spout, handle; blue/brown flowers; brown triangles	225	150.00	190.00	75.00

SHAPE 92
Jugs, 1935-c.1945

Backstamp: A. Black ink stamp "Wadeheath Ware England"
        B. Black ink stamp "Made in England"

No.	Description	Colourways	Size	U.S.$	Can.$	U.K.£
JU-13a	Shape 92	Yellow/orange bowl, flowers; mottled dark brown foot, handle	204	80.00	110.00	40.00
JU-13b	Shape 92	Orange/brown/yellow streaks; yellow foot, handle	204	80.00	110.00	40.00
JU-13c	Shape 92	Brown foot, handle; yellow/orange/grey streaks	204	80.00	110.00	40.00

SHAPE 93

Elite Jugs, 1934-1937

Backstamp: A. Black ink stamp "WadeHeath England" with a lion and embossed "Elite No 93," 1934-1935
B. Black ink stamp "Flaxman Ware Hand Made Pottery by Wadeheath England" with embossed "Elite 93"

No.	Description	Colourways	Size	U.S.$	Can.$	U.K.£
JU-14a	Elite 93	Cream; green/brown base, handle; maroon/ mauve flowers	285	170.00	225.00	85.00
JU-14b	Elite 93	Cream; orange spout, handle; blue/orange/ brown flames	295	170.00	225.00	85.00
JU-14c	Elite 93	Yellow; orange spout, base; brown handle; green leaves	295	170.00	225.00	85.00
JU-14d	Elite 93	Cream; green handle; blue/yellow flowers; brown/green tree; bird outlined in brown	295	170.00	225.00	85.00

Peony Series Jug, c.1948-c.1952

The flowers on this jug were hand painted, so no two are identical.

Photograph not available
at press time

Backstamp: Black ink stamp "Harvest Ware Wade England" with the impressed "93"

No.	Description	Colourways	Size	U.S.$	Can.$	U.K.£
JU-15	Harvest Ware 93	Cream; multi-coloured flowers	280	90.00	120.00	45.00

Imperial Jugs, 1955

These jugs are decorated with large white seed cases highlighted in burnished gold.

Photograph not available
at press time

Backstamp: Circular print "Wade Made in England Hand Painted" and embossed "Elite 93"

No.	Description	Colourways	Size	U.S.$	Can.$	U.K.£
JU-16	Imperial 93	Burgundy; white seed; gold highlights	285	130.00	175.00	65.00

SHAPE 98/2
Jug, c.1928

The spout of this jug is short, and there are raised ribs running around the bowl.

Backstamp: Impressed "98/2 Made in England"

No.	Description	Colourways	Size	U.S.$	Can.$	U.K.£
JU-17	Shape 98/2	Mottled turquoise/green/cream	205	110.00	145.00	55.00

SHAPE 106
Jugs, 1934-c.1948

These jugs were either decorated with hand-painted designs or produced in an all-over mottled colours. There is a drainage hole inside the base under the handle.

Backstamp:
A. Black ink stamp "Wadeheath England" with a lion and impressed "106/30"
B. Black ink stamp "Flaxman Ware Hand Made Pottery by Wadeheath England" with impressed "106"
C. Black ink stamp "Flaxman Wade Heath England" with impressed "106"
D. Black ink stamp "Wadeheath Ware England" with impressed "106"
E. Black ink stamp "Made in England" with impressed "106"

Shape No.: 106 — Miniature, large
106/30 — Medium

No.	Description	Colourways	Size	U.S.$	Can.$	U.K.£
JU-18a	Flaxman 106	Dark blue	Miniature/140	70.00	95.00	35.00
JU-18b	Shape 106	Cream; green base, handle; large blue/yellow/orange flowers	Miniature/140	70.00	95.00	35.00
JU-18c	Shape 106	Cream; green base, handle; light brown leaves; small pink flower	Miniature/140	70.00	95.00	35.00
JU-18d	Shape 106	Orange	Miniature/140	70.00	95.00	35.00
JU-18e	Shape 106	Cream; orange base; red/yellow/orange flowers	Miniature/140	70.00	95.00	35.00
JU-18f	Shape 106	Mottled blue	Miniature/140	60.00	80.00	30.00
JU-18g	Shape 106	Mottled green	Miniature/140	60.00	80.00	30.00
JU-18h	Shape 106	Mottled orange/grey	Miniature/140	60.00	80.00	30.00
JU-18i	Shape 106	Cream; grey base; brown handle; large blue/yellow/orange flowers	Miniature/140	60.00	80.00	30.00
JU-19a	Shape 106/30	Cream; yellow flowers; green leaves	Medium/190	130.00	175.00	65.00
JU-19b	Shape 106/30	White; dark blue handle; orange/dark blue flowers; gold lustre leaves	Medium/190	130.00	175.00	65.00
JU-19c	Shape 106/30	Cream; yellow/orange flowers; green leaves	Medium/190	130.00	175.00	65.00
JU-19d	Shape 106/30	Blue; brown trees	Medium/190	60.00	90.00	30.00
JU-19e	Shape 106/30	Mottled dark green	Medium/190	80.00	110.00	40.00
JU-19f	Shape 106/30	Mottled cream/blue	Medium/190	80.00	110.00	40.00
JU-19g	Shape 106/30	Cream; three multi-coloured flowers	Medium/190	130.00	175.00	65.00
JU-20a	Flaxman 106	Cream; orange handle, parrot	Large/222	130.00	175.00	65.00
JU-20b	Flaxman 106	Yellow; orange handle; orange/brown flowers; green leaves	Large/222	130.00	175.00	65.00
JU-20c	Flaxman 106	Blue; brown base, handle; brown/blue trees	Large/222	130.00	175.00	65.00
JU-20d	Flaxman 106	Dull mustard/green/yellow; mottled orange bands	Large/222	100.00	135.00	50.00

SHAPE 110
Jugs, 1934–1935

There are four ribbed bands around the waist of these jugs.

| Shape 110 (JU-21a) | Shape 110 (JU-21d) |

Backstamp: Black ink stamp "Wadeheath England" with a lion and embossed "110"

No.	Description	Colourways	Size	U.S.$	Can.$	U.K.£
JU-21a	Shape 110	Cream; grey rim, spout, handle, base; mauve flowers; brown gate, cottage	230	110.00	145.00	55.00
JU-21b	Shape 110	Cream; large orange/blue/green flowers	230	110.00	145.00	55.00
JU-21c	Shape 110	Orange/yellow/brown streaks; brown base	230	80.00	110.00	40.00
JU-21d	Shape 110	Yellow; brown streaks	230	70.00	95.00	35.00
JU-21e	Shape 110	Beige; rust spout; green flowers; outlined butterfly	230	90.00	120.00	45.00
JU-21f	Shape 110	Yellow; orange scrolls	230	70.00	95.00	35.00
JU-21g	Shape 110	Mottled yellow/green	230	70.00	95.00	35.00
JU-21h	Shape 110	Cream; purple/lilac/grey/yellow flowers; green grasses; orange-lustre spout, handle	230	70.00	95.00	35.00

SHAPE 112
Jugs, 1934–1935

These tall slender, hand-painted jugs, which taper at the top, have a handle consisting of a small and large triangle.

Photograph not available
at press time

Backstamp: Black ink stamp "Wadeheath England" with a lion

No.	Description	Colourways	Size	U.S.$	Can.$	U.K.£
JU-22a	Shape 112	Off white; blue/brown base, handle; pink/blue hollyhocks	285	170.00	225.00	85.00
JU-22b	Shape 112	Off white; green handle; yellow corn; blue cornflowers; red poppies	285	170.00	225.00	85.00
JU-22c	Shape 112	Brown; yellow/green/grey leaves	285	90.00	120.00	45.00
JU-22d	Shape 112	Cream; red house; red/orange flowers	285	90.00	120.00	45.00

SHAPE 113
Jugs, 1934-c.1945

The body of these jugs is ribbed.

Backstamp: A. Black ink stamp "Wadeheath England" with a lion and impressed "113"
B. Black ink stamp "Flaxman Ware Hand Made—Pottery by Wadeheath England"
C. Black ink stamp "Made in England" with impressed "113"

No.	Description	Colourways	Size	U.S.$	Can.$	U.K.£
JU-23a	Flaxman 113	Orange/green	Miniature/130	50.00	70.00	25.00
JU-23b	Shape 113	Cream; orange base; black/cream handle; black vine; orange/blue/green leaves	Miniature/130	70.00	95.00	35.00
JU-23c	Shape 113	Cream; green base, handle; pink/yellow flowers	Miniature/130	70.00	95.00	35.00
JU-23d	Shape 113	Green/mottled brown	Miniature/130	50.00	70.00	25.00
JU-23e	Shape 113	Yellow/mottled brown	Miniature/130	50.00	70.00	25.00
JU-23f	Shape 113	Off white; orange flowers	Miniature/130	50.00	70.00	25.00
JU-23g	Shape 113	Cream; pearlised orange base; cream/orange handle; orange/red/blue flowers; silver lustre	Miniature/130	70.00	95.00	35.00
JU-23h	Shape 113	Green	Miniature/130	50.00	70.00	25.00
JU-24a	Flaxman 113	Green; yellow base, handle; yellow/blue fruit	Medium/190	110.00	145.00	55.00
JU-24b	Shape 113	Cream; orange base; cream/orange handle; orange/blue/yellow/orange flowers; green leaves	Medium/190	110.00	145.00	55.00

SHAPE 114
Jugs, 1934-1935

The tail of the moulded bird on the bowl of these jugs extends upward to form the handle.

Backstamp: Black ink stamp "Wadeheath England" with a lion

No.	Description	Colourways	Size	U.S.$	Can.$	U.K.£
JU-25a	Shape 114	Yellow; orange spout, base, butterfly; mauve/ orange flowers; light green/orange bird	180	180.00	240.00	90.00
JU-25b	Shape 114	Yellow; orange butterfly, flowers; green/yellow bird	180	180.00	240.00	90.00

SHAPE 119
Jugs, 1935-1937

Backstamp: **A.** Black ink stamp "Flaxman Ware Hand Made Pottery by Wadeheath England" with embossed "119" and black ink stamp "Wadeheath England Registration No 812659" with impressed "119"
B. Black ink stamp "Flaxman Ware Hand Made Pottery by Wadeheath England" with impressed "119"

No.	Description	Colourways	Size	U.S.$	Can.$	U.K.£
JU-26a	Flaxman 119	Mottled cream/green	229	110.00	145.00	55.00
JU-26b	Flaxman 119	Green; blue/yellow/green fruit	229	110.00	145.00	55.00

SHAPE 120
Jugs, 1934-1937

A broad band runs diagonally down the jug from the spout to the base of the handle. It separates two panels of horizontal ridges.

Backstamp: A. Black ink stamp "Wadeheath England" with a lion
B. Black ink stamp "Flaxman Ware Hand Made Pottery by Wadeheath England" with embossed "120"

No.	Description	Colourways	Size	U.S.$	Can.$	U.K.£
JU-27a	Flaxman 120	Mottled orange	215	110.00	145.00	55.00
JU-27b	Flaxman 120	Mottled green	215	110.00	145.00	55.00
JU-27c	Flaxman 120	Mottled green/cream	215	110.00	145.00	55.00
JU-27d	Shape 120	Mottled yellow/golden brown	215	130.00	175.00	65.00
JU-27e	Shape 120	Cream; orange rim, base; orange/yellow flowers	215	130.00	175.00	65.00

SHAPE 121
Jugs, 1934–1940

Backstamp: **A.** Grey ink stamp "Wadeheath England Registration No 812930" and embossed "121A"
B. Black ink stamp "Wadeheath England" with a lion and impressed "121A"
C. Black ink stamp "Flaxman Ware Hand Made Pottery by Wadeheath England" with embossed "121"
D. Black ink stamp "Wade Heath England" with embossed "121"

No.	Description	Colourways	Size	U.S.$	Can.$	U.K.£
JU-28a	Flaxman 121	Cream; brown handle; grey/green trees; brown cottage; grey hill; orange/blue flowers	230	150.00	200.00	75.00
JU-28b	Shape 121	Cream top; mottled turquoise bottom	230	150.00	200.00	75.00
JU-28c	Shape 121	Mottled yellow/golden brown	230	150.00	200.00	75.00
JU-28d	Shape 121	Cream; orange handle; blue/yellow tree; orange/blue flowers	230	150.00	200.00	75.00
JU-28e	Shape 121	Mottled orange	230	150.00	200.00	75.00
JU-28f	Shape 121	Mottled green	230	150.00	200.00	75.00

SHAPE 122
Jugs, 1937-c.1945

Raised ribs run across the handle side of these jugs.

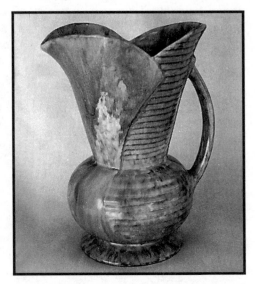

Backstamp: A. Black ink stamp "Wade Heath England" with embossed "122"
B. Black ink stamp "Flaxman Wade Heath England" with embossed "122"

No.	Description	Colourways	Size	U.S.$	Can.$	U.K.£
JU-29a	Flaxman 122	Mottled turquoise/blue/beige	205	120.00	160.00	60.00
JU-29b	Flaxman 122	Mottled orange; mottled grey/brown base	205	120.00	160.00	60.00
JU-29c	Shape 122	Mottled orange; blue/pink flowers	205	120.00	160.00	60.00

SHAPE 123
Jugs, 1934-1937

These jugs have three embossed spirals extending down the body from the spout, with horizontal bands on the handle side.

Backstamp: **A.** Black ink stamp "Wadeheath England" with a lion and embossed "123"
B. Black ink stamp "Flaxman Ware Hand Made Pottery by Wadeheath England" with impressed "123"

No.	Description	Colourways	Size	U.S.$	Can.$	U.K.£
JU-30a	Flaxman 123	Mottled grey/turquoise	229	110.00	145.00	55.00
JU-30b	Flaxman 123	Mottled orange	229	110.00	145.00	55.00
JU-30c	Shape 123	Cream; black/purple tree top; orange/yellow flowers; yellow/green cross bands	229	110.00	145.00	55.00

SHAPE 124
Jugs, 1934-1937

These jugs have a broad band angled across the middle and a ribbed design around the body.

Backstamp: **A.** Black ink stamp "Wadeheath England" with a lion and embossed "124"
B. Black ink stamp "Flaxman Ware Hand Made Pottery by Wadeheath England" with impressed "124"

No.	Description	Colourways	Size	U.S.$	Can.$	U.K.£
JU-31a	Flaxman 124	Pale yellow	75	60.00	80.00	30.00
JU-31b	Flaxman 124	Pale orange	75	60.00	80.00	30.00
JU-31c	Shape 124	Mottled green/yellow	75	60.00	80.00	30.00
JU-31d	Shape 124	Mottled green/mauve/cream	75	60.00	80.00	30.00
JU-31e	Shape 124	Green/cream; silver diagonal stripe, flowers	75	60.00	80.00	30.00

SHAPE 127
Jugs, 1934-1937

Shape 127 (JU-32b)   Shape 127 (JU-32c)

Backstamp: **A.** Black ink stamp "Wadeheath England" with a lion and embossed "127"
  B. Black ink stamp "Flaxman Ware Hand Made Pottery by Wadeheath England" with impressed "127"

No.	Description	Colourways	Size	U.S.$	Can.$	U.K.£
JU-32a	Flaxman 127	Mottled blue	190	110.00	145.00	55.00
JU-32b	Shape 127	Cream; yellow/orange flowers; green/yellow grass	190	110.00	145.00	55.00
JU-32c	Shape 127	Cream; lilac/pink grasses; blue/yellow flowers; silver lustre	190	110.00	145.00	55.00
JU-32d	Shape 127	Cream; maroon rim, handle; maroon/green/ orange streaks	190	110.00	145.00	55.00

SHAPE 128
Flaxman Ware Jugs, 1935-1937

These tall jugs have a wavy handle consisting of three loops.

Photograph not available
at press time

Backstamp: Black ink stamp "Flaxman Ware Hand Made Pottery by Wadeheath England" with impressed "128"

No.	Description	Colourways	Size	U.S.$	Can.$	U.K.£
JU-33a	Flaxman 128	Cream; orange spout, handle; orange/ green trees; orange cottage, flowers	220	130.00	175.00	65.00
JU-33b	Flaxman 128	Cream; grey/orange tree; brown cottage; mauve flower	220	130.00	175.00	65.00

SHAPE 131
Jugs, 1934-1940

These jugs have horizontal ribs running around the body and base.

Backstamp: A. Black ink stamp "WadeHeath England" with a lion and impressed "131"
B. Black ink stamp "Flaxman Ware Hand Made Pottery by Wadeheath, England" and impressed "131MIN"

No.	Description	Colourways	Size	U.S.$	Can.$	U.K.£
JU-34a	Flaxman 131	Mottled grey	Miniature/135	60.00	80.00	30.00
JU-34b	Flaxman 131	Mottled blue	Miniature/135	60.00	80.00	30.00
JU-34c	Flaxman 131MIN	Mottled green	Miniature/135	60.00	80.00	30.00
JU-34d	Shape 131	Cream; blue base; green band; blue flowers; brown leaves, branches	Miniature/135	70.00	95.00	35.00
JU-35a	Flaxman 131	Yellow; green crossed bands	Medium/184	60.00	80.00	30.00
JU-35b	Flaxman 131	Mottled green/orange on yellow	Medium/184	60.00	80.00	30.00
JU-35c	Shape 131	Grey; blue/brown crossed bands	Medium/184	60.00	80.00	30.00
JU-36a	Flaxman 131	Mottled grey/mauve; mottled brown handle, base	Large/215	90.00	120.00	45.00
JU-36b	Flaxman 131	Mottled yellow/green/orange	Large/215	90.00	120.00	45.00
JU-36c	Shape 131	Cream; bright yellow base, handle; multi-coloured flowers	Large/215	150.00	200.00	75.00
JU-36d	Shape 131	Off white; bright orange base, handle, cottage; brown tree	Large/215	150.00	200.00	75.00

SHAPE 132
Flaxman Ware Jugs, 1935-1937

These round jugs have an impressed design of wavy lines and swirls, except for style JU-38b, which has no impressed design.

Backstamp: Black ink stamp "Flaxman Ware Hand Made Pottery by Wadeheath, England" and an embossed "132"

No.	Description	Colourways	Size	U.S.$	Can.$	U.K.£
JU-37a	Flaxman 132	Mottled brown/green	Miniature/130	70.00	95.00	35.00
JU-37b	Flaxman 132	Mottled amber; brown leaves	Miniature/130	70.00	95.00	35.00
JU-38a	Flaxman 132	Pale matt blue; dull yellow crossed lines	Medium/192	120.00	160.00	60.00
JU-38b	Flaxman 132	White; yellow sunflower, crossed lines	Medium/192	120.00	160.00	60.00
JU-39	Flaxman 132	Matt grey; dull yellow patches	Large/230	120.00	160.00	60.00

SHAPE 133
Jugs, 1934-1937

These jugs have a raised band at the waist and an impressed cross-hatch design at the neck and base.

Backstamp: A. Black ink stamp "WadeHeath England" with a lion and embossed "133 MIN"
 B. Black ink stamp "Flaxman Ware Hand Made Pottery by Wadeheath, England" and embossed "133 MIN"
 C. Black ink stamp "Flaxman Ware Hand Made Pottery by Wadeheath, England" and embossed "133"

No.	Description	Colourways	Size	U.S.$	Can.$	U.K.£
JU-40a	Shape 133	Mottled pink; green stems, handle; lilac flowers	Miniature/135	70.00	95.00	35.00
JU-40b	Shape 133	Yellow; green handle; orange tulips	Miniature/135	70.00	95.00	35.00
JU-40c	Shape 133	Cream; grey neck band; green/orange flowers; green waist band	Miniature/135	70.00	95.00	35.00
JU-40d	Flaxman 133	Mottled orange	Miniature/135	60.00	80.00	30.00
JU-40e	Flaxman 133	Mottled green/orange	Miniature/135	60.00	80.00	30.00
JU-40f	Shape 133	Mottled green/beige	Miniature/135	60.00	80.00	30.00
JU-41a	Flaxman 133	Mottled blue/green	Large/230	90.00	120.00	45.00
JU-41b	Flaxman 133	Mottled orange/brown	Large/230	90.00	120.00	45.00

SHAPE 134
Flaxman Ware Jugs, 1935-1937

These six-sided jugs have four panels of raised lines and two framed panels in the centre.

__**Backstamp:**__ Black ink stamp "Flaxman Ware Hand Made Pottery by Wadeheath, England" with embossed "134"

No.	Description	Colourways	Size	U.S.$	Can.$	U.K.£
JU-42a	Flaxman 134	Mottled orange bands; mottled turquoise bands	215	80.00	110.00	40.00
JU-42b	Flaxman 134	Mottled green	215	80.00	110.00	40.00
JU-42c	Flaxman 134	Mottled green; blue/black windmill	215	80.00	110.00	40.00
JU-42d	Flaxman 134	Mottled orange/brown	215	80.00	110.00	40.00
JU-42e	Flaxman 134	Mottled brown/green	215	80.00	110.00	40.00
JU-42f	Flaxman 134	Mottled blue/green	215	80.00	110.00	40.00

SHAPE 135
Jugs, 1934-1937

These unusual jugs have four spouts around the rim.

Backstamp: A. Black ink stamp "WadeHeath England" with a lion and embossed "135"
B. Black ink stamp "Flaxman Ware Hand Made Pottery by Wadeheath, England" with embossed "135"

No.	Description	Colourways	Size	U.S.$	Can.$	U.K.£
JU-43a	Flaxman 135	Pale blue; brown trees, rabbits	216	150.00	200.00	75.00
JU-43b	Shape 135	Pale yellow top; light green bottom	216	130.00	175.00	65.00
JU-43c	Shape 135	Pale yellow; large mauve flower; small red/yellow flowers	216	130.00	175.00	65.00

SHAPE 143

These jugs are shaped like a birdbath and are embossed with a brick design. A budgerigar sits on the rim, his tail and a rose stem form the handle. There are variations of the corner piece on which the budgie sits. It can be either a round corner, a small straight diagonal or a large straight diagonal platform.

Round-Corner Platform, 1935

Budgie sits on round platform

Backstamp: **A.** Black ink stamp "Flaxman Ware Hand Made Pottery by Wadeheath England"
B. Black ink stamp "Wadeheath Ware England"
C. Black ink stamp "Flaxman Wade Heath England" impressed No 143
D. Black ink stamp "Wade Heath England" with impressed No 143)
E. Black ink stamp "Wade England"

No.	Description	Colourways	Size	U.S.$	Can.$	U.K.£
JU-44	Flaxman 143	Pale green; green bird with blue/yellow/ black markings; pale blue/yellow flowers	Extra large/266	110.00	145.00	55.00

Small Diagonal Corner Platform, 1935-1939

Large diagonal platform; small diagonal platform

No.	Description	Colourways	Size	U.S.$	Can.$	U.K.£
JU-45a	Shape 143	Light blue; blue/green bird; blue flowers	Small/159	50.00	70.00	25.00
JU-45b	Shape 143	Yellow; green/yellow bird; blue flowers	Small/159	50.00	70.00	25.00
JU-45c	Shape 143	Yellow; yellow/blue bird; pink flowers	Small/159	50.00	70.00	25.00
JU-46a	Flaxman 143	Creamy yellow; grey bird; blue flowers; brown handle	Medium/195	70.00	95.00	35.00
JU-46b	Flaxman 143	Grey; grey/blue bird; blue flowers	Medium/195	70.00	95.00	35.00
JU-46c	Shape 143	Green; green/blue bird; orange flowers	Medium/195	70.00	95.00	35.00
JU-46d	Shape 143	Pale blue; blue/dark blue bird; dark blue flowers	Medium/195	70.00	95.00	35.00
JU-47a	Flaxman143	Grey; grey/blue bird; blue flowers	Large/225	90.00	120.00	45.00
JU-47b	Flaxman 143	Pale blue; blue/green bird; blue flowers	Large/225	90.00	120.00	45.00
JU-47c	Shape 143	Yellow; grey bird; mauve flowers; brown handle	Large/225	90.00	120.00	45.00
JU-47d	Shape 143	Grey; brown handle; yellow bird; mauve/purple flowers	Large/225	90.00	120.00	45.00
JU-48a	Flaxman 143	Yellow; yellow/blue bird; mauve flowers; green leaves	Extra large/266	110.00	145.00	55.00
JU-48b	Flaxman 143	Blue; blue/dark blue bird; dark/yellow flowers	Extra large/266	110.00	145.00	55.00
JU-48c	Flaxman 143	Pale green; green/brown bird; blue/yellow flowers	Extra large/266	110.00	145.00	55.00
JU-48d	Shape 143	White; yellow/green bird; purple flowers	Extra large/266	110.00	145.00	55.00
JU-48e	Flaxman 143	Pale green; blue/dark blue bird; blue/yellow flowers	Extra large/266	110.00	145.00	55.00
JU-48f	Shape 143	Honey jug, bird; deep red flowers	Extra large/266	110.00	145.00	55.00

Large Diagonal Corner Platform, c.1948-1953

Except for version JU-51d, these jugs were produced in one-colour glazes.

Budgie sits on large diagonal platform

No.	Description	Colourways	Size	U.S.$	Can.$	U.K.£
JU-49a	Shape 143	Blue	Small/159	50.00	70.00	25.00
JU-49b	Shape 143	Cream	Small/159	50.00	70.00	25.00
JU-49c	Shape 143	Green	Small/159	50.00	70.00	25.00
JU-49d	Shape 143	Yellow	Small/159	50.00	70.00	25.00
JU-50a	Shape 143	Blue	Medium/195	60.00	80.00	30.00
JU-50b	Shape 143	Cream	Medium/195	60.00	80.00	30.00
JU-50c	Shape 143	Green	Medium/195	60.00	80.00	30.00
JU-50d	Shape 143	Orange	Medium/195	60.00	80.00	30.00
JU-50e	Shape 143	Pale orange	Medium/195	60.00	80.00	30.00
JU-50f	Shape 143	Yellow	Medium/195	60.00	80.00	30.00
JU-51a	Shape 143	Blue	Large/225	80.00	110.00	40.00
JU-51b	Shape 143	Green	Large/225	80.00	110.00	40.00
JU-51c	Shape 143	Turquoise	Large/225	80.00	110.00	40.00
JU-51d	Shape 143	Turquoise; dark blue handle	Large/225	80.00	110.00	40.00
JU-51e	Shape 143	Yellow	Large/225	80.00	110.00	40.00
JU-52	Shape 143	Green	Extra large/266	80.00	110.00	40.00

SHAPE 144
Jugs, c.1948

This jug has an all-over design of embossed flowers, with a ribbed spout and rim.

Backstamp: Black ink stamp "Wade England"

No.	Description	Colourways	Size	U.S.$	Can.$	U.K.£
JU-53a	Shape 144	White; green/red flower	215	140.00	185.00	70.00
JU-53b	Shape 144	Pale green; blue brown highlighted flowers	215	120.00	160.00	60.00
JU-53c	Shape 144	Pale green	215	120.00	160.00	60.00
JU-53d	Shape 144	Pale orange	215	120.00	160.00	60.00
JU-53e	Shape 144	Mottled yellow/green	215	120.00	160.00	60.00

SHAPE 145
Flaxman Ware Jugs, 1937-1939

There are ribs running around the body and base of these jugs.

Backstamp: Black print "Flaxman Wade Heath, England" with embossed "145"

No.	Description	Colourways	Size	U.S.$	Can.$	U.K.£
JU-54a	Flaxman 145	Cream; pale green/brown leaves; yellow berries	242	120.00	160.00	60.00
JU-54b	Flaxman 145	Mottled lilac/turquoise	242	120.00	160.00	60.00

SHAPE 146
Jugs, 1935-c.1945

This jug has an embossed design of sycamore seed balls, leaves and small flowers.

Backstamp: A. Black ink stamp "Flaxman Ware Hand Made Pottery by Wadeheath England" with embossed "146"
B. Black ink stamp "Flaxman Wade Heath, England" with embossed "146"
C. Green ink stamp "Wade Heath England" with embossed "146"

No.	Description	Colourways	Size	U.S.$	Can.$	U.K.£
JU-55a	Flaxman 146	Pale yellow; brown handle, leaves, seeds	230	110.00	145.00	55.00
JU-55b	Flaxman 146	Mauve; light brown leaves; purple seeds	230	110.00	145.00	55.00
JU-55c	Shape 146	Brown; dark brown handle, leaves, seeds	230	90.00	120.00	45.00

SHAPE 147
Jugs, 1933-c.1940

These jugs have wavy, ribbed lines around the bowl.

Backstamp: **A.** Black ink stamp "WadeHeath England" with a lion and embossed "147"
B. Black ink stamp "Flaxman Wade Heath England"
C. Green ink stamp "Wade Heath England" with embossed "147"
D. Black ink stamp "Flaxman Ware Hand Made Pottery Wadeheath England" and impressed "147MIN"

No.	Description	Colourways	Size	U.S.$	Can.$	U.K.£
JU-56a	Shape 147	Green base; green/yellow/cream handles; yellow/green flowers; black leaves	Miniature/145	70.00	95.00	35.00
JU-56b	Shape 147	Grey base; orange/cream handles; orange/grey flowers; black leaves	Miniature/145	70.00	95.00	35.00
JU-56c	Shape 147	Mottled brown/green/cream	Miniature/145	70.00	95.00	35.00
JU-56d	Shape 147	Mottled green	Miniature/145	50.00	70.00	25.00
JU-56e	Shape 147	Green/purple	Miniature/145	50.00	70.00	25.00
JU-57a	Shape 147	Blue base; blue/yellow/cream handles; blue/blue/yellow flowers; black leaves	Medium/185	100.00	135.00	50.00
JU-57b	Flaxman 147	Mottled cream/orange	Medium/185	80.00	110.00	40.00
JU-57c	Flaxman 147	Mottled dull green/orange	Medium/185	80.00	110.00	40.00
JU-57d	Flaxman 147	Mottled pink/cream top; mottledgreen/blue bottom	Medium/185	80.00	110.00	40.00
JU-57e	Flaxman 147	Cream; blue/pink flowers; orange butterfly	Medium/185	100.00	135.00	50.00
JU-57f	Shape 147	Cream; orange band; orange/black flowers; black leaves	Medium/185	100.00	150.00	50.00
JU-58	Shape 147	Cream; pink/blue flowers; orange butterfly	Large/225	120.00	160.00	60.00

SHAPE 148
Jugs, 1935-c.1945

There are four rows of indented ribs around the bowl of these jugs.

Backstamp: **A.** Black ink stamp "Flaxman Ware Hand Made Pottery by Wadeheath England"
B. Black ink stamp "Flaxman Wade Heath England"
C. Black ink stamp "Wade Heath England" with embossed "148" or "148MS"
D. Black ink stamp "Wade Heath England"

No.	Description	Colourways	Size	U.S.$	Can.$	U.K.£
JU-59a	Flaxman 148	Mottled brown/green	Miniature/140	60.00	80.00	30.00
JU-59b	Flaxman 148	Mottled green/orange	Miniature/140	60.00	80.00	30.00
JU-59c	Flaxman 148	Mottled yellow/green	Miniature/140	60.00	80.00	30.00
JU-59d	Flaxman 148	Mottled blue/brown	Miniature/140	60.00	80.00	30.00
JU-59e	Flaxman 148	Mottled blue/orange	Miniature/140	60.00	80.00	30.00
JU-59f	Shape 148	Cream; black base; green/cream handle; green rim; orange/yellow flowers	Miniature/140	70.00	95.00	35.00
JU-59g	Shape 148	Mottled blue/brown	Miniature/140	60.00	80.00	30.00
JU-60a	Flaxman 148	Mottled blue/brown/cream	Medium/195	70.00	95.00	35.00
JU-60b	Flaxman 148	Mottled green/brown	Medium/195	70.00	95.00	35.00
JU-60c	Flaxman 148	Mottled green	Medium/195	70.00	95.00	35.00
JU-60d	Flaxman 148	Mottled yellow	Medium/195	70.00	95.00	35.00
JU-60e	Shape 148	Beige; red stripe; multi-coloured flowers	Medium/195	70.00	95.00	35.00
JU-61	Shape 148	Cream; orange/cream handle; large orange/ yellow/black flowers	Large/229	90.00	120.00	45.00

SHAPE 149
Jugs, 1935-c.1945

Two embossed bands with an impressed loop design run around the neck and the bottom of the body of these jugs. Style JU-62f has a verse on the back, entitled "Memories Gardens," within an oval surrounded by flowers.

Backstamp: A. Black ink stamp "Flaxman Ware Hand Made Pottery by Wade Heath England" with impressed "149 Min"
B. Black ink stamp "Flaxman Wade Heath England" with impressed "149 Min"
C. Green ink stamp "Wade Heath England" with impressed "149"

No.	Description	Colourways	Size	U.S.$	Can.$	U.K.£
JU-62a	Flaxman 149	Pale mottled turquoise/brown	Miniature/145	50.00	70.00	25.00
JU-62b	Flaxman 149	Pale yellow	Miniature/145	50.00	70.00	25.00
JU-62c	Flaxman 149	Mottled blue	Miniature/145	50.00	70.00	25.00
JU-62d	Flaxman 149	Mottled green	Miniature/145	50.00	70.00	25.00
JU-62e	Shape 149	Cream; green base; green/cream handle; maroon/blue flowers	Miniature/145	50.00	70.00	25.00
JU-62f	Flaxman 149	Cream; green trim; green oval (back) with flowers, verse	Miniature/145	50.00	70.00	25.00
JU-63a	Flaxman 149	Cream; mottled green/cream	Medium/190	60.00	80.00	30.00
JU-63b	Flaxman 149	Mottled yellow	Medium/190	60.00	80.00	30.00
JU-63c	Shape 149	Mottled brown/orange	Medium/190	60.00	80.00	30.00

SHAPE 150
Jug, 1934-1935

This large round-bodied jug has a round handle.

Photograph not available
at press time

Backstamp: Black ink stamp "WadeHeath England" with a lion and impressed "150"

No.	Description	Colourways	Size	U.S.$	Can.$	U.K.£
JU-64	Shape 150	Orange; yellow handle; orange/grey leaves	195	120.00	160.00	60.00

SHAPE 154
Jugs, 1936-c.1948

The style JU-65 jugs have a moulded squirrel sitting under a tree holding a nut. A pair of birds are perched on top of the tree branch that forms the handle.

The style JU-66 jugs were issued in the late 1940s. They were produced in one-colour glazes and do not have the birds on the handle.

Two birds on handle, JU-65   **No birds on handle, JU-66**

Backstamp: **A.** Black ink stamp "Flaxman Wade Heath England" with impressed "154"
B. Brown ink stamp "Flaxman Wade Heath England" with impressed "154"
C. Black ink stamp "Wade Heath England"
D. Black print "Wade England"

No.	Description	Colourways	Size	U.S.$	Can.$	U.K.£
JU-65a	Squirrel/birds	Amber; honey brown squirrel, birds; green leaves	220	140.00	195.00	75.00
JU-65b	Squirrel/birds	Turquoise jug, birds; light brown squirrel	220	140.00	195.00	75.00
JU-65c	Squirrel/birds	Beige; brown squirrel, birds	220	140.00	195.00	75.00
JU-65d	Squirrel/birds	Blue; blue/brown squirrel, birds	220	170.00	230.00	85.00
JU-65e	Squirrel/birds	Green jug, birds; green/brown squirrel	220	140.00	195.00	75.00
JU-65f	Squirrel/birds	Orange; grey squirrel, birds	220	142.00	195.00	75.00
JU-65g	Squirrel/birds	Honey brown; honey/dark brown squirrel, birds	220	140.00	195.00	75.00
JU-66a	Squirrel	Blue	215	130.00	175.00	65.00
JU-66b	Squirrel	Brown	215	130.00	175.00	65.00
JU-66c	Squirrel	Green	215	130.00	175.00	65.00
JU-66d	Squirrel	Orange	215	130.00	175.00	65.00
JU-66e	Squirrel	Pale orange	215	130.00	175.00	65.00
JU-66f	Squirrel	Yellow	215	130.00	175.00	65.00

SHAPE 155
Gothic Ware Jugs, 1937-1939, 1953

These jugs are embossed with a design of swirling leaves and tulips. They were first decorated with matt colours, then reissued in 1953 in gloss colours with gold highlights.

Shape 155 (JU-67a)

Shape 155 (JU-67e)

Backstamp: **A.** Black ink stamp "Gothic Wade Heath England" with impressed "155"
B. Gold transfer print "Wade made in England - hand painted - Gothic" with impressed "155"

No.	Description	Colourways	Size	U.S.$	Can.$	U.K.£
JU-67a	Gothic 155	Pale green; yellow/brown leaves; blue flowers	230	100.00	145.00	55.00
JU-67b	Gothic 155	Pale yellow; green leaves/flowers	230	100.00	145.00	55.00
JU-67c	Gothic 155	Pale green; cream leaves/flowers	230	100.00	145.00	55.00
JU-67d	Gothic 155	Brown; dark brown leaves/flowers	230	100.00	145.00	55.00
JU-67e	Gothic 155	Cream; lilac/pink flowers; green/yellow leaves; gold highlights	230	100.00	145.00	55.00

SHAPE 157
Gothic Ware Jugs, 1937-1939, 1953

These jugs are embossed with a design of swirling leaves and tulips. They were first glazed in matt colours, then reissued in 1953 in gloss colours with gold highlighting.

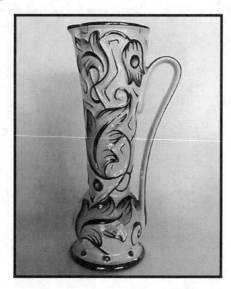

Backstamp: A. Black ink stamp "Gothic Wade Heath England" with impressed "157," 1937-1939
B. Gold transfer print "Wade made in England - hand painted - Gothic" with impressed "157," 1953

No.	Description	Colourways	Size	U.S.$	Can.$	U.K.£
JU-68a	Gothic 157	Pale orange	290	90.00	130.00	45.00
JU-68b	Gothic 157	Cream; lilac/pink flowers; green/yellow leaves; gold highlights	290	100.00	145.00	55.00

SHAPE 164
Jug, 1936-1940

This art-deco jug has a small square handle that is crossed by a long loop handle. It stands on a square foot.

Photograph not available
at press time

Backstamp: Black ink stamp "Wade Heath England"

No.	Description	Colourways	Size	U.S.$	Can.$	U.K.£
JU-69	Shape 164	Cream; black/green rim, handle, base; green bands; orange/blue/yellow flowers	300	255.00	350.00	125.00

SHAPE 168
Jugs, 1936-c.1940

These jugs were moulded in the shape of a wooden dovecote on a pole; the bird forms the top of the handle. Large lupines grow under the birdhouse; one flower forming the bottom of the handle.

Backstamp: A. Black ink stamp "Flaxman Wade Heath England" with impressed "168"
B. Black ink stamp "Wade Heath England" with impressed "168"

No.	Description	Colourways	Size	U.S.$	Can.$	U.K.£
JU-70a	Flaxman 168	Green jug, birds; dark brown pole; blue/yellow flowers; blue/green handle	223	180.00	240.00	90.00
JU-70b	Flaxman 168	Green jug, bird; green/yellow bird; brown pole; yellow/blue flowers; yellow/green handle	223	180.00	240.00	90.00
JU-70c	Shape 168	Yellow jug, birds; golden brown pole; pink/blue flowers; pink/yellow handle	223	180.00	240.00	90.00
JU-70d	Shape 168	Blue jug, birds; dark brown pole; yellow/dark blue flowers; yellow handle	223	180.00	240.00	90.00
JU-70e	Shape 168	Yellow jug, birds; brown pole; blue/yellow flowers; blue handle	223	180.00	240.00	90.00

SHAPE 169
Jugs, 1936-c.1948

In style JU-71 a moulded rabbit sits under a tree. The handle is shaped like a tree branch with a moulded bird feeding the chicks in a nest. The style JU-72 jugs were issued in the late 1940s in one-colour glazes; they do not have the bird on the handle.

| Bird on handle (JU-71b) | No bird on handle (JU-72e) |

Backstamp: A. Green ink stamp "Wade Heath England" with impressed "169"
B. Black ink stamp "Wade England"

No.	Description	Colourways	Size	U.S.$	Can.$	U.K.£
JU-71a	Rabbit/bird	Yellow; brown leaves, rabbit; blue/brown bird	190	150.00	200.00	75.00
JU-71b	Rabbit/bird	Yellow jug, rabbit; green leaves; blue/yellow bird	190	150.00	200.00	75.00
JU-71c	Rabbit/bird	Blue jug, bird; green leaves; grey rabbit	190	150.00	200.00	75.00
JU-71d	Rabbit/bird	Orange; grey rabbit; blue bird	190	150.00	200.00	75.00
JU-72a	Rabbit	Blue	190	150.00	200.00	65.00
JU-72b	Rabbit	Dark blue	190	150.00	200.00	65.00
JU-72c	Rabbit	Green	190	150.00	200.00	65.00
JU-72d	Rabbit	Orange	190	150.00	200.00	65.00
JU-72e	Rabbit	Yellow	190	150.00	200.00	65.00
JU-72f	Rabbit	Cream	190	150.00	200.00	65.00

SHAPE 172
Flaxman Ware Jugs, 1937-1939

This footed jug has a design of loops on one side above the handle.

Photograph not available
at press time

Backstamp: Ink stamp "Flaxman Wade Heath England" with impressed "172"

No.	Description	Colourways	Size	U.S.$	Can.$	U.K.£
JU-73	Flaxman 172	Mottled blue/orange	190	110.00	145.00	55.00

SHAPE 173
Jugs, 1937-c.1940

These jugs have an embossed basket-weave pattern on the body, an ornamental projection under the spout and above the handle and three wavy lines running around the foot.

Backstamp: **A** Black ink stamp "Flaxman Wade Heath England" with impressed "173"
B. Black ink stamp "Wade Heath England" with impressed "173"

No.	Description	Colourways	Size	U.S.$	Can.$	U.K.£
JU-74	Shape 173	Mottled grey/blue/brown	177	110.00	145.00	55.00
JU-75	Flaxman 173	Mottled green	228	110.00	145.00	55.00

SHAPE 301
Flaxman Ware Jug, 1937-1939

Backstamp: Black ink stamp "Flaxman Wade Heath England" with impressed "301"

No.	Description	Colourways	Size	U.S.$	Can.$	U.K.£
JU-76	Flaxman 301	Mottled blue	229	80.00	110.00	40.00

SHAPE 302
Flaxman Ware Jugs, 1937-1939

These jugs have a band of slanted ribs around the middle.

Backstamp: Black ink stamp "Flaxman Wade Heath England" with impressed "S302"

No.	Name	Colourways	Size	U.S.$	Can.$	U.K.£
JU-77a	Flaxman 302	Light green	230	80.00	110.00	40.00
JU-77b	Flaxman 302	Mottled blue	230	80.00	110.00	40.00
JU-77c	Flaxman 302	Mottled green/orange	230	80.00	110.00	40.00
JU-77d	Flaxman 302	Mottled yellow	230	80.00	110.00	40.00

SHAPE 334

Flaxman Jug, 1937-1939

Backstamp: Black ink stamp "Flaxman Wade Heath England"

No.	Description	Colourways	Size	U.S.$	Can.$	U.K.£
JU-78	Flaxman 334	Mottled cream/yellow	229	80.00	110.00	40.00

Imperial Series Jug, 1955

These jugs are decorated with large white seed cases highlighted in burnished gold.

Photograph not available
at press time

Backstamp: Circular print "Wade Made in England Hand Painted" and impressed "334"

No.	Description	Colourways	Size	U.S.$	Can.$	U.K.£
JU-79	Imperial 334	Burgundy; white seed; gold highlights	229	80.00	110.00	40.00

SHAPE 371
Jugs, c.1948-c.1952

These jugs are embossed with a flower design on the top and five wavy bands running diagonally across the bottom.

Backstamp: Black ink stamp "Wade England" with impressed "371"

No.	Description	Colourways	Size	U.S.$	Can.$	U.K.£
JU-80a	Shape 371	Dark blue	225	110.00	145.00	55.00
JU-80b	Shape 371	Orange	225	110.00	145.00	55.00
JU-80c	Shape 371	Pale orange	225	110.00	145.00	55.00
JU-80d	Shape 371	Pale blue	225	110.00	145.00	55.00
JU-80e	Shape 371	Dark green	225	110.00	145.00	55.00
JU-80f	Shape 371	Light green	225	110.00	145.00	55.00
JU-80g	Shape 371	Beige	225	110.00	145.00	55.00

SHAPE 401

Empress Jugs, c.1948-1952

Version JU-81a was issued in the late 1940s, JU-81b circa 1950 and versions JU-81c to e in 1952.

Backstamp: **A.** Circular ink stamp "Royal Victoria Pottery Wade England"
B. Black ink stamp "Wade England"
C. Black ink stamp "Wade Empress England" with impressed "401"

No.	Series	Colourways	Size	U.S.$	Can.$	U.K.£
JU-81a	Empress 401	Mottled green	170	80.00	110.00	40.00
JU-81b	Empress 401	White	170	80.00	110.00	40.00
JU-81c	Empress 401	Blue; gold/cream stripes; gold handle	170	130.00	175.00	65.00
JU-81d	Empress 401	Green; gold stripes, handle	170	130.00	175.00	65.00
JU-81e	Empress 401	Maroon; gold stripes, handle	170	130.00	175.00	65.00

Regency Series Jug, 1959-1961

Backstamp: **A.** Red print "Wade England"
B. Black print "Wade England"

No.	Series	Colourways	Size	U.S.$	Can.$	U.K.£
JU-82	Regency 401	White; gold handle, stripes on base	Miniature/110	30.00	40.00	15.00

SHAPE 405 — Jug, c.1948-1953

Backstamp: Black ink stamp "Wade England" with impressed "405"

No.	Description	Colourways	Size	U.S.$	Can.$	U.K.£
JU-83a	Shape 405	Orange; orange/black acorns; green handle, leaves	138	40.00	55.00	20.00
JU-83b	Shape 405	Blue	138	30.00	40.00	15.00
JU-83c	Shape 405	Cream	138	30.00	40.00	15.00
JU-83d	Shape 405	Green	138	30.00	40.00	15.00
JU-83e	Shape 405	Orange	138	30.00	40.00	15.00

SHAPE 406 — Jugs, c.1948-1953

Backstamp: Grey ink stamp "Wade England" with impressed "406"

No.	Description	Colourways	Size	U.S.$	Can.$	U.K.£
JU-84a	Shape 406	Cream; gold flowers	145	40.00	55.00	20.00
JU-84b	Shape 406	Orange; gold flowers	145	40.00	55.00	20.00
JU-84c	Shape 406	Green; gold flowers	145	40.00	55.00	20.00
JU-84d	Shape 406	Cream; pink/yellow flowers	145	40.00	55.00	20.00
JU-84e	Shape 406	Pearlised mauve/yelllow flowers; gold highlights	145	40.00	55.00	20.00
JU-84f	Shape 406	Green	145	30.00	40.00	15.00
JU-84g	Shape 406	Pale orange	145	30.00	40.00	15.00
JU-84h	Shape 406	Blue	145	30.00	40.00	15.00

SHAPE 407

Jugs, c.1948-c.1952

These jugs are embossed with a pebble design, curved diagonal bands and horizontal bands .

Backstamp: Grey ink stamp "Wade England" and impressed "407"

No.	Description	Colourways	Size	U.S.$	Can.$	U.K.£
JU-85a	Shape 407	Cream; gold bands	140	40.00	55.00	20.00
JU-85b	Shape 407	Cream; orange bands	140	40.00	55.00	20.00
JU-85c	Shape 407	Cream; orange/yellow/black bands	140	40.00	55.00	20.00
JU-85d	Shape 407	White; dark green bands	140	40.00	55.00	20.00
JU-85e	Shape 407	Green	140	30.00	40.00	15.00
JU-85f	Shape 407	Blue	140	30.00	40.00	15.00
JU-85g	Shape 407	Yellow	140	30.00	40.00	15.00
JU-85h	Shape 407	Orange	140	30.00	40.00	15.00

Jugs, c.1948-1953

These jugs are the same shape as those above, but without the pebbled finish. There are curved bands on one side.

Photograph not available
at press time

Backstamp: Black ink stamp "Wade England" and impressed "407"

No.	Description	Colourways	Size	U.S.$	Can.$	U.K.£
JU-86a	Shape 407	Beige; orange bands	140	40.00	55.00	20.00
JU-86b	Shape 407	Beige; orange/yellow bands	140	40.00	55.00	20.00
JU-86c	Shape 407	Beige; gold bands	140	40.00	55.00	20.00
JU-86d	Shape 407	Beige	140	40.00	55.00	20.00
JU-86e	Shape 407	Blue	140	30.00	40.00	15.00
JU-86f	Shape 407	Green	140	30.00	40.00	15.00
JU-86g	Shape 407	Orange	140	30.00	40.00	15.00
JU-86h	Shape 407	Yellow	140	30.00	40.00	15.00

SHAPE 411
Gothic Ware Jug, 1953

This jug is embossed with a design of swirling leaves and tulips and is glazed in gloss colours.

Backstamp: A. Black ink stamp "Gothic Wade Heath England" with impressed "411"
B. Gold transfer print "Wade made in England - hand painted - Gothic" with impressed "411"

No.	Description	Colourways	Size	U.S.$	Can.$	U.K.£
JU-87	Gothic 411	Cream; lilac/pink flowers; green/gold leaves	160	101.00	145.00	55.00

SHAPE 433
Harmony Ware Jugs, 1957-c.1962

Backstamp: **A**. Red print "Wade England" with impressed "England" and "433"
B. Red print "Wade England Fern" with impressed "England" and "433"
C. Black print "Wade England Parasol" with impressed "England" and "433"
D. Black print "Wade England" with impressed "England" and "433"
E. Black print "Wade England" and green shooting stars with impressed "England" and "433"
F. Impressed "Wade England" and "433"
G. Impressed "Wade England"

No.	Description	Colourways	Size	U.S.$	Can.$	U.K.£
JU-88a	Harmony 433	White; yellow/red/green flower	150	50.00	70.00	25.00
JU-88b	Harmony 433	White; black/red ferns	150	50.00	70.00	25.00
JU-88c	Harmony 433	White; multi-coloured parasols	150	50.00	70.00	25.00
JU-88d	Harmony 433	White; multi-coloured stars	150	50.00	70.00	25.00
JU-88e	Harmony 433	Black	150	40.00	55.00	20.00
JU-88f	Harmony 433	White	150	40.00	55.00	20.00
JU-88g	Harmony 433	Green	150	40.00	55.00	20.00
JU-88h	Harmony 433	Yellow	150	40.00	55.00	20.00
JU-88i	Harmony 433	Grey; pink inside	150	40.00	55.00	20.00
JU-88j	Harmony 433	Green; peach inside	150	40.00	55.00	20.00

SHAPE 435
Harmony Ware Jugs, 1957-c.1962

Carnival (JU-89a)	Fern (JU-89b)

Backstamp: **A**. Red print "Wade England" with impressed "England" and "435"
B. Red print "Wade England Fern" with impressed "England" and "435"
C. Black print "Wade England Parasol" with impressed "England" and "435"
D. Black print "Wade England" with impressed "England" and "435"
E. Black print "Wade England" and green shooting stars with impressed "England" and "435"
F. Impressed "Wade England" and "435"
G. Impressed "Wade England"

No.	Description	Colourways	Size	U.S.$	Can.$	U.K.£
JU-89a	Carnival	White; yellow/red/green flower	225	80.00	110.00	40.00
JU-89b	Fern	White; black/red ferns	225	80.00	110.00	40.00
JU-89c	Parasols	White; multi-coloured parasols	225	80.00	110.00	40.00
JU-89d	Shooting stars	White; multi-coloured stars	225	80.00	110.00	40.00
JU-89e	Solid colour	Black	225	60.00	80.00	30.00
JU-89f	Solid colour	White	225	60.00	80.00	30.00
JU-89g	Solid colour	Green	225	60.00	80.00	30.00
JU-89h	Solid colour	Yellow	225	60.00	80.00	30.00
JU-89i	Two-tone	Grey; pink inside	225	60.00	80.00	30.00
JU-89j	Two-tone	Green; peach inside	225	60.00	80.00	30.00

SHAPE 436
Harmony Ware Jugs, 1957-c.1962

The mouth of these jugs juts upward.

Photograph not available
at press time

Backstamp: **A**. Red print "Wade England" with impressed "England" and "436"
B. Red print "Wade England Fern" with impressed "England" and "436"
C. Black print "Wade England Parasol" with impressed "England" and "436"
D. Black print "Wade England" with impressed "England" and "436"
E. Black print "Wade England" and green shooting stars with impressed "England" and "436"
F. Impressed "Wade England" and "436"
G. Impressed "Wade England"

No.	Description	Colourways	Size	U.S.$	Can.$	U.K.£
JU-90a	Carnival	White; yellow/red/green flower	177	60.00	80.00	30.00
JU-90b	Fern	White; black/red ferns	177	60.00	80.00	30.00
JU-90c	Parasols	White; multi-coloured parasols	177	60.00	80.00	30.00
JU-90d	Shooting stars	White; multi-coloured stars	177	60.00	80.00	30.00
JU-90e	Solid colour	Black	177	50.00	70.00	25.00
JU-90f	Solid colour	White	177	50.00	70.00	25.00
JU-90g	Solid colour	Green	177	50.00	70.00	25.00
JU-90h	Solid colour	Yellow	177	50.00	70.00	25.00
JU-90i	Two-tone	Grey/pink	177	50.00	70.00	25.00
JU-90j	Two-tone	Green/peach	177	50.00	70.00	25.00

SHAPE 453
Harmony Ware Jugs, 1957-c.1962

Backstamp: **A**. Red print "Wade England" with impressed "England" and "453"
B. Red print "Wade England Fern" with impressed "England" and "453"
C. Black primt "Wade England Parasol" with impressed "England" and "453"
D. Black print "Wade England" with impressed "England" and "453"
E. Black print "Wade England" and green shooting stars with impressed "England" and "453"
F. Impressed "Wade England" and"453"
G. Impressed "Wade England"

No.	Description	Colourways	Size	U.S.$	Can.$	U.K.£
JU-91a	Carnival	White; yellow/red/green flower	Miniature/130	25.00	35.00	12.00
JU-91b	Fern	White; black/red ferns	Miniature/130	25.00	35.00	12.00
JU-91c	Parasols	White; multi-coloured parasols	Miniature/130	25.00	35.00	12.00
JU-91d	Shooting stars	White; multi-coloured stars	Miniature/130	25.00	35.00	12.00
JU-91e	Two-tone	Grey; pink inside	Miniature/130	15.00	20.00	8.00
JU-91f	Two-tone	Green; peach inside	Miniature/130	15.00	20.00	8.00

Souvenir Jugs, c.1958-c.1962

Backstamp: A. Black transfer print "A Dee Cee Souvenir by Wade"
B. Impressed "Wade 453 England" and a blue transfer print "A Desmond Cooper Souvenir by Wade"
C. Impressed "Wade 453 England" and a black transfer print "A Dee Cee Souvenir by Wade"
D. Red transfer print "Wade England"

No.	Description	Colourways	Size	U.S.$	Can.$	U.K.£
JU-92a	Bognor Regis	White; red sail; blue water	130	25.00	35.00	12.00
JU-92b	Cardiff	White; multi-coloured parasols	130	25.00	35.00	12.00
JU-92c	Dunnose cottage, I.W.	White; multi-coloured parasols	130	25.00	35.00	12.00
JU-92d	Eastbourne	White; multi-coloured parasols	130	25.00	35.00	12.00
JU-92e	Jersey	White; multi-coloured parasols	130	25.00	35.00	12.00
JU-92f	New Brunswick map	White; gold rim, handle; multi-coloured map; violet flowers	130	25.00	35.00	15.00
JU-92g	Nova Scotia map	White; gold rim, handle; multi-coloured map; violet flowers	130	25.00	35.00	15.00
JU-92h	Truro	White; red sail; blue water	130	25.00	35.00	12.00

SHAPE 465
Jugs, 1957-c.1962

The Black Frost Series jug was issued from 1957 to c.1962 and the Zamba Series jug was issued in 1957 only.

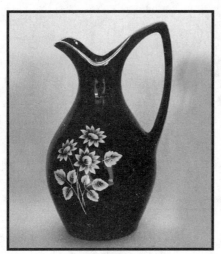
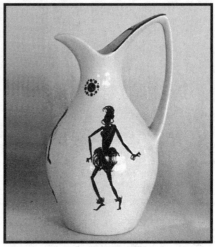

Black Frost (JU-93a)   Zamba (JU-93b)

Backstamp: A. White "Wade England"
B. Red transfer print "Wade England"

No.	Description	Colourways	Size	U.S.$	Can.$	U.K.£
JU-93a	Black Frost 465	Black; white flowers; gold rim	145	50.00	70.00	25.00
JU-93b	Zamba 465	White; black print	145	70.00	95.00	35.00

SHAPE 470
Zamba Series Jug, 1957

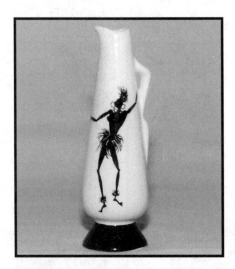

Backstamp: **A.** Red transfer print "Wade England" with impressed "England 470"
           B. Black transfer print "Wade England" with impressed "England 470"

No.	Description	Colourways	Size	U.S.$	Can.$	U.K.£
JU-94	Zamba 470	White; black print	Miniature/124	40.00	55.00	20.00

BIG BAD WOLF AND THE THREE LITTLE PIGS JUGS, 1937-1939

The Big Bad Wolf forms the handle of these cartoon jugs, which can be found with or without a musical box fitted in the base. The jug is hand painted, so no two are identical (for example, the top of the door on the pig's house is square on one jug, rounded on another). The musical jug plays "Whose Afraid of the Big Bad Wolf" or "The Teddy Bear's Picnic."

Musical jug - round door (JU-96a)

Musical jug - square door (JU-96b)

Backstamp: Black hand painted "Wadeheath England"

No.	Description	Colourways	Size	U.S.$	Can.$	U.K.£
JU-95	Jug	Cream/multi-coloured; brown wolf; orange trousers; green braces	245	1,200.00	1,600.00	600.00
JU-96a	Musical jug, round door	Cream/multi-coloured; brown wolf; orange trousers; green braces; round door	260	1,400.00	1,850.00	700.00
JU-96b	Musical jug, square door	Cream/multi-coloured; brown wolf; orange trousers; green braces; square door	260	1,400.00	1,850.00	700.00

FLOWER-HANDLED JUGS, 1934-1935

These jugs have a large embossed seven-petal flower on the top of the handle and three large flowers on the neck. There are embossed leaves and a pebble design in the background.

Backstamp: Black ink stamp "Wadeheath England" with a black lion and a small impressed triangle

No.	Description	Colourways	Size	U.S.$	Can.$	U.K.£
JU-97a	Flower handle	Pale yellow; pale green flowers; pale orange stems	240	110.00	145.00	55.00
JU-97b	Flower handle	Yellow; dark blue/pale blue flowers; brown stems	240	110.00	145.00	55.00
JU-97c	Flower handle	Cream; yellow, brown and orange flowers; green stems	240	110.00	145.00	55.00

GALLERY COLLECTION JUGS, 1995

There were five jug designs in this series: "nouvelle" is an art-deco design with a lily-type flower; the "Japanese garden" features a tall tree with flowers around the base; the "orange grove" consists of large oranges; "sunburst" has large orange marigold-type flowers and the "paradise" design includes a large blue bird with oranges. The price direct from the Wade Shop for versions JU-98a, 98b and 98c was £19.50 and £17.50 for versions JU-98d and 98e.

Nouvelle (JU-98d)

Sunburst (JU-98e)

Backstamp: Black and orange print "The Gallery Collection inspired by original 1930s Wade Heath Designs - Wade made in England" with the pattern name and two red lines, all within a frame composed of elements of the pattern

No.	Description	Colourways	Size	U.S.$	Can.$	U.K.£
JU-98a	Japanese garden	White; blue/green/orange design	180	50.00	70.00	25.00
JU-98b	Orange grove	White; orange/green/black design	180	50.00	70.00	25.00
JU-98c	Paradise	White; blue/orange/green/black design	180	50.00	70.00	25.00
JU-98d	Nouvelle	White; orange/green/yellow/black design	180	50.00	70.00	25.00
JU-98e	Sunburst	White; orange/black design	180	50.00	70.00	25.00

HORSE'S HEAD JUGS, 1935-1937

These jugs were moulded in the shape of a horse's head tilted forward onto its chest.

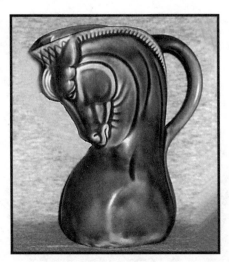

Backstamp: **A.** Black ink stamp "Flaxman Ware Hand Made Pottery by Wadeheath England," 1935-1937
B. Black ink stamp "Flaxman Wade Heath England," 1937

No.	Description	Colourways	Size	U.S.$	Can.$	U.K.£
JU-99a	Horse's head	Blue	100	50.00	70.00	25.00
JU-99b	Horse's head	Green	100	50.00	70.00	25.00
JU-99c	Horse's head	Pale yellow	100	50.00	70.00	25.00
JU-99d	Horse's head	White	100	50.00	70.00	25.00

IMPERIAL SERIES JUGS, 1955

These jugs are decorated with large white seed cases highlighted in burnished gold. The handle of style JU-101 is shaped like the number 3.

Imperial, round foot (JU-100)

Backstamp: Circular print "Wade Made in England Hand Painted"

No.	Description	Colourways	Size	U.S.$	Can.$	U.K.£
JU-100	Round foot	Burgundy; white seed; gold highlights	140	60.00	80.00	30.00
JU-101	3-shaped handle	Burgundy; white seed; gold highlights	140	70.00	95.00	35.00

LEANING JUGS, 1935

The body of these jugs curves inward at the handle, while the mouth juts upward in three steps.

Photograph not available
at press time

Backstamp: Black ink stamp "Flaxman Ware Hand Made Pottery by Wadeheath"

No.	Description	Colourways	Size	U.S.$	Can.$	U.K.£
JU-102a	Leaning	Yellow; orange fruit	160	170.00	225.00	85.00
JU-102b	Leaning	Off white; orange flowers; brown bird; green leaves; blue branch	160	170.00	225.00	85.00

MEDALLION JUGS, c.1948-c.1952

These jugs have flattened sides and are embossed with two circular rows of dots around the edges of each side. They were either hand painted or glazed in matt colours.

Backstamp: Black ink stamp "Wade England"

No.	Description	Colourways	Size	U.S.$	Can.$	U.K.£
JU-103a	Medallion	Cream; brown outline of fawn; orange flowers	Small/125	60.00	80.00	30.00
JU-103b	Medallion	Cream; orange flowers	Small/125	60.00	80.00	30.00
JU-103c	Medallion	Blue	Small/125	50.00	70.00	25.00
JU-103d	Medallion	Cream	Small/125	50.00	70.00	25.00
JU-103e	Medallion	Green	Small/125	50.00	70.00	25.00
JU-104a	Medallion	Copper lustre; yellow barley ears	Medium/153	90.00	120.00	45.00
JU-104b	Medallion	Cream; gold ring	Medium/153	90.00	120.00	45.00
JU-104c	Medallion	Blue	Medium/153	60.00	80.00	30.00
JU-104d	Medallion	Cream	Medium/153	60.00	80.00	30.00
JU-104e	Medallion	Green	Medium/153	60.00	80.00	30.00
JU-105a	Medallion	Copper lustre; yellow barley ears	Large/175	100.00	145.00	55.00
JU-105b	Medallion	Cream; gold ring	Large/175	70.00	95.00	35.00
JU-105c	Medallion	Blue	Large/175	70.00	95.00	35.00
JU-105d	Medallion	Cream	Large/175	70.00	95.00	35.00
JU-105e	Medallion	Green	Large/175	70.00	95.00	35.00

OIL JUGS

South Africa, c.1962

These miniature oil jugs have transfer prints of African animals on the front.

Eland oil jug (JU-106a)

Backstamp: Red transfer print "Wade England"

No.	Description	Colourways	Size	U.S.$	Can.$	U.K.£
JU-106a	Eland	Amber; silver lustre; brown/white print	95	25.00	35.00	12.00
JU-106b	Lion	Amber; silver lustre; multi-coloured print	95	25.00	35.00	12.00
JU-106c	Zebra	Amber; multi- coloured print	95	25.00	35.00	12.00

Souvenirs of London, 1956-c.1962

These oil jugs were decorated with black transfer prints of London landmarks.

Trafalgar Square (JU-107d)

Backstamp: A. Red transfer print "Wade England"
B. Red transfer print "Wade Ireland"

No.	Description	Colourways	Size	U.S.$	Can.$	U.K.£
JU-107a	Big Ben	Amber; silver lustre; black print	95	30.00	40.00	15.00
JU-107b	Eros, Piccadilly Circus	Amber; silver lustre; black print	95	30.00	40.00	15.00
JU-107c	Tower Bridge	Amber; silver lustre; black print	95	30.00	40.00	15.00
JU-107d	Trafalgar Square	Amber; silver lustre; black print	95	30.00	40.00	15.00

Veteran Car Series, c.1958-c.1975

These jugs were produced in the same amber glaze used for the Veteran Car Series tankards and have silver lustre rims, handles and bases. They are decorated on the front with transfer prints of veteran and vintage racing cars and were produced in the Wade England and Wade Ireland potteries. Printed on the base is "Authenticated by the Veteran Car Club of Great Britain."

Ford; series 1 (JU-108c)   Sunbeam; series 2 (JU-108f)

Backstamp: A. Black print "A Moko product by Wade of England"
B. Black print "An RK Product by Wade of Ireland"

Series 1

No.	Description	Colourways	Size	U.S.$	Can.$	U.K.£
JU-108a	Benz	Amber; silver lustre; black print	90	20.00	30.00	10.00
JU-108b	Darracq	Amber; silver lustre; black print	90	20.00	30.00	10.00
JU-108c	Ford	Amber; silver lustre; black print	90	20.00	30.00	10.00

Series 2

No.	Description	Colourways	Size	U.S.$	Can.$	U.K.£
JU-108d	Baby Peugeot	Amber; silver lustre; black print	90	20.00	30.00	10.00
JU-108e	Rolls-Royce	Amber; silver lustre; black print	90	20.00	30.00	10.00
JU-108f	Sunbeam	Amber; silver lustre; black print	90	20.00	30.00	10.00

Series 3

No.	Description	Colourways	Size	U.S.$	Can.$	U.K.£
JU-108g	De Dion Bouton	Amber; silver lustre; black print	90	20.00	30.00	10.00
JU-108h	Lanchester	Amber; silver lustre; black print	90	20.00	30.00	10.00
JU-108i	Spyker	Amber; silver lustre; black print	90	20.00	30.00	10.00

Series 4

No.	Description	Colourways	Size	U.S.$	Can.$	U.K.£
JU-108j	Cadillac	Amber; silver lustre; black print	90	20.00	30.00	10.00
JU-108k	Oldsmobile	Amber; silver lustre; black print	90	20.00	30.00	10.00
JU-108l	White Steam Car	Amber; silver lustre; black print	90	20.00	30.00	10.00

Series 5

No.	Description	Colourways	Size	U.S.$	Can.$	U.K.£
JU-108m	Bugatti	Amber; silver lustre; multi-coloured print	90	20.00	30.00	10.00
JU-108n	Itala	Amber; silver lustre; multi-coloured print	90	20.00	30.00	10.00
JU-108o	Sunbeam, 1914	Amber; silver lustre; multi-coloured print	90	20.00	30.00	10.00

Series 6

No.	Description	Colourways	Size	U.S.$	Can.$	U.K.£
JU-108p	Alfa Romeo	Amber; silver lustre; multi-coloured print	90	20.00	30.00	10.00
JU-108q	Bentley	Amber; silver lustre; multi-coloured print	90	20.00	30.00	10.00
JU-108r	Bugatti, 1927	Amber; silver lustre; multi-coloured print	90	20.00	30.00	10.00

ORCADIA WARE JUGS, 1933-1935

Orcadia Ware was produced in vivid streaked glazes which were allowed to run over the rims and down the inside and outside of the item.

Backstamp: **A.** Orange ink stamp "Wadeheath Orcadia Ware"
B. Black ink stamp "Wadeheath Orcadia Ware British Made"

No.	Description	Colourways	Shape/Size	U.S.$	Can.$	U.K.£
JU-109a	Orcadia	Orange/dark green; grey base	Wide mouth/180	142.00	195.00	75.00
JU-109b	Orcadia	Orange/yellow green; grey-blue base	Wide mouth/180	142.00	195.00	75.00

PINCHED-MOUTH JUGS, 1935-1937

The mouth of these jugs is pinched in at the centre.

Backstamp: Black ink stamp "Wadeheath Ware Regd Shape No. 787794 Made in England"

No.	Description	Colourways	Size	U.S.$	Can.$	U.K.£
JU-110a	Pinched mouth	Cream; orange base, handle; brown/orange flowers	Small/140	120.00	160.00	60.00
JU-110b	Pinched mouth	Cream; brown base; orange handle; brown/orange/blue/greens bands	Small/140	120.00	160.00	60.00
JU-111a	Pinched mouth	Cream; brown neck; cream/brown handle; blue/yelloworange fruit; orange/yellow/blue squares	Medium/185	140.00	185.00	70.00
JU-111b	Pinched mouth	Cream; black base; blue/yellow orange flowers	Medium/185	140.00	185.00	70.00
JU-111c	Pinched mouth	Green; orange drip design	Medium/185	140.00	185.00	70.00
JU-112a	Pinched mouth	Cream; black/orange bands at bottom; cream/orange handle; blue/green/yellow squares; orange/blue balls	Large/205	160.00	215.00	80.00
JU-112b	Pinched mouth	Blue/brown/yellow; orange drip design	Large/205	160.00	215.00	80.00
JU-112c	Pinched mouth	Brown; orange/yellow flowers	Large/205	160.00	215.00	80.00
JU-112d	Pinched mouth	Orange/yellow/brown drip design	Large/205	160.00	215.00	80.00
JU-112e	Pinched mouth	Maroon/green/yellow/orange drip design	Large/205	160.00	215.00	80.00

PLYMOUTH JUG, 1953-c.1962

This jug resembles a wooden keg.

Photograph not available
at press time

Backstamp: Red transfer print "Wade England"

No.	Description	Colourways	Size	U.S.$	Can.$	U.K.£
JU-113	New Brunswick coat of arms	Amber; silver-lustre bands; multi-coloured print	95	15.00	20.00	12.00

PYRAMID JUGS, 1933-1935

These art-deco style jugs are wide at the base and narrow at the top, thus resembling a pyramid. The long straight handle steps in at the bottom of the jug.

Photograph not available
at press time

Backstamp: Black ink stamp "Flaxman Ware Hand Made Pottery by Wadeheath"

No.	Description	Colourways	Size	U.S.$	Can.$	U.K.£
JU-114a	Pyramid	White; royal blue spout, handle; royal blue/gold centre panel	215	160.00	215.00	80.00
JU-114b	Pyramid	Green; orange spout, handle; pink rose; cream centre panel	215	160.00	215.00	80.00

SCALLOPED, WIDE-MOUTH JUGS, 1933-c.1940

The rim of these jugs is scalloped, and they have a round curved-edge foot.

Six-panel neck, Eros (JU-116a)   Smooth neck (JU-117a)

Six-panel Neck, Eros

Backstamp: Red ink stamp "Wadeheath England" with a lion

No.	Description	Colourways	Size	U.S.$	Can.$	U.K.£
JU-115	Eros	Yellow; blue rim, base; large purple/blue flowers	Small/165	90.00	120.00	45.00
JU-116a	Eros	Cream; black rim, base; large orange leaves	Medium/190	90.00	120.00	45.00
JU-116b	Eros	Grey-green; green handle, base; large orange flowers	Medium/190	90.00	120.00	45.00
JU-116c	Eros	Cream; royal blue handle, leaves; gold/orange wavy lines	Medium/190	90.00	120.00	45.00

Smooth Neck

Backstamp: Red ink stamp "Wadeheath England" with a lion

No.	Description	Colourways	Size	U.S.$	Can.$	U.K.£
JU-117a	Smooth neck	Cream; black base; large orange leaves; grey/black flowers	Medium/190	90.00	120.00	45.00
JU-117b	Smooth neck	Cream; large orange/yellow/blue flowers green leaves	Medium/190	90.00	120.00	45.00

SNOW WHITE AND THE SEVEN DWARFS JUG, 1938

This musical jug has Snow White and the Seven Dwarfs moulded around the front with the dwarfs' cottage on the back. A squirrel and a pair of bluebirds sit on the handle. Two tunes have been reported, "Whistle While You Work" and "Someday My Prince Will Come."

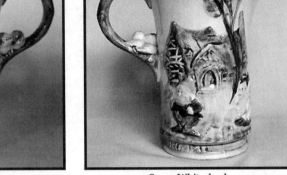

Snow White, face   Snow White, back

Backstamp: Black ink stamp "Wade Heath England"

No.	Description	Colourways	Size	U.S.$	Can.$	U.K.£
JU-118	Snow White	Cream; multi-coloured figures	225	1,200.00	1,600.00	600.00

VICTORIAN WATER JUG AND BOWL

This set was created in the style of a Victorian water jug and wash basin.

Backstamp: Red print "Wade England" with two red lines

No.	Name	Colourways	Size	U.S.$	Can.$	U.K.£
JU-119a	Floral fayre	White; pink/green print	153	25.00	35.00	12.00
JU-119b	Fuchsia	White; pink/yellow/grey print	153	25.00	35.00	12.00

WIDE-MOUTH JUGS, 1933-1934

These jugs are similar to the woodpecker jug, shape 13.

Wide-mouth jug (JU-120a)

Wide-mouth jug (JU-120b)

Backstamp: Red ink stamp "Wadeheath England" with a lion

No.	Description	Colourways	Size	U.S.$	Can.$	U.K.£
JU-120a	Wide mouth	Cream; brown rim; cream/brown base; large orange/ yellow/purple fruit; green leaves	180	90.00	120.00	45.00
JU-120b	Wide mouth	Cream; cream/brown base; large orange/yellow/ blue fruit; small orange/brown/blue squares	180	90.00	120.00	45.00

ZEBRA-STRIPED JUGS, 1955

Squat jug (JU-121)

3-shaped handle (JU-122)

Backstamp: Circular transfer print "Royal Victoria Pottery Wade England"

No.	Description	Colourways	Size	U.S.$	Can.$	U.K.£
JU-121	Squat jug	Bright yellow/black stripes	140	70.00	95.00	35.00
JU-122a	3-shaped handle	Blue/black stripes	140	70.00	95.00	35.00
JU-122b	3-shaped handle	Bright yellow/black stripes	140	70.00	95.00	35.00

Empress

404

402

400

401

403

A range of outstanding ornamental pieces; the classical shapes
are decorated in Regency style with rich underglaze colours and
burnished gold finish.

LAMPS
1959-1995

The majority of Wade lamps were produced from 1991 to 1995 for sale in British department stores. They are listed here in alphabetical order.

BACKSTAMPS

Transfer Prints

All the known backstamps on Wade lamps are transfer prints. They were used from 1959 to 1995. The many series of lamps that were produced from 1991 to 1995 are all marked with a gold "Wade" transfer print.

BARREL LAMP, c.1962

Backstamp: Red transfer print "Wade England"

No.	Description	Colourways	Size	U.S.$	Can.$	U.K.£
LA-1	Barrel	Amber; silver bands	Unknown	50.00	70.00	25.00

BUTTERFLY LAMPS, 1991

These rectangular lamps have a decorative band around the top and base and were produced with a wooden plinth.

Butterfly and flowers (LA-2a)   Butterfly, swallow and flowers (LA-2b)

Backstamp: Unknown

No.	Description	Colourways	Size	U.S.$	Can.$	U.K.£
LA-2a	Butterfly and flowers	White; yellow/white/green butterfly; multi-coloured flowers	405	80.00	110.00	40.00
LA-2b	Butterfly, swallow and flowers	White; blue butterfly, bird, flowers	405	80.00	110.00	40.00

EMPRESS LAMP, c.1953-c.1955

Backstamp: Transfer print "Wade 'Empress' England" inside a scalloped frame

No.	Description	Colourways	Size	U.S.$	Can.$	U.K.£
LA-3	Empress	Maroon; gold/ white stripes	220	130.00	175.00	65.00

ENGLISH BOUQUET LAMPS, 1991-1995

These lamps are fitted with a brass lampholder and riser and a gold cable. They are banded in 24-karat gold and sit on a hardwood plinth.

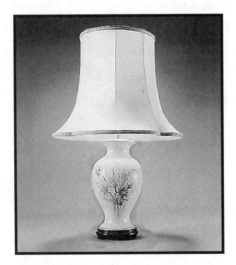

Backstamp: Gold transfer print "Wade"

No.	Description	Colourways	Size	U.S.$	Can.$	U.K.£
LA-4	English bouquet	White; gold bands; pale pink/blue/beige flowers	Small/355	80.00	110.00	40.00
LA-5	English bouquet	White; gold bands; pale pink/blue/beige flowers	Medium/405	100.00	135.00	50.00
LA-6	English bouquet	White; gold bands; pale pink/blue/beige flowers	Large/455	110.00	145.00	55.00

GILBEY'S GIN WINE BARREL LAMPS, 1959-1961

These lamps were made from Gilbey's Gin wine barrels, which had the name of a different spirit printed on the front. A lamp kit and five Gilbey lamp shades were first sold at the Ideal Home Exhibition in London in March 1959 and went on sale to the general public the next month.

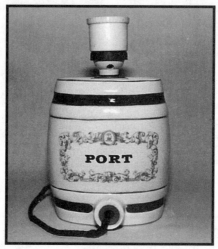

Port (LA-7b)

Backstamp: Transfer print "Royal Victoria Pottery, Wade England"

No.	Description	Colourways	Size	U.S.$	Can.$	U.K.£
LA-7a	Gin	White; gold/blue bands; grey border; black lettering	Half bottle/115	40.00	55.00	20.00
LA-7b	Port	White; gold/maroon bands; grey border; black lettering	Half bottle/115	40.00	55.00	20.00
LA-7c	Scotch	White; gold/red bands; brown border; black lettering	Half bottle/115	40.00	55.00	20.00
LA-7d	Sherry	White; gold/green bands; brown border; black lettering	Half bottle/115	40.00	55.00	20.00
LA-8	Cognac	Black; gold bands, frame, lettering	Quart/133	50.00	70.00	25.00

HANA LAMPS, 1991-1995

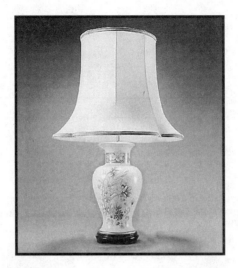

Backstamp: Gold transfer print "Wade"

No.	Description	Colourways	Size	U.S.$	Can.$	U.K.£
LA-9	Hana	White; mauve band; gold bands; multi-coloured flowers	Small/355	90.00	120.00	45.00
LA-10	Hana	White; mauve band; gold bands; multi-coloured flowers	Medium/405	110.00	145.00	55.00
LA-11	Hana	White; mauve band; gold bands; multi-coloured flowers	Large/455	120.00	160.00	60.00

JACOBEAN LAMPS, 1991-1995

Backstamp: Gold transfer print "Wade"

No.	Description	Colourways	Size	U.S.$	Can.$	U.K.£
LA-12	Jacobean	White; gold bands; rust/black flowers	Small/355	110.00	145.00	55.00
LA-13	Jacobean	White; gold bands; rust/black flowers	Medium/405	120.00	160.00	60.00
LA-14	Jacobean	White; gold bands; rust/black flowers	Large/455	140.00	185.00	70.00

KAWA LAMPS, 1991-1995

These lamps are shaped like an oriental ginger jar and are decorated with large peonies and bamboo leaves. They are part of a giftware line that was all decorated in this style.

Photograph not available
at press time

Backstamp: Unknown

No.	Description	Colourways	Size	U.S.$	Can.$	U.K.£
LA-15	Kawa	White; pale pink flowers; pale green bamboo	Miniature/305	110.00	145.00	55.00
LA-16	Kawa	White; pale pink flowers; pale green bamboo	Small/355	120.00	160.00	60.00
LA-17	Kawa	White; pale pink flowers; pale green bamboo	Medium/405	140.00	185.00	70.00

KO-EDA LAMPS, 1991-1995

These oriental-style lamps were produced in a craquelle glaze of pale blue or mushroom and are decorated with small flowers and a medallion design around the rim and base, as well as two bands of 24-karat gold. They are fitted with a brass lampholder and riser and a gold cable and sit on a hardwood plinth.

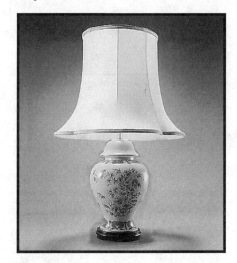

Backstamp: Gold transfer print "Wade"

No.	Description	Colourways	Size	U.S.$	Can.$	U.K.£
LA-18a	Ko-eda	Pale blue; pastel pink/blue flowers;	Small/355	110.00	145.00	55.00
LA-18b	Ko-eda	Mushroom; pastel pink/blue flowers; gold medallions	Small/355	110.00	145.00	55.00
LA-19a	Ko-eda	Pale blue; pastel pink/blue flowers; gold medallions	Medium/405	120.00	160.00	60.00
LA-19b	Ko-eda	Mushroom; pastel pink/blue flowers; gold medallions	Medium/405	120.00	160.00	60.00
LA-20a	Ko-eda	Pale blue; pastel pink/blue flowers; gold medallions	Large/455	140.00	185.00	70.00
LA-20b	Ko-eda	Mushroom; pastel pink/blue flowers; gold medallions	Large/455	140.00	185.00	70.00

MARIKO LAMPS, 1991-1995

These oriental-style lamps were produced in a craquelle glaze of pale blue or mushroom and are decorated with peonies and a floral band around the neck and base, as well as two bands of 24-karat gold. They are fitted with a brass lampholder and riser and a gold cable and sit on a hardwood plinth.

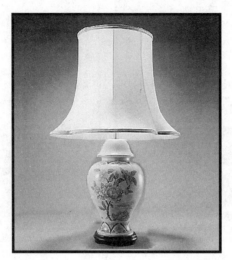

Backstamp: Gold transfer print "Wade"

No.	Description	Colourways	Size	U.S.$	Can.$	U.K.£
LA-21a	Mariko	Pale blue; pale pink/yellow peonies; blue/yellow band	Small/355	110.00	145.00	55.00
LA-21b	Mariko	Mushroom; pale pink/yellow peonies; blue/yellow band	Small/355	110.00	145.00	55.00
LA-22a	Mariko	Pale blue; pale pink/yellow peonies; blue/yellow band	Medium/405	120.00	160.00	60.00
LA-22b	Mariko	Mushroom; pale pink/yellow peonies; blue/yellow band	Medium/405	120.00	160.00	60.00
LA-23a	Mariko	Pale blue; pale pink/yellow peonies; blue/yellow band	Large/455	140.00	185.00	70.00
LA-23b	Mariko	Mushroom; pale pink/yellow peonies; blue/yellow band	Large/455	140.00	185.00	70.00

VINTAGE CARS LAMP

The base of this tubular-shaped lamp is decorated with transfer prints of Rolls-Royce, Ford and Morris vintage cars.

Vintage cars lamp, face   Vintage cars lamp, back

Backstamp: Red transfer print "Wade England"

No.	Description	Colourways	Size	U.S.$	Can.$	U.K.£
LA-24	Vintage cars	White/black; multi-coloured prints	165	70.00	95.00	35.00

ZAKURO LAMPS, 1991-1995

These lamps were produced in a mushroom craquelle glaze and are decorated with flowers and seed pods, with a floral band around the neck, as well as two bands of 24-karat gold. They are fitted with a brass lampholder and riser and a gold cable and sit on a hardwood plinth.

Backstamp: Gold transfer print "Wade"

No.	Description	Colourways	Size	U.S.$	Can.$	U.K.£
LA-25	Zakuro	Mushroom; pale yellow/pink flowers; blue/green leaves; gold/blue band	Small/355	110.00	145.00	55.00
LA-26	Zakuro	Mushroom; pale yellow flowers; blue/green leaves; gold/blue band	Medium/405	120.00	160.00	60.00
LA-27	Zakuro	Mushroom; pale yellow flowers; blue/green leaves; gold/blue band	Large/455	140.00	185.00	70.00

EXECUTIVE DESK SET
IN HIGH QUALITY CERAMIC BY WADE

MANUFACTURERS SINCE 1810

Available: Desk Tidy, Pencil Holder, Letter Rack, Ink Well, Trinket Box, Ash Tray, Bosuns Decanter, Half Pint Tankard.

MISCELLANEOUS DECORATIVE WARE c.1955-1993

The items in this section vary from clocks to photo frames to brooches to bells. The potteries in England and Ireland are represented here. The items are listed in alphabetical order.

BACKSTAMPS

Impressed Backstamps

Wade Ireland used impressed backstamps on its ink stand, produced in the mid 1950s , and in 1962 on its rhinoceros decanter.

Transfer Prints

Wade used transfer-printed backstamps on a variety of miscellaneous items from the late 1950s to 1992.

Embossed Backstamps

Embossed backstamps appear on the 1962 Wade Ireland rhinoceros decanter and on the Romance Series photo frames and pomanders, produced from 1983 to 1985.

BELLS OF IRELAND, 1983-1986

These seven porcelain bells are decorated on the front with transfer prints, mostly of Irish scenes.

Backstamp: Unknown
Shape No.: SR03

No.	Description	Colourways	Shape No./Size	U.S.$	Can.$	U.K.£
MD-1a	Blarney Castle	White; gold bands; multi-coloured print	SR03/1/146	60.00	80.00	30.00
MD-1b	Bunratty Castle	White; gold bands; multi-coloured print	SR03/3/146	60.00	80.00	30.00
MD-1c	Christmas tree	White; gold bands; multi-coloured print	SR03/7/146	50.00	70.00	25.00
MD-1d	Ross Castle	White; gold bands; multi-coloured print	SR03/2/146	60.00	80.00	30.00
MD-1e	Shamrocks	White; gold bands; green shamrocks	SR03/5/146	50.00	70.00	25.00
MD-1f	Spinning wheel	White; gold bands; multi-coloured print	SR03/4/146	60.00	80.00	30.00
MD-1g	Thatched cottage	White; gold bands; multi-coloured print	SR03/8/146	60.00	80.00	30.00

EXECUTIVE DESK SET, 1993

These items were part of an eight-piece executive desk set produced by Wade for companies to present to their clients. They have a stylized lily emblem in the centre of each item. The inkwell is similar in shape to the Pusser's miniature rum jug.

For an illustration of
these items see page 198

Backstamp: Unknown

No.	Description	Colourways	Size	U.S.$	Can.$	U.K.£
MD-2	Desk tidy	Black; gold edge, emblem	Unknown		Unknown	
MD-3	Inkwell	Black; gold edge, emblem	63		Unknown	
MD-4	Letter rack	Black; gold edge, emblem	100		Unknown	
MD-5	Pencil holder pot	Black; gold edge, emblem	100		Unknown	

GOLD-LUSTRE MINIATURES, c.1962

Backstamp: Black transfer print "Wade England"

No.	Description	Colourways	Size	U.S.$	Can.$	U.K.£
MD-6	Coal scuttle	Gold	90	25.00	35.00	12.00
MD-7	Coal box	Gold	45	25.00	35.00	12.00
MD-8	Flagon	Gold	90	25.00	35.00	12.00
MD-9	Oil jug	Gold	90	25.00	35.00	12.00

INK STAND, c.1955

This small rectangular ink stand from Wade Ireland has an embossed design of shamrocks on it. It includes a round lid and two grooves for pens.

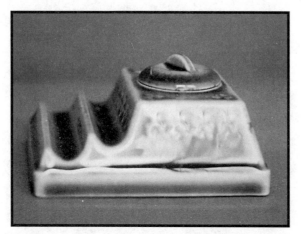

Backstamp: Impressed "Irish Porcelain" curved over a shamrock leaf with "Made in Ireland" in a straight line underneath

No.	Description	Colourways	Size	U.S.$	Can.$	U.K.£
MD-10	Ink stand	Blue-grey	55	50.00	70.00	25.00

JACOBEAN AND KAWA CLOCK, 1990-1992

The Jacobean design is of enamelled exotic flowers and kawa is a Japanese design of peonies and bamboo stems.

Kawa clock

Backstamp: **A.** Red transfer print "Wade England" with two red lines and "Jacobean"
B. Gold transfer print "Wade England" with two gold lines and "Kawa"

No.	Description	Colourways	Size	U.S.$	Can.$	U.K.£
MD-11a	Jacobean	White; red/black print, clock face	160	50.00	70.00	25.00
MD-11b	Kawa	White; pastel pink/green print; gold highlights, clock face	160	50.00	70.00	25.00

PHOTOGRAPH FRAME, 1986-1990

This rectangular frame has a curved top rim.

Photograph not available
at press time

Backstamp: Red "Wade England" with two red lines

No.	Description	Colourways	Size	U.S.$	Can.$	U.K.£
MD-12a	Floral fayre	White; pink/green print	140	25.00	35.00	12.00
MD-12b	Fuchsia	White; pink/yellow/grey print	140	25.00	35.00	12.00

RHINOCEROS DECANTERS, 1962

These are novelty models of a comic rhinoceros with a wide-open mouth. A design fault (especially prominant in the large version, with its front toes curled upward) causes them to be top heavy, and they topple over unless filled with liquid or sand to keep them upright. They have a black stopper in the hole in the base, which has "Chekaleke Regd No 698795" and "14" impressed in it.

Backstamp: **A.** Embossed "Irish Porcelain Made in Ireland" in an Irish knot oval frame
B. Impressed "Irish Porcelain Made in Ireland" with a shamrock leaf

No.	Description	Colourways	Size	U.S.$	Can.$	U.K.£
MD-13	Rhinoceros	Blue/grey/green	Small/140	120.00	160.00	60.00
MD-14	Rhinoceros	Blue/grey/green	Large/220	170.00	225.00	85.00

ROMANCE SERIES PHOTO FRAMES AND POMANDERS, 1983-1985

The Romance Series is decorated with embossed flowers and leaves and, on the rectangular photograph frames, a butterfly. These items are difficult to find. The original price for the small rectangular frame was £3.99 and the large frame was £4.99. The heart-shaped frames originally sold for £4.50.

The round pomander has a mottled glaze on the top, with fluted ribs around the body and lid. It was sold with a sachet of herbs or lavender. The top of the lid, which is embossed with a pebbled design, has vents in it to allow the scent to escape. The original price was £2.50.

Backstamp: Raised "Wade Made in England"

No.	Description	Colourways	Size	U.S.$	Can.$	U.K.£
MD-15a	Frame	Fawn; grey/yellow/white flowers	Rectangular/142	60.00	80.00	30.00
MD-15b	Frame	Cream; blue/grey/fawn flowers	Rectangular/142	60.00	80.00	30.00
MD-16a	Frame	Fawn; grey/yellow/white flowers	Rectangular/170	70.00	95.00	35.00
MD-16b	Frame	Cream; blue/grey/fawn flowers	Rectangular/170	70.00	95.00	35.00
MD-17a	Frame	Fawn; grey/yellow/white flowers	Heart/150	80.00	110.00	40.00
MD-17b	Frame	Cream; blue/grey/fawn flowers	Heart/150	80.00	110.00	40.00
MD-18a	Pomander	Mottled grey/yellow/white top; fawn bottom	Round/52	25.00	35.00	12.00
MD-18b	Pomander	Mottled blue/grey/fawn top; cream bottom	Round/52	25.00	35.00	12.00

TEENAGE GUITAR BROOCHES, 1960

First issued in August 1960, this set of brooches depict the British teenage heart throbs of the time. For matching cameo plaques, see Plaques; for matching heart-shaped caskets, see Boxes.

Backstamp: Black print "Wade Porcelain Made in England"

No.	Description	Colourways	Size	U.S.$	Can.$	U.K.£
MD-19a	Cliff Richard	White; multi-coloured portrait; gold trim	60		Rare	
MD-19b	Frankie Vaughan	White; multi-coloured portrait; gold trim	60		Rare	
MD-19c	Marty Wilde	White; multi-coloured portrait; gold trim	60		Rare	
MD-19d	Tommy Steele	White; multi-coloured portrait; gold trim	60		Rare	

VETERAN CAR MINIATURE OIL FUNNEL, c.1958

A small quantity of miniature oil funnels were produced in the Veteran Car Series during the late 1950s. They are in the same amber glaze as the oil jugs. They are decorated with transfer prints of veteran cars.

Backstamp: A. Black print "A Moko product by Wade of England"
B. Black print "An RK Product by Wade of Ireland

Series 1

No.	Description	Colourways	Size	U.S.$	Can.$	U.K.£
MD-20a	Benz	Amber; silver lustre; black print	92	30.00	40.00	15.00
MD-20b	Darracq	Amber; silver lustre; black print	92	30.00	40.00	15.00
MD-20c	Ford	Amber; silver lustre; black print	92	30.00	40.00	15.00

Series 2

No.	Description	Colourways	Size	U.S.$	Can.$	U.K.£
MD-20d	Baby Peugeot	Amber; silver lustre; black print	92	30.00	40.00	15.00
MD-20e	Rolls-Royce, 1907	Amber; silver lustre; black print	92	30.00	40.00	15.00
MD-20f	Sunbeam	Amber; silver lustre; black print	92	30.00	40.00	15.00

Series 3

No.	Description	Colourways	Size	U.S.$	Can.$	U.K.£
MD-20g	De Dion Bouton	Amber; silver lustre; black print	92	30.00	40.00	15.00
MD-20h	Lanchester	Amber; silver lustre; black print	92	30.00	40.00	15.00
MD-20i	Spyker	Amber; silver lustre; black print	92	30.00	40.00	15.00

WADE (IRELAND) LTD

ONE OF THE WADE GROUP

Registered Office:

WATSON STREET
PORTADOWN
CO. ARMAGH BT 63 5AH
NORTHERN IRELAND

TELEPHONE:
(0762) 332288
TELEX: 747128

SHAMROCK RANGE
1. SR09 Bud Vase
3. SR11 Oval Vase

2. SR10 Round Vase
5. SR19 Shamrock Urn

SHEET S4

4. SR20 Shamrock Cooking Pot

PLANTERS AND FLOWER POTS
1935-1992

Most of these planters and flower pots were made in England, although a couple were produced at Wade Ireland beginning in the 1950s. Several items were part of a series that included matching bowls, dishes or vases. They are listed in alphabetical order.

BACKSTAMPS

Ink Stamps

From 1935 to 1937, Wade Heath used an ink stamp on its Flaxman Ware tulip planter. From the mid 1950s to the 1980s, Wade Ireland used an ink stamp on some of its jardinieres.

Impressed Backstamps

Wade Ireland used impressed backstamps on its flower pot holder and on some of its jardinieres, from the early 1950s to the 1980s.

Embossed Backstamp

As well as using ink stamps and impressed backstamps, Wade Ireland also put an embossed backstamp on some of its jardinieres.

Transfer Prints

Most of the items in this section were marked with a transfer-printed backstamp. They were used from 1957 to 1992.

BLACK FROST SERIES FLOWER POT AND WATER TRAY, 1957-c.1962

Backstamp: Red or white transfer print "Wade England"

No.	Description	Colourways	Size	U.S.$	Can.$	U.K.£
PF-1	Black Frost	Black; white flowers; gold rim	60 x 65	20.00	28.00	8.00

CLEMENTINE, DAUPHINE AND PLAIN PLANTERS, 1986-1988

The Clementine design consists of flowers and leaves; the Dauphine design is of orchids.

Photograph not available
at press time

Backstamp: Red transfer print "Wade England" with two red lines

No.	Description	Colourways	Size	U.S.$	Can.$	U.K.£
PF-2a	Clementine	White; pale pink/grey print	Small/88	13.00	18.00	5.00
PF-2b	Dauphine	White; cream/yellow print	Small/88	13.00	18.00	5.00
PF-2c	Plain	White	Small/88	13.00	18.00	5.00
PF-3a	Clementine	White; pale pink/grey print	Medium/108	20.00	28.00	8.00
PF-3b	Dauphine	White; cream/yellow print	Medium/108	20.00	28.00	8.00
PF-3c	Plain	White	Medium/108	20.00	28.00	8.00
PF-4a	Clementine	White; pale pink/grey print	Large/127	25.00	35.00	10.00
PF-4b	Dauphine	White; cream/yellow print	Large/127	25.00	35.00	10.00
PF-4c	Plain	White	Large/127	25.00	35.00	10.00

EDWARDIAN PLANTERS

The floral fayre design consists of small pink flowers; the fushia design is of fushias and leaves. These planters have two handles.

Fushia planters

Backstamp: Red transfer print "Wade England" with two red lines

No.	Description	Colourways	Size	U.S.$	Can.$	U.K.£
PF-5a	Floral fayre	White; pink/green print	Small/88	20.00	30.00	10.00
PF-5b	Fuchsia	White; pink/yellow/grey print	Small/88	20.00	30.00	10.00
PF-6a	Floral fayre	White; pink/green print	Medium/108	40.00	55.00	20.00
PF-6b	Fuchsia	White; pink/yellow/grey print	Medium/108	40.00	55.00	20.00
PF-7a	Floral fayre	White; pink/green print	Large/127	40.00	55.00	20.00
PF-7b	Fuchsia	White; pink/yellow/grey print	Large/127	40.00	55.00	20.00

FLOWER POTS, c.1958–c.1962

These flower pots were produced by the Wade Heath Pottery and could be purchased with a matching water tray. Styles PF-8, PF-10 and PF-12 are footed pots.

Backstamp: Red transfer print "Wade England"

No.	Description	Colourways	Shape/Size	U.S.$	Can.$	U.K.£
PF-8a	Cherry blossom	White; pink flowers; pink inside	Small, footed/67	10.00	15.00	5.00
PF-8b	Ivy	White; light/dark green; black inside	Small, footed/67	10.00	15.00	5.00
PF-9a	Banded	Unknown	Small/67	10.00	15.00	5.00
PF-9b	Bella Donna	White; green/yellow leaves; red berries; yellow inside	Small/67	10.00	15.00	5.00
PF-9c	Bella Donna	White; green/yellow leaves; red berries; red inside	Small/67	10.00	15.00	5.00
PF-9d	Bella Donna	White; green/yellow leaves; red berries; black inside	Small/67	10.00	15.00	5.00
PF-9e	Etched	Unknown	Small/67	10.00	15.00	5.00
PF-9f	White rose	Black; white rose; pink inside	Small/67	10.00	15.00	5.00
PF-10	Cherry blossom	White; pink flowers; pink inside	Medium, footed/108	20.00	30.00	10.00
PF-11a	Banded	Unknown	Medium/108	20.00	30.00	10.00
PF-11b	Bella Donna	White; green/yellow leaves; red berries; green inside	Medium/108	10.00	15.00	5.00
PF-11c	Etched	Unknown	Medium/108	25.00	35.00	12.00
PF-11d	Virginia creeper	White; green/white vine; green inside	Medium/108	25.00	35.00	12.00
PF-11e	White rose	Black; white rose; pink inside	Medium/108	25.00	35.00	12.00
PF-12a	Cherry blossom	White; pink flowers; pink inside	Large, footed/133	25.00	35.00	12.00
PF-12b	Ivy	White; light/dark green; black inside	Large, footed/133	25.00	35.00	12.00
PF-13a	Etched	Unknown	Large/133	25.00	35.00	12.00
PF-13b	Virginia creeper	White; green/white vine; green inside	Large/133	25.00	35.00	12.00
PF-13c	White rose	Black; white rose; pink inside	Large/133	25.00	35.00	12.00

IRISH PORCELAIN FLOWER POT HOLDER, c.1952-1979

This flower pot holder has five rows of knurls and shamrock leaves on it. It was reissued in the 1970s and discontinued in 1979.

Backstamp: Impressed "Irish Porcelain" curved over a shamrock with "Made in Ireland" impressed in a straight line underneath
Shape No.: I.P.37

No.	Description	Colourways	Size	U.S.$	Can.$	U.K.£
PF-14	Shape I.P.37	Brown/blue	101	40.00	55.00	20.00

JACOBEAN AND KAWA PLANTERS, 1990-1992

The Jacobean design consists of enamelled exotic flowers, and Kawa is a Japanese design of peonies and bamboo stems.

Photograph not available
at press time

Backstamp: A. Red "Wade England" with two red lines and "Jacobean"
B. Gold "Wade England" with two gold lines and "Kawa"

No.	Description	Colourways	Size	U.S.$	Can.$	U.K.£
PF-15a	Jacobean	White; enamelled red/black print	Small/88	30.00	40.00	15.00
PF-15b	Kawa	White; pastel pink/green print; gold highlights	Small/88	30.00	40.00	15.00
PF-16a	Jacobean	White; enamelled red/black print	Medium/108	40.00	55.00	20.00
PF-16b	Kawa	White; pastel pink/green print; gold highlights	Medium/108	40.00	55.00	20.00
PF-17a	Jacobean	White; enamelled red/black print	Large/127	50.00	70.00	25.00
PF-17b	Kawa	White; pastel pink/green print; gold highlights	Large/127	50.00	70.00	25.00

JARDINIERES, c.1955–c.1985

These two-handled jardinieres have an embossed design of raindrops around the bottom of the oval bowl. They originally came packaged in a brown cardboard box with a green label that reads "Irish Porcelain Created by Wade of Ireland." They were first issued in the mid 1950s, then again in the 1970s and 1980s.

Backstamp: **A.** Impressed "Irish Porcelain" over a shamrock and "Wade Co Armagh" impressed underneath
B. Embossed "Irish Porcelain" over a small shamrock with embossed "Made in Ireland," all inside a wreath of Irish knots
C. Black ink stamp "Irish Porcelain" over a shamrock with black ink stamp "Made in Ireland" underneath
Shape No.: C.302

No.	Description	Colourways	Size	U.S.$	Can.$	U.K.£
PF-18	Shape C.302	Grey/blue/green	Small/65	20.00	30.00	10.00
PF-19	Shape C.302	Grey/blue/green	Large/100	30.00	40.00	15.00

ROSE TRELLIS PLANTER

Backstamp: Red transfer print "Wade England" with two red lines

No.	Description	Colourways	Size	U.S.$	Can.$	U.K.£
PF-20	Rose trellis	White; dark pink/green print	Small/88	20.00	30.00	10.00
PF-21	Rose trellis	White; dark pink/green print	Medium/108	20.00	30.00	10.00
PF-22	Rose trellis	White; dark pink/green print	Large/127	30.00	40.00	15.00

TULIP PLANTER, 1935-1937

This rectangular planter is embossed with tulips and leaves, which form the top rim.

Photograph not available
at press time

Backstamp: Black ink stamp "Flaxman Ware Hand Made Pottery by Wadeheath England," 1935-1937

No.	Description	Colourways	Size	U.S.$	Can.$	U.K.£
PF-23	Tulip planter	Mottled green/orange	115 x 255	150.00	200.00	75.00

VENETIAN FLOWER POTS, c.1958-c.1962

These pots have a fluted rib design running down the outside of the pot.

Photograph not available
at press time

Backstamp: Red transfer print "Wade England"

No.	Description	Colourways	Size	U.S.$	Can.$	U.K.£
PF-24	Venetian	Black; red inside	Small/67	20.00	30.00	10.00
PF-25	Venetian	Black; red inside	Medium/108	20.00	30.00	10.00
PF-26	Venetian	Black; grey inside	Large/133	30.00	40.00	15.00

PLAQUES AND WALL DECORATIONS
1935-1993

The earliest plaques and wall decorations were made by Wade Heath in the 1930s, followed by Gothic Ware wall pockets and by wall masks. In the 1940s Wade produced Regency and Romance wall plates and Harvest Ware Peony Series wall plaques. Beginning in the 1950s, transfer prints were commonly used to decorate plaques and wall decorations.

This section is divided into plaques, wall masks, wall plates and wall pockets. The items are listed in alphabetical order.

BACKSTAMPS

Ink Stamps

Transfer Prints

Wade Heath wall decorations were marked with black and green ink stamps from 1935 until circa 1940. Items from Wade Ireland can be found with ink stamps from 1960 until 1964.

From 1953 to 1991, most plaques and wall decorations were marked with transfer-printed backstamps.

Embossed Backstamps

Beginning in 1958 the exotic fish wall plaques were marked with embossed backstamp. In 1960 embossed backstamps from Wade England and Wade Ireland were used on the yacht wall plaques.

PLAQUES

BOTTLES AND JARS WALL PLAQUE, 1963-1964

This was produced at the same time as the pearlstone plaques, but made to look like carved wood. It has a contemporary design of glass bottles and jars.

Photograph not available at press time

Backstamp: Black ink stamp "Made in Ireland by Wade Co Armagh"

No.	Description	Colourways	Size	U.S.$	Can.$	U.K.£
PW-1	Bottles and jars	Brown; red/green/blue/orange jars	380 x 245	120.00	165.00	60.00

EXOTIC FISH WALL PLAQUES, 1958-1959

Backstamp: Embossed "Wade Porcelain Made in England"

No.	Description	Colourways	Size	U.S.$	Can.$	U.K.£
PW-2a	Tropical fish	Pink head; white/yellow body; green tail	65 x 95		Rare	
PW-2b	Tropical fish	Green head; white/pink body; yellow tail	65 x 95		Rare	
PW-2c	Tropical fish	Blue head; white/orange body; pink tail	65 x 95		Rare	
PW-2d	Tropical fish	Green head; white/maroon body; yellow tail	65 x 95		Rare	
PW-2e	Tropical fish	Green head; white/maroon body; pink tail	65 x 95		Rare	
PW-2f	Tropical fish	Green head; white/pink body; yellow tail	65 x 95		Rare	
PW-2g	Tropical fish	Green head; green/pink body; yellow tail	65 x 95		Rare	
PW-2h	Tropical fish	Grey head; white/pink body; green tail	65 x 95		Rare	

IRELAND PLAQUES, c.1960

This series of square wall plaques was produced by Wade Ireland with multi-coloured transfer prints of typical Irish scenes.

Photograph not available at press time

Backstamp: **A.** Black ink stamp "Irish Porcelain Wade County Armagh" with a shamrock leaf
B. Unmarked

No.	Description	Colourways	Size	U.S.$	Can.$	U.K.£
PW-3a	Colleen and cottage	Grey-green; multi-coloured print	75	50.00	70.00	25.00
PW-3b	Irish jaunting car	Grey-green; multi-coloured print	75	50.00	70.00	25.00
PW-3c	Giants Causeway	Grey-green; multi-coloured print	75	50.00	70.00	25.00
PW-3d	Irish fisherman	Grey-green; multi-coloured print	75	50.00	70.00	25.00

PEARLSTONE WALL PLAQUES, 1963-1964

Two styles of backs are found on these plaques. One has large irregular hollows in the back for setting into a stone fireplace or wall by filling with cement. It also has holes into which wire or cord could be strung for hanging, if preferred. Other plaques with Patio Ware labels have a flat back with a large hole on the top edge for hanging on a wall hook.

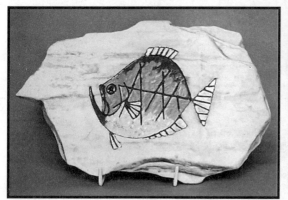

Prehistoric fish (PW-5a)

Rainbow trout (PW-6b); spotted fish (PW-8)

Stallion, running (PW-9b)

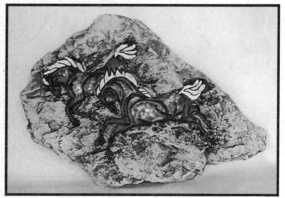

Stallions, running side by side (PW-11)

Siamese cats (PW-7)

Backstamp: A. Black ink stamp "Made in Ireland by Wade Co Armagh," hollowed back
          B. Black ink stamp "Made in Ireland by Wade Co Armagh" and a gold foil label shaped like a sombrero
             with "Patio Ware" Irish Porcelain by Wade Co Armagh," flat back
          C. Unmarked

No.	Description	Colourways	Size	U.S.$	Can.$	U.K.£
PW-4	Bison	Stone; brown bison	185 x 300	200.00	265.00	100.00
PW-5a	Prehistoric fish	Creamy beige; turquoise fish	180 x 300	200.00	265.00	100.00
PW-5b	Prehistoric fish	Dark grey; turquoise/white fish	180 x 300	200.00	265.00	100.00
PW-6a	Rainbow trout	Beige; red/white/black fish	205 x 425	200.00	265.00	100.00
PW-6b	Rainbow trout	Beige; pink/green/black/white fish	205 x 425	200.00	265.00	100.00
PW-7	Siamese cats	Stone; chocolate brown/cream cats; blue eyes	400 x 290	400.00	530.00	200.00
PW-8	Spotted fish	Beige; white/orange/grey fish with red spots	185 x 300	200.00	265.00	100.00
PW-9a	Stallion, running	Beige/cream; green stallion; yellow mane, tail	310 x 400	300.00	400.00	150.00
PW-9b	Stallion, running	Beige/cream; turquoise stallion; white mane, tail	310 x 400	300.00	400.00	150.00
PW-10	Stallions, one behind the other	Beige/cream; green stallions; white manes, tails	150 x 325	400.00	530.00	200.00
PW-11	Stallions, running side by side	Beige/cream; brown stallions; white manes, tails	195 x 290	400.00	530.00	200.00

PEONY SERIES WALL PLAQUE, c.1948

Produced as part of a series with a number of vases, this heavy, ribbed wall plaque is similar to the ribbed wall plaques (p.223).

Backstamp: Black ink stamp "Harvest Ware Wade England" with impressed "398"
Shape No.: 398

No.	Description	Colourways	Size	U.S.$	Can.$	U.K.£
PW-12	Harvest Ware 398	Cream; bright mauve/red/green flowers	30 x 265	90.00	120.00	45.00

PHOTO-HOLDER PLAQUE, c.1988

This plain, oval plaque has a foot at the back for it to stand. A photograph is meant to be glued into the recessed face.

Photograph not available
at press time

Backstamp: Unmarked

No.	Description	Colourways	Size	U.S.$	Can.$	U.K.£
PW-13	Photo holder	Blue/grey	105 x 85	Unknown		

RIBBED WALL PLAQUES, 1935-1937

A small number of heavy, ribbed wall plaques were produced from 1935 to 1937. Owing to their high production costs, not many of these plaques were made. There are three holes in the back for hanging.

Two large butterflies are flying over flowers on the style PW-14a plaque. Style PW-14c depicts a scene of hills and trees with hellebore flowers in the foreground. An owl sits on a branch with a large moon rising behind him on style PW-14d. Style PW-14e has three rabbits sitting under trees on top of a hill, watching the sun set.

Heron ribbed wall plaque (PW-14b)

Backstamp: Black ink stamp "Flaxman Ware Hand Made Pottery by Wadeheath England"

No.	Description	Colourways	Size	U.S.$	Can.$	U.K.£
PW-14a	Butterflies plaque	Creamy yellow; yellow/orange butterflies, flowers; green leaves	30 x 265	142.00	195.00	75.00
PW-14b	Heron plaque	Dull yellow; brown heron, chrysanthemums; green leaves	30 x 265	142.00	195.00	75.00
PW-14c	Hellebore flowers plaque	Dull yellow; dark purple flowers; brown hills; green trees	30 x 265	142.00	195.00	75.00
PW-14d	Owl and moon plaque	Pale blue; brown owl; green tree; grey moon	30 x 265	142.00	195.00	75.00
PW-14e	Rabbits and sunset plaque	Pale blue; dark brown rabbits; dull yellow sun; green trees	30 x 265	142.00	195.00	75.00

SEAGULL WALL PLAQUE, 1960

This model of a flying seagull was produced as a bathroom wall decoration.

Backstamp: Unmarked

No.	Description	Colourways	Size	U.S.$	Can.$	U.K.£
PW-15	Seagull	White; black wing tips; yellow beak, feet	225 x 80	90.00	120.00	45.00

SHOP-COUNTER PLAQUES, c.1960, 1993

The Irish Porcelain plaque, produced circa 1960, was meant to be displayed with Wade Ireland figures. Dealers who purchased a quantity of 1993 Whimsey-in-the-Vale models (see *The Charlton Standard Catalogue of Wade WhimsicalCollectables*) were able to purchase the Royal Victoria Pottery plaque to display with them.

Irish Porcelain plaque

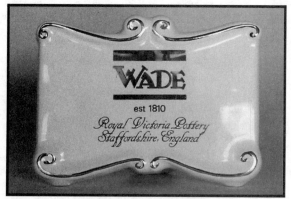

Royal Victoria Pottery plaque

Backstamp: Unmarked

No.	Description	Colourways	Size	U.S.$	Can.$	U.K.£
PW-16	Irish Porcelain plaque	Green/grey	135 x 98	40.00	55.00	20.00
PW-17	Royal Victoria Pottery plaque	White; gold lettering	65 x 94	25.00	30.00	12.00

TEENAGE POTTERY CAMEO PLAQUES, 1960

First issued in 1960, the original was 12/6.

PW-18a

Backstamp: Embossed "Wade Porcelain Made in England"

No.	Description	Colourways	Size	U.S.$	Can.$	U.K.£
PW-18a	Cliff Richard	Maroon; gold edge, multi-coloured print	95 x 70	160.00	215.00	80.00
PW-18b	Marty Wilde	Maroon; gold edge, multi-coloured print	95 x 70	160.00	215.00	80.00

VICTORIAN LADIES CAMEO PORTRAIT PLAQUES, c.1988–c.1990

A number of oval Victorian ladies cameo portraits were produced by Wade Ireland, possibly at the same time as the Gray Fine Art plaques (see volume one). These plaques have a slotted porcelain stand for the plaque to sit in. Style PW-21e has a plaited rim; the others are plain. Some of these plaques were used on the lids of trinket boxes (see Boxes section).

Plaque Stand

Plaque (PW-21e) with stand; plaque (PW-21j)

Backstamp: Unmarked

No.	Description	Colourways	Size	U.S.$	Can.$	U.K.£
PW-19	Plaque stand	Grey/blue/green	20 x 105	10.00	14.00	3.00

Plaques

Backstamp: Unmarked

No.	Description	Colourways	Size	U.S.$	Can.$	U.K.£
PW-20a	Hair band	Green background, dress	65	30.00	40.00	15.00
PW-20b	Pearl necklace, folded hands	Green; grey dress	65	30.00	40.00	15.00
PW-21a	Cowboy hat	Brown-black; brown hat, dress	85	30.00	40.00	15.00
PW-21b	Cowboy hat	Brown background, hat; green dress	85	30.00	40.00	15.00
PW-21c	Cross and chain necklace	Grey-brown; blue-grey dress	85	30.00	40.00	15.00
PW-21d	Hair in bun	Green-brown; blue-grey dress	85	30.00	40.00	15.00
PW-21e	Holding flowers	Green; blue-grey dress; yellow flowers	85	30.00	40.00	15.00
PW-21f	Holding flowers	Blue-grey background, dress; yellow flowers	85	30.00	40.00	15.00
PW-21g	Holding flowers	Blue-grey; brown dress; yellow flowers	85	30.00	40.00	15.00
PW-21h	Knotted collar	Green; blue-grey dress	85	30.00	40.00	15.00
PW-21i	Pearl and cross necklace	Brown; dark grey-blue dress	85	30.00	40.00	15.00
PW-21j	Pearl necklace	Browny green; blue-grey dress	85	30.00	40.00	15.00
PW-21k	Pearl necklace, facing left	Grey; brown hair; flesh-coloured lady	85	30.00	40.00	15.00
PW-21l	Pearl necklace, facing left	Brown; sepia lady	85	30.00	40.00	15.00
PW-21m	Pearl necklace, frilled collar	Brown; blue-grey dress	85	30.00	40.00	15.00

WEE WILLIE WINKIE NURSERY WALL PLAQUES, 1959-1960

These four nursery wall plaques were only produced for a short time. They depict scenes from the children's nursery rhyme, "Wee Willie Winkie," on the recessed face. Each plaque has a different illustration and two lines from the rhyme. There is a recessed hole in the back for hanging on a wall. They were originally sold with black and gold "Genuine Wade Porcelain" labels on the backs. These plaques are extremely hard to find.

Backstamp: Black transfer print "Wade England"

No.	Description	Colourways	Size	U.S.$	Can.$	U.K.£
PW-22a	Wee Willie Winkie runs through the town	White; multi-coloured print	133	200.00	265.00	100.00
PW-22b	Upstairs and downstairs in his night gown	White; multi-coloured print	133	200.00	265.00	100.00
PW-22c	Tapping at the window, peeping through the lock	White; multi-coloured print	133	200.00	265.00	100.00
PW-22d	Are the children in their beds, it's past 8 o'clock	White; multi-coloured print	133	200.00	265.00	100.00

WILDFOWL WALL PLAQUES, 1960

This set includes four duck wall plaques in natural colours. A loop is provided for hanging.

Mallard drake (PW-23)

Shoveller drake (PW-25)

Pintail (PW-24)

Backstamp: **A.** Black transfer print "Wildfowl by Wade of England" and model name
B. Black transfer print "Wildfowl by Wade of England," model name and signature of Peter Scott
C. Unmarked

No.	Description	Colourways	Size	U.S.$	Can.$	U.K.£
PW-23	Mallard drake	Grey; green head; brown neck; white/beige wings; orange feet	230 x 245	150.00	200.00	75.00
PW-24	Pintail	Green/black head; beige/grey/white wings; grey feet	240 x 205	150.00	200.00	75.00
PW-25	Shoveller drake	White/black body; black/green head; beige/white wings	190 x 220	150.00	200.00	75.00
PW-26	Shoveller female	Grey/brown body; green head	175 x 200	150.00	200.00	75.00

YACHT WALL PLAQUES, 1960

These brightly coloured racing yachts, designed for decoration in a bathroom, have a number on their sails. At some time in late 1960, the production of these plaques was moved to Wade Ireland. The original price was 9/11d.

Yachts PW-27a, 28a, 29a

Backstamp: A. Embossed "Wade England" in recess
B. Embossed "Wade Ireland" in recess

No.	Description	Colourways	Size	U.S.$	Can.$	U.K.£
PW-27a	Yacht, no. 7	Blue hull; brown roof; white/grey striped sails	Small/85 x 20	65.00	85.00	30.00
PW-27b	Yacht, no. 7	Green hull; blue roof; beige/mauve sails	Small/85 x 20	50.00	70.00	25.00
PW-27c	Yacht, no. 7	Dark green hull; dark blue roof; pink sails	Small/85 x 20	50.00	70.00	25.00
PW-28a	Yacht, no. 3	Blue hull; brown roof; white/grey striped sails	Medium/110 x 26	66.00	85.00	30.00
PW-28b	Yacht, no. 3	Blue hull; dark green roof; pale green sails	Medium/110 x 26	50.00	70.00	25.00
PW-28c	Yacht, no. 3	Dark blue hull; dark green roof; pale green sails	Medium/110 x 26	50.00	70.00	25.00
PW-29a	Yacht, no. 9	Blue hull; brown roof; white/grey striped sails	Large/115 x 30	65.00	85.00	30.00
PW-29b	Yacht, no. 9	Red hull; yellow roof; blue sails	Large/115 x 30	50.00	70.00	25.00
PW-29c	Yacht, no. 9	Red hull;brown roof; dark blue sails	Large/115 x 30	50.00	70.00	25.00
	Set of three (small, medium and large)			150.00	200.00	75.00

WALL MASKS, c.1938-c.1948

These wall masks have been found in three glaze types—cellulose, matt and high gloss. The masks all have cellulose glazed backs, with a backstamp from the late 1930s. This suggests the cellulose glaze was used first, then the unsold masks were reglazed in matt or high-gloss glaze at a later date in order to increase sales.

Dyllis (PW-30b)

Frolic (PW-31a)

Sonia (PW-33a)

Pan (PW-32a, 32b)

Backstamp: Black ink stamp "Wade Figures," a red leaping deer over "Made in England" and the model name handwritten in black

No.	Description	Colourways	Size	U.S.$	Can.$	U.K.£
PW-30a	Dyllis	Black hair; cream face; pink flowers; cellulose glaze	180 x 95	300.00	400.00	150.00
PW-30b	Dyllis	Black hair; cream face; pink flowers; high-gloss glaze	180 x 95	380.00	500.00	190.00
PW-31a	Frolic	Pale yellow; high-gloss glaze	180 x 160	380.00	500.00	190.00
PW-31b	Frolic	Green; matt glaze	180 x 160	380.00	500.00	190.00
PW-32a	Pan	Cream; matt glaze	180 x 115	380.00	500.00	190.00
PW-32b	Pan	Green; matt glaze	180 x 115	380.00	500.00	190.00
PW-33a	Sonia	Black hair; flesh-coloured face; pink flowers; cellulose glaze	220 x 110	300.00	400.00	150.00
PW-33b	Sonia	Black hair; flesh-coloured face; pink flowers; high-gloss glaze	220 x 110	380.00	500.00	190.00

WALL PLATES

ENGLISH LIFE WALL PLATES, 1992-1993

Only six plates were issued in the English Life Series. Each plate was produced in two sizes and was white with multi-coloured transfer prints of village shops, etc., similar to those of the English Life teapots.

Photograph not available
at press time

Backstamp: Black transfer print "English Life Collector Plates, designs by Barry Smith and Barbara Wootton for Wade U.K."

No.	Description	Caption	Size	U.S.$	Can.$	U.K.£
PW-34a	Antique shop	"Second-hand Rose"	Small/190	10.00	15.00	5.00
PW-34b	Fish and chip shop	"Three penny worth please"	Small/190	10.00	15.00	5.00
PW-34c	Flories flowers	"Say it with flowers"	Small/190	10.00	15.00	5.00
PW-34d	Post office	"Please write Soon"	Small/190	10.00	15.00	5.00
PW-34e	Primrose Junction	"All change please"	Small/190	10.00	15.00	5.00
PW-34f	The Queen Victoria	"Time gentleman please"	Small/190	10.00	15.00	5.00
PW-35a	Antique shop	"Second-hand Rose"	Large/240	20.00	30.00	10.00
PW-35b	Fish and chip shop	"Three penny worth please"	Large/240	20.00	30.00	10.00
PW-35c	Flories flowers	"Say it with flowers"	Large/240	20.00	30.00	10.00
PW-35d	Post office	"Please write soon"	Large/240	20.00	30.00	10.00
PW-35e	Primrose Junction	"All change please"	Large/240	20.00	30.00	10.00
PW-35f	The Queen Victoria	"Time gentleman please"	Large/240	20.00	30.00	10.00

MIRROR WALL PLATE, c.1950

A mirror framed in solid brass was riveted into the centre of a Regency-style plate. Wade did not assemble this plate with the mirror.

Backstamp: Gold transfer print "Royal Victoria Pottery, Wade England"

No.	Description	Colourways	Size	U.S.$	Can.$	U.K.£
PW-36	Mirror wall plate	Pale green plate; brass-framed mirror	265	30.00	40.00	15.00

NURSERY WALL PLATES, c.1970

These nursery wall plates, with a design of a cuckoo clock and a stork holding a baby on scales, were intended as birth commemoratives. The time of birth and the baby's weight were hand painted on the clock and the scales.

Backstamp: Black transfer print "Wade England, Made in England, Red Cherry Pie Potteries, Farnborough, Hampshire England, Limited Edition"

No.	Description	Colourways	Size	U.S.$	Can.$	U.K.£
PW-37a	Nursery	Blue; white/black/yellow print	240	50.00	70.00	25.00
PW-37b	Nursery	Pink; white/black/yellow print	240	50.00	70.00	25.00

REGENCY AND ROMANCE WALL PLATES, c.1940-c.1950

The plates have a fluted band of colour around the rim. The Regency Series features flowers, fruits and berries; the Romance Series portrays a Georgian couple.

Regency Series

Rose spray (PW-38f)

Backstamp: Green ink stamp "Wade England"

No.	Description	Colourways	Size	U.S.$	Can.$	U.K.£
PW-38a	Assorted flowers	Maroon band; pink/yellow/blue flowers	265	30.00	40.00	15.00
PW-38b	Assorted flowers	Turquoise band; pink/yellow/blue flowers	265	30.00	40.00	15.00
PW-38c	Assorted flowers	Mottled pale grey band; pink/yellow/blue flowers	265	30.00	40.00	15.00
PW-38d	Fruits and berries	White band; purple/red/blue fruits, berries	265	30.00	40.00	15.00
PW-38e	Plums	White band; purple/blue fruit	265	30.00	40.00	15.00
PW-38f	Rose spray	Mottled pale blue band; pink flowers	265	30.00	40.00	15.00
PW-38g	Rose spray	Mottled pale yellow band; pink flowers	265	30.00	40.00	15.00

Romance Series

This series begins with a Georgian couple meeting, the lady curtsies, they walk in a garden, lean on a wall, sit on a bench talking and finally the lady is alone with a bouquet of flowers.

Lady curtsying (PW-39a)

Leaning on wall (PW-39c)

Sitting talking (PW-39g)

Walking (PW-39i)

Backstamp: A. Green ink stamp "Wade England"
B. Gold transfer print "Royal Victoria Pottery, Wade England"

No.	Description	Colourways	Size	U.S.$	Can.$	U.K.£
PW-39a	Lady curtsying	Dark green band; multi-coloured print	265	30.00	40.00	15.00
PW-39b	Lady with bouquet	Maroon band; multi-coloured print	265	30.00	40.00	15.00
PW-39c	Leaning on wall	Yellow band; multi-coloured print	265	30.00	40.00	15.00
PW-39d	Leaning on wall	Maroon band; multi-coloured print	265	30.00	40.00	15.00
PW-39e	Leaning on wall	Dark green band; multi-coloured print	265	30.00	40.00	15.00
PW-39f	Sitting talking	Dark green band; multi-coloured print	265	30.00	40.00	15.00
PW-39g	Sitting talking	Maroon band; multi-coloured print	265	30.00	40.00	15.00
PW-39h	Walking	Dark blue band; multi-coloured print	265	30.00	40.00	15.00
PW-39i	Walking	Maroon band; multi-coloured print	265	30.00	40.00	15.00

SOMERSET COTTAGE WALL PLATE, c.1950

This plate has a print of a thatched cottage in a garden of flowers.

Photograph not available
at press time

Backstamp: Gold transfer print "Royal Victoria Pottery, Wade England"

No.	Description	Colourways	Size	U.S.$	Can.$	U.K.£
PW-40	Somerset cottage	Maroon band; multi-coloured print	265	30.00	40.00	15.00

SOUVENIR WALL PLATES, 1957-c.1960

Canadian Provinces Wall Plates

This series of white wall plates with multi-coloured transfer prints depict items related to each province. They were produced for the Canadian tourist industry and were not sold in England.

Backstamp: Red transfer print "Wade England"

No.	Description	Description	Size	U.S.$	Can.$	U.K.£
PW-41a	British Columbia	R.C.M.P., totem pole, dogwood, shield	240	25.00	35.00	20.00
PW-41b	Dominion of Canada	Map, maple leaves	240	25.00	35.00	20.00
PW-41c	Gaspesie, P.Q. Canada	Map, maple leaf, seagulls	240	25.00	35.00	20.00
PW-41d	Historic Nova Scotia	Flag, provincial flower, history of flag	240	25.00	35.00	20.00
PW-41e	Maritime lobster and trap	Lobster, trap, shield	240	25.00	35.00	20.00
PW-41f	New Brunswick Canada	Map, crest, provincial flower	240	25.00	35.00	20.00
PW-41g	Niagara Falls	Niagara Falls, legend	240	25.00	35.00	20.00
PW-41h	Nova Scotia Canada	Map, crest, provincial flower	240	25.00	35.00	20.00
PW-41i	Prince Edward Island	Map, crest, provincial flower	240	25.00	35.00	20.00
PW-41j	Province of Alberta	Map, R.C.M.P., Indian chief	240	25.00	35.00	20.00
PW-41k	Province of Ontario	Map, Parliament Buildings, crest, trillium	240	25.00	35.00	20.00

Isle of Wight and London Souvenir Wall Plates

The first plate has a reproduction of an early 17th-century map of the Isle of Wight in the centre. The other illustrates brightly coloured views of the Thames and the tourist attractions of London.

Photograph not available
at press time

Backstamp: **A.** Black transfer print "Royal Victoria Pottery Wade England"
B. Red transfer print "Wade England"

No.	Description	Colourways	Size	U.S.$	Can.$	U.K.£
PW-42	Isle of Wight	White; multi-coloured print	240	30.00	40.00	15.00
PW-43	London souvenir	White; red band; multi-coloured prints	200	30.00	40.00	15.00

VETERAN CAR WALL PLATES, c.1965

In the latter half of the long-running Veteran Car Series, Wade Ireland produced the last sets of the Veteran Car tankards with coloured transfers of competition cars. The same transfers are in the centre of these souvenir plates which were produced for the tourist trade.

Photograph not available
at press time

Backstamp: Black transfer print "An RK product by Wade of Ireland"

No.	Description	Colourways	Size	U.S.$	Can.$	U.K.£
PW-44a	Fiat F2, 1907	White; red/yellow print	180	30.00	40.00	15.00
PW-44b	Dusenbourg, 1933	White; blue/black print	180	30.00	40.00	15.00
PW-44c	Wolseley, 6hp, 1904	White; red/black/cream print	180	30.00	40.00	15.00
PW-44d	Austin Seven, 1926	White; red/black print	180	30.00	40.00	15.00

WELLYPHANT WALL PLATE, 1991

This wall plate was part of an intended series, called Wellyphant World. It was designed by Stuart Hampson and issued in a limited edition of 5,000.

Backstamp: Black transfer print "Wellyphant World, a limited edition of 5,000 designed by Stuart Hampson, Wade Made in England"

No.	Description	Colourways	Size	U.S.$	Can.$	U.K.£
PW-45	Wellyphant	White; red/yellow prints	190	50.00	70.00	25.00

WALL POCKETS

Wall pockets are flat-backed vases that have a hole in the back top edge so they can be hung on a wall. They are glazed inside to hold water.

SHAPE 159

Gothic Ware Wall Pockets, 1937-1939, 1953

These triangular-shaped wall pockets are decorated with an embossed design of swirling leaves and tulips characteristic of Gothic Ware.

Backstamp: A. Black ink stamp "Gothic Wade Heath England" and impressed "159"
B. Gold transfer print "Wade made in England - hand painted - Gothic" and impressed "159"
Shape No.: 159

No.	Description	Colourways	Size	U.S.$	Can.$	U.K.£
PW-46a	Gothic 159	Pale yellow	165 x 165	60.00	80.00	30.00
PW-46b	Gothic 159	Cream; lilac/pink flowers; green/gold leaves	165 x 165	70.00	90.00	35.00
PW-46c	Gothic 159	Creamy orange; pale pink flower; pale green leaves	165 x 165	60.00	80.00	30.00

SHAPE 224

Wall Pockets, 1935-c.1940

Backstamp: Black ink stamp "Wadeheath Ware England"
Shape No.: 224

No.	Description	Colourways	Size	U.S.$	Can.$	U.K.£
PW-47a	Round top with embossed flowers	Mottled white/blue/yellow	180 x 153	50.00	70.00	25.00
PW-47b	Round top with embossed flowers	Mottled orange/yellow/brown; blue/orange/pink flowers	180 x 153	50.00	70.00	25.00

SHAPE 225

Wall Pockets, 1935-c.1940

Backstamp: Black ink stamp "Flaxman Wade Heath England," with impressed "225"
Shape No.: 225

No.	Description	Colourways	Size	U.S.$	Can.$	U.K.£
PW-48	Fleur-de-lis	Pale yellow	220 x 118	50.00	70.00	25.00

SHAPE 226

Wall Pockets, 1935-c.1940

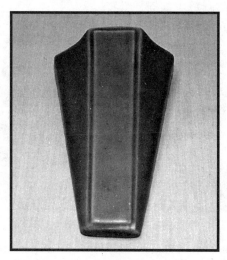

Backstamp: Black ink stamp "Wadeheath Ware England," with impressed "226"
   Shape No.: 226

No.	Description	Colourways	Size	U.S.$	Can.$	U.K.£
PW-49a	Fan	Mottled blue/orange	Medium/145 x 90	51.00	70.00	25.00
PW-49b	Fan	Mottled orange/grey	Medium/145 x 90	51.00	70.00	25.00
PW-49c	Fan	Mottled green/orange	Medium/145 x 90	40.00	55.00	20.00
PW-50	Fan	White; turquoise criss-cross stripes	Large/150 x 150	60.00	80.00	30.00

SHAPE 249

Wall Pockets, 1935-c.1940

Backstamp: Black ink stamp "Wade Heath England," with impressed shape number
   Shape No.: 249

No.	Description	Colourways	Size	U.S.$	Can.$	U.K.£
PW-51	Basket ware	Cream; grey/pink/yellow flowers; green leaves	145 x 185	51.00	70.00	25.00

MISCELLANEOUS WALL POCKETS, 1935-c.1940

Round top (PW-54)   Three-sided with scroll design (PW-55)

Backstamp: **A.** Black ink stamp "Flaxman Ware Hand Made Pottery by Wadeheath England"
B. Black ink stamp "Wade Heath England"

No.	Description	Colourways	Size	U.S.$	Can.$	U.K.£
PW-52	Daffodil	Grey daffodils; green leaves	205 x 100	90.00	120.00	45.00
PW-53	Rose	Yellow; pink roses; green leaves	205 x 100	90.00	120.00	45.00
PW-54	Round top	Mottled yellow/green/lilac	140 x 88	30.00	40.00	15.00
PW-55	Three-sided with scroll design	Mottled green/grey	180 x 153	50.00	70.00	25.00
PW-56	Tulip	Yellow tulips; green leaves	205 x 100	90.00	120.00	45.00

POSY BOWLS AND LOGS
1934-1988

Posy bowls and logs are low containers meant to hold short-stemmed flowers. The items in this section range from 28-millimetres to 120-millimetres high. They come in several novelty shapes, including a caterpillar posy bowl, a donkey and cart and a duck posy bowl.

The first measurement given in the listings is the height of the piece, the second is its width or length. The items are listed in alphabetical order.

BACKSTAMPS

Ink Stamps

Most of the ink stamps found on posy bowls are from Wade Heath and range from 1934 to 1937. Wade Ireland used a black ink stamp on some of its duck posy bowls from 1954 to the 1960s.

Impressed Backstamps

All the impressed backstamps used on posy bowls were produced by Wade Ireland. They range in dates from the early 1950s to the mid 1980s.

Embossed Backstamps

The majority of backstamps used on posy bowls are embossed, and most of them read "Wade England." They were primarily used in the 1950s, but also appear on the log posy bowl produced in 1988. Wade Ireland used an embossed backstamp for its 1957 to 1958 Valencia posy bowls.

ASCOT POSY BOWLS, 1957-1958

These fluted bowls have a 25-millimetre-high model of a horse standing on a plinth in the centre. They were created by Paul Zalman, who also designed the cherub posy bowls. They were first issued in August 1957 and withdrawn in January 1958.

Backstamp: Embossed "Wade Porcelain Made in England"

No.	Description	Colourways	Size	U.S.$	Can.$	U.K.£
PB-1a	Ascot	Brown; white horse	50 x 105	80.00	110.00	40.00
PB-1b	Ascot	Grey; white horse	50 x 105	80.00	110.00	40.00
PB-1c	Ascot	Blue; white horse	50 x 105	80.00	110.00	40.00

BARGE POSY BOWLS

1954 Issue

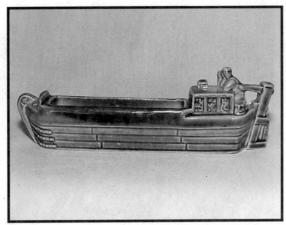

Barge posy bowl, 1954 issue

Backstamp: Embossed "Wade England Regd in Gt Britain No 871886"

No.	Description	Colourways	Size	U.S.$	Can.$	U.K.£
PB-2a	Barge	Green	60 x 195	30.00	40.00	15.00
PB-2b	Barge	Beige	60 x 195	30.00	40.00	15.00

1972 Issue

Barge posy bowl, 1972 issue

Backstamp: Embossed "Wade England"

No.	Description	Colourways	Size	U.S.$	Can.$	U.K.£
PB-3	Barge	Beige	40 x 198	50.00	70.00	25.00

BRIDGE POSY BOWLS, 1954-1958

Two styles of bridge posy bowls were produced due to the replacement of a broken die. The top of the bridge on style PB-4 is curved and has a swallow on it. The bridge on style PB-5 has a straight top and the bird has been omitted. They were withdrawn in January 1958.

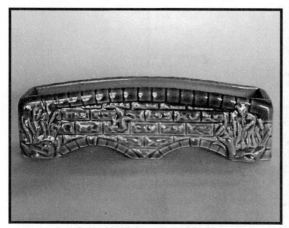

Curved bridge/swallow (PB-4b)

Straight bridge/no swallow (PB-5b)

Backstamp: Embossed "Wade England Regd in Gt Britain No 871653"

No.	Description	Colourways	Size	U.S.$	Can.$	U.K.£
PB-4a	Curved bridge/swallow	Beige	43 x 150	30.00	40.00	15.00
PB-4b	Curved bridge/swallow	Green	43 x 150	30.00	40.00	15.00
PB-4c	Curved bridge/swallow	Honey brown/brown	43 x 150	40.00	55.00	20.00
PB-5a	Straight bridge	Beige	43 x 150	30.00	40.00	15.00
PB-5b	Straight bridge	Green	43 x 150	30.00	40.00	15.00

C-SHAPED POSY LOGS, 1954-1959

These posy logs are finished with a bark and wood-knots design. They originally sold for 2/3d.

Backstamp: Embossed "Wade England"

No.	Description	Colourways	Size	U.S.$	Can.$	U.K.£
PB-6a	C-shape	Beige	30 x 140	10.00	15.00	5.00
PB-6b	C-shape	Green	30 x 140	10.00	15.00	5.00
PB-6c	C-shape	Pale blue	30 x 140	10.00	15.00	5.00

C-SHAPED POSY LOGS WITH RABBIT OR SQUIRREL, 1954-1959

These posy logs are similar to the C-shaped posy logs with the addition of a rabbit or squirrel sitting on one end of the log. The rabbit model was first produced in January 1954, and the squirrel was added in 1955. The original price was 2/11d.

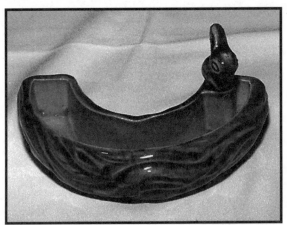

C-shaped posy log with squirrel (PB-8b)

Backstamp: Embossed "Wade England"

No.	Description	Colourways	Size	U.S.$	Can.$	U.K.£
PB-7a	Rabbit	Beige	60 x 140	20.00	30.00	10.00
PB-7b	Rabbit	Green	60 x 140	20.00	30.00	10.00
PB-8a	Squirrel	Beige	60 x 140	20.00	30.00	10.00
PB-8b	Squirrel	Green	60 x 140	20.00	30.00	10.00

CATERPILLAR POSY BOWLS, 1935-1937

Backstamp: Black ink stamp "Flaxman Ware Hand Made Pottery by Wadeheath"

No.	Description	Colourways	Size	U.S.$	Can.$	U.K.£
PB-9a	Caterpillar	Pale orange	73 x 290	90.00	120.00	45.00
PB-9b	Caterpillar	Beige	73 x 290	90.00	120.00	45.00

CHERUB POSY BOWLS, 1957-1959

These bowls were modelled by Paul Zalman. They were first issued in August 1957 for a price of 4/6d, then withdrawn in January 1959. For similar bowls without the cherub and swan, see primrose posy bowls.

Backstamp: Embossed "Wade Porcelain Made in England"

No.	Description	Colourways	Size	U.S.$	Can.$	U.K.£
PB-10a	Cherub	Green outside; yellow inside; flesh-coloured cherub; white swan	100 x 100	90.00	120.00	45.00
PB-10b	Cherub	Grey outside; yellow inside; flesh-coloured cherub; white swan	100 x 100	90.00	120.00	45.00

CHEVALINE POSY BOWLS, 1955-1959

These crescent-shaped bowls have an embossed design of horses and leafy branches on both sides and handles that resemble curled knots. They were first issued in September 1955.

Backstamp: Embossed "Wade England"

No.	Description	Colourways	Size	U.S.$	Can.$	U.K.£
PB-11a	Chevaline	Beige	65 x 155	25.00	35.00	12.00
PB-11b	Chevaline	Green	65 x 155	25.00	35.00	12.00

CHIMPANZEE POSY BOWL, 1959-1960

This posy bowl was first issued in September 1959 for an original price of 3/6d.

Backstamp: Embossed "Wade Porcelain Made in England"

No.	Description	Colourways	Size	U.S.$	Can.$	U.K.£
PB-12	Chimpanzee	Green trunk; grey-brown chimpanzee	80 x 90	50.00	70.00	25.00

DONKEY AND CART POSY BOWLS, 1956-1961

These items are part of the Shamrock Pottery Series, with included the pink elephant, the Irish comical pig, the shamrock cottage and the pixie dish (see *The Charlton Standard Catalogue of Wade Whimsical Collectables*). The first style of this posy bowl has an open back on the cart with the shafts not touching the neck, and the second style has a solid back with the shafts touching the neck.

Open back (PB-13)   Closed back (PB-14)

Backstamp: Embossed "Shamrock Pottery Made in Ireland"
Shape No.: C. 338

No.	Description	Colourways	Size	U.S.$	Can.$	U.K.£
PB-13	Open back	Grey/blue/green	100 x 158	90.00	120.00	45.00
PB-14	Closed back	Grey/blue/green	91 x 168	70.00	95.00	35.00

DUCK POSY BOWLS, 1954-c.1965

Backstamp: A. Impressed "Irish Porcelain Made in Ireland" with a shamrock leaf
B. Black ink stamp "Irish Porcelain Made in Ireland" with a shamrock leaf
C. Unmarked

No.	Description	Colourways	Size	U.S.$	Can.$	U.K.£
PB-15a	Duck	Grey/blue	105 x 173	60.00	80.00	30.00
PB-15b	Duck	Grey/blue/green	100 x 180	60.00	80.00	30.00

GLOBE POSY BOWLS, 1934-1937

These bowls have six flower pockets around the outside. The 1934 bowls were hand painted; from 1935 they were issued in mottled Flaxman glazes.

Backstamp: A. Black ink stamp "WadeHeath England" with a lion and impressed "216"
B. Black ink stamp "Flaxman Ware Hand Made Pottery by Wadeheath England" with impressed "216"
Shape No.: 216

No.	Description	Colourways	Size	U.S.$	Can.$	U.K.£
PB-16a	Globe	Cream; blue/pink/yellow flowers; yellow/brown butterfly	120 x 150	130.00	175.00	65.00
PB-16b	Globe	Cream/orange; blue/pink/orange flowers	120 x 150	130.00	175.00	65.00
PB-16c	Globe	White; orange/yellow cottage, flowers	120 x 150	130.00	175.00	65.00
PB-16d	Globe	Mottled orange/dark green	120 x 150	90.00	120.00	45.00
PB-16e	Globe	Mottled green/brown	120 x 150	90.00	120.00	45.00
PB-16f	Globe	Mottled blue/dark blue flecks	120 x 150	90.00	120.00	45.00
PB-16g	Globe	Mottled green/dark green flecks	120 x 150	90.00	120.00	45.00
PB-16h	Globe	Mottled dark brown/light brown	120 x 150	90.00	120.00	45.00
PB-16i	Globe	Brown/yellow/green	120 x 150	90.00	120.00	45.00

GRECIAN URN POSY BOWLS, 1955-1959

These posy bowls have an embossed decoration of oval stones and dots around the top rim and the stem. They also have a six-sided foot. The bowl shown has a fitted double-wire frame which holds small flowers in place. Some of these bowls have been found with small holes in the top rim. These are for a single-wire flower frame.

Backstamp: Embossed "Wade" in the hollow of the base

No.	Description	Colourways	Size	U.S.$	Can.$	U.K.£
PB-17a	Grecian urn	Marbled blue	80 x 110	32.00	45.00	20.00
PB-17b	Grecian urn	Green	80 x 110	32.00	45.00	20.00
PB-17c	Grecian urn	Beige	80 x 110	32.00	45.00	20.00

IRISH COOKING POT POSY BOWLS, c.1955, c.1975-1986

The Irish cooking pot was first issued in the 1950s as souvenir ware, then again in the 1970s until the 1980s. The Shamrock Range pot was issued from 1983 to 1986.

Irish cooking pot (PB-18)   Shamrock Range (PB-19)

Backstamp: Impressed "Irish Porcelain" curved over a shamrock with "Made in Ireland, Wade Co. Armagh" underneath
Shape No.: I.P.603—shape PB-18
          SR 20—shape PB-19

No.	Description	Colourways	Size	U.S.$	Can.$	U.K.£
PB-18	Irish cooking pot	Greenish brown/blue	60 x 70	10.00	15.00	5.00
PB-19	Shamrock Range	White; green shamrocks	60 x 70	30.00	40.00	15.00

KILLARNEY URN POSY BOWLS, c.1953–c.1985

These posy bowls are decorated with an embossed design of knurls, dots and shamrocks.

Backstamp: A. Impressed "Irish Porcelain" over a shamrock and "Made in Ireland" underneath in a curved shape
B. Impressed "Irish Porcelain" curved above a shamrock and "Made in Ireland" in a straight line underneath
C. Impressed "Made in Ireland Irish Porcelain Wade eire tir a dheanta" in a circle with a small crown and shamrock in the centre
Shape No.: I.P.40—Large
I.P.41—Medium
I.P.42—Small
I.P.43—Miniature

No.	Description	Colourways	Shape No./Size	U.S.$	Can.$	U.K.£
PB-20	Killarney urn	Grey/blue	I.P.40/Large/202	30.00	40.00	15.00
PB-21	Killarney urn	Grey/blue	I.P.41/Medium/153	20.00	30.00	10.00
PB-22	Killarney urn	Grey/blue	I.P.42/Small/114	20.00	30.00	10.00
PB-23	Killarney urn	Grey/blue	I.P.43/Miniature/78	10.00	15.00	5.00

KOALA BEAR POSY BOWL, 1957-1959

This bowl was first issued in March 1957, when it sold for 2/11d, and was withdrawn in January 1959.

Backstamp: Embossed "Wade Porcelain Made in England"

No.	Description	Colourways	Size	U.S.$	Can.$	U.K.£
PB-24	Koala bear	Green; brown koala	55 x 80	70.00	95.00	35.00

LOG POSY BOWLS, 1988

Two log-shaped posy bowls were produced by Wade in early February 1988.

Backstamp: Embossed "Wade England"

No.	Description	Colourways	Size	U.S.$	Can.$	U.K.£
PB-25	Log	Light brown/dark brown/grey	Small /57 x 177	20.00	30.00	10.00
PB-26	Log	Light brown/dark brown/grey	Large/101 x 255	30.00	40.00	15.00

MERMAID POSY BOWLS, 1955-1959

These bowls have an embossed design of starfish, seahorses and seaweed on them. Mermaids form the handles of the bowl, each one looking to her right. These bowls were first issued in September 1955.

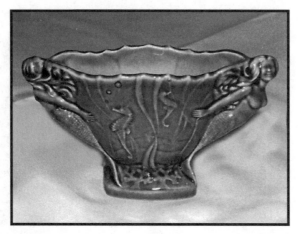

Backstamp: Embossed "Wade England"

No.	Description	Colourways	Size	U.S.$	Can.$	U.K.£
PB-27a	Mermaid	Beige	Small/60 x 100	20.00	30.00	10.00
PB-27b	Mermaid	Green	Small/60 x 100	20.00	30.00	10.00
PB-28a	Mermaid	Beige	Large/90 x 150	30.00	40.00	15.00
PB-28b	Mermaid	Green	Large/90 x 150	30.00	40.00	15.00

PALERMO POSY BOWLS, 1957-1959

These posy bowls were first issued in August 1957 and withdrawn in January 1959.

Backstamp: Embossed "Wade Porcelain Made in England"

No.	Description	Colourways	Size	U.S.$	Can.$	U.K.£
PB-29a	Palermo	Beige	85 x 155	30.00	40.00	15.00
PB-29b	Palermo	Green	85 x 155	30.00	40.00	15.00
PB-29c	Palermo	White	85 x 155	30.00	40.00	15.00

PEGASUS POSY BOWL, 1958-1959

The open wings of this mythical flying horse form the posy bowl. It was first issued in January 1958 and sold for 10/6d. It was withdrawn in January 1959.

Backstamp: Embossed "Wade Porcelain Made in England"

No.	Description	Colourways	Size	U.S.$	Can.$	U.K.£
PB-30	Pegasus	Yellow; blue mane, hooves, tail	110 x 145	130.00	175.00	65.00

POPPY POSY BOWLS, 1957-1959

These small bowls are shaped in the form of an open four-petalled poppy with embossed petals and stamens.

Backstamp: Unmarked

No.	Description	Colourways	Size	U.S.$	Can.$	U.K.£
PB-31a	Poppy	Red/white; green stamens	45	50.00	70.00	25.00
PB-31b	Poppy	Bright yellow/white; green stamens	45	50.00	70.00	25.00
PB-31c	Poppy	Dull yellow/white; black stamens	45	50.00	70.00	25.00

POSY RING, 1937

This posy ring has a trough for short-stemmed flowers and is decorated with a rolling scroll design around the outside.

Photograph not available
at press time

Backstamp: Black ink stamp "Flaxman Ware Hand Made Pottery by Wadeheath England"

No.	Description	Colourways	Size	U.S.$	Can.$	U.K.£
PB-32	Posy ring	Mottled green/grey	70 x 229	50.00	70.00	25.00

PRIMROSE POSY BOWLS, 1957-1959

These are the same shape as the cherub posy bowls above, but without the centre pillar and cherub. The first style still has the square indentation in the middle where the pillar would fit; there is no indentation in the second style. They were first issued in August 1957 and withdrawn in January 1959.

Primrose bowl with indentation   Primrose bowl without indentation

Backstamp: Embossed "Wade Porcelain Made in England"

No.	Description	Colourways	Size	U.S.$	Can.$	U.K.£
PB-33	Indentation	Pale blue outside; yellow inside	50 x 100	30.00	40.00	15.00
PB-34a	No indentation	Cream outside; light green inside	50 x 100	30.00	40.00	15.00
PB-34b	No indentation	Cream outside; pale blue inside	50 x 100	30.00	40.00	15.00
PB-34c	No indentation	Dark green outside; pink inside	50 x 100	30.00	40.00	15.00

S-SHAPED POSY LOGS, 1954-1959

These posy logs are embossed with a bark and wood-knots design. When they were first issued, they sold for 2/3d. They were withdrawn in January 1959.

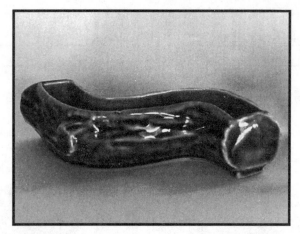

Backstamp: Embossed "Wade England"

No.	Description	Colourways	Size	U.S.$	Can.$	U.K.£
PB-35a	S-shape	Brown	30 x 140	10.00	15.00	5.00
PB-35b	S-shape	Green	30 x 140	10.00	15.00	5.00
PB-35c	S-shape	Pale blue	30 x 140	10.00	15.00	5.00
PB-35d	S-shape	Salmon pink	30 x 140	10.00	15.00	5.00

S-SHAPED POSY LOGS WITH RABBIT OR SQUIRREL, 1954-1959

These logs combine the S-shaped posy logs with a model of a sitting rabbit or squirrel. The rabbit model was used first; in 1955 the squirrel was added to the range. They originally sold for 2/11d. These models were withdrawn in January 1959.

Backstamp: Embossed "Wade England"

No.	Description	Colourways	Size	U.S.$	Can.$	U.K.£
PB-36a	Rabbit	Beige	60 x 140	20.00	30.00	10.00
PB-36b	Rabbit	Green	60 x 140	20.00	30.00	10.00
PB-37a	Squirrel	Beige	60 x 140	20.00	30.00	10.00
PB-37b	Squirrel	Green	60 x 140	20.00	30.00	10.00

STRAIGHT POSY LOGS, 1954-1959

Backstamp: Embossed "Wade England"

No.	Description	Colourways	Size	U.S.$	Can.$	U.K.£
PB-38a	Straight log	Beige	28 x 120	10.00	15.00	5.00
PB-38b	Straight log	White	28 x 120	10.00	15.00	5.00
PB-38c	Straight log	Green	28 x 120	10.00	15.00	5.00
PB-38d	Straight log	Light green	28 x 120	10.00	15.00	5.00
PB-38e	Straight log	Royal blue	28 x 120	10.00	15.00	5.00
PB-38f	Straight log	Turquoise	28 x 120	10.00	15.00	5.00
PB-38g	Straight log	Pale blue	28 x 120	10.00	15.00	5.00
PB-38h	Straight log	Salmon pink	28 x 120	10.00	15.00	5.00

STRAIGHT POSY LOGS WITH RABBIT OR SQUIRREL, 1954-1959

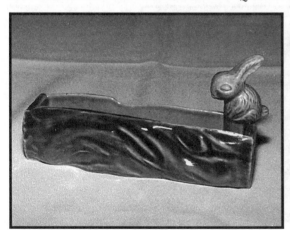

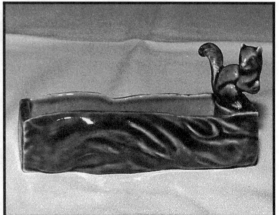

Straight log posy bowl with rabbit (PB-39b)   Straight log posy bowl with squirrel (PB-40b)

Backstamp: Embossed "Wade England"

No.	Description	Colourways	Size	U.S.$	Can.$	U.K.£
PB-39a	Rabbit	Beige	60 x 120	20.00	30.00	10.00
PB-39b	Rabbit	Green	60 x 120	20.00	30.00	10.00
PB-40a	Squirrel	Beige	60 x 120	20.00	30.00	10.00
PB-40b	Squirrel	Green	60 x 120	20.00	30.00	10.00

SWALLOW POSY BOWLS, 1957-1961

These bowls were first issued in August 1957 and sold for 4/6d.

Backstamp: Unknown

No.	Description	Colourways	Size	U.S.$	Can.$	U.K.£
PB-41a	Swallow	Green; blue/white bird	105 x 105	60.00	80.00	30.00
PB-41b	Swallow	Brown; blue/white bird	105 x 105	60.00	80.00	30.00
PB-41c	Swallow	White; blue/white/green bird	105 x 105	60.00	80.00	30.00

THREE-LEGGED POSY BOWL, c.1955, c.1975-c.1985

The three-legged posy bowl has an impressed design of shamrocks around the middle.

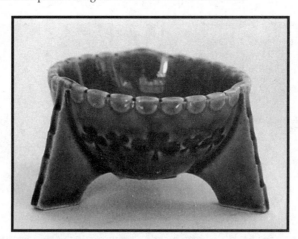

Backstamp: Impressed "Irish Porcelain" curved over a shamrock with "Made in Ireland" impressed in a straight line underneath
Shape: I.P.602

No.	Description	Colourways	Size	U.S.$	Can.$	U.K.£
PB-42a	Three legs	Blue/green	45 x 65	10.00	15.00	5.00
PB-42b	Three legs	Light brown	45 x 65	10.00	15.00	5.00

TRADITIONAL POSY BOWLS, 1954-1959

The first advertisement which mentions these posy bowls is dated January 1954. The small bowl originally cost 2/3d, and the large bowl cost 3/11d. They were withdrawn in January 1959.

Backstamp: Embossed "Wade England"

No.	Description	Colourways	Size	U.S.$	Can.$	U.K.£
PB-43a	Traditional	Beige	Small/45 x 100	10.00	15.00	5.00
PB-43b	Traditional	Green	Small/45 x 100	10.00	15.00	5.00
PB-43c	Traditional	White	Small/45 x 100	10.00	15.00	5.00
PB-44a	Traditional	Beige	Large/70 x 155	20.00	30.00	10.00
PB-44b	Traditional	Green	Large/70 x 155	20.00	30.00	10.00
PB-44c	Traditional	White	Large/70 x 155	20.00	30.00	10.00
PB-44d	Traditional	Ming green	Large/70 x 155	20.00	30.00	10.00
PB-44e	Traditional	Pink	Large/70 x 155	20.00	30.00	10.00

VALENCIA POSY BOWLS, 1957-1958

Valencia posy bowls were produced by Wade and Wade Ireland during the same period. The slight size variation is due to the replacement of worn dies. They were first issued in August 1957 for a price of 3/6d, and withdrawn in January 1958.

Backstamp: **A.** Embossed "Wade Porcelain made in England"
B. Embossed "Irish Porcelain" over a shamrock," embossed "Made in Ireland" underneath and "S" in the centre of the shamrock
C. Impressed "Irish Porcelain" over a shamrock," embossed "Made in Ireland by Wade Co Armagh" underneath and a gold foil shamrock-shaped label with "Irish Porcelain" in green letters stuck onto the front

No.	Description	Colourways	Size	U.S.$	Can.$	U.K.£
PB-45a	Valencia	Beige	65 x 148	10.00	15.00	5.00
PB-45b	Valencia	Green	65 x 148	10.00	15.00	5.00
PB-45c	Valenicia	White	65 x 148	10.00	15.00	5.00
PB-45d	Valencia	Blue-grey	67-70 x 148	10.00	15.00	5.00

VIOLET POSY BOWL, c.1952, c.1975-c.1985

This miniature model has three rows of impressed and embossed knurls, dots and shamrocks on it. Although it is actually a thistle-shaped vase, it was catalogued as a bowl by Wade Ireland.

Photograph not
available at press time

Backstamp: Impressed "Irish Porcelain" over a shamrock, impressed "Made in Ireland" underneath, with "H" inside the shamrock
Shape No.: I.P.34

No.	Description	Colourways	Size	U.S.$	Can.$	U.K.£
PB-46	Violet	Grey/blue	65 x 40	10.00	15.00	5.00

VASES AND URNS
1933-1992

All of the vases produced up to World War II were made by Wade Heath. When production of decorative ware resumed following the war, production was spread out amongst all Wade's potteries, including Wade Ireland beginning in the 1950s.

Those items with shape numbers are listed first, in number order. The rest of the vases and urns follow in alphabetical order.

BACKSTAMPS

Ink Stamps

Transfer Prints

From 1957 to 1992 Wade used a variety of black, black and red, red and gold transfer prints. Some of these backstamps incorporated impressed marks, often the shape number, as well.

Impressed Backstamps

Impressed backstamps can be found on some Harmony Ware vases produced from 1957 to the early 1960s. Wade Ireland used impressed marks on its vases from 1950 to the mid 1980s.

Embossed Backstamps

Wade England began using embossed backstamps in 1962, and by 1959 they could also be found on Wade Ireland vases until 1982.

Many of the vases in this section were produced in the 1930s and are marked with a Wade Heath backstamp, which often includes a lion and an impressed shape number. These stamps are predominantly black, but may also be found in orange, red and green.

From the late 1940s to the early 1950s, black Harvest Ware and green Gothic Ware ink stamps were used. The standard Wade England ink stamps, in green or black, appeared from the late 1940s to the mid 1960s. Wade Ireland used an ink stamp intermittently until the mid 1980s.

SHAPE 11

Vases, 1935-1937

These vases have a moulded foot on each corner.

Backstamp: Black ink stamp "Flaxman Ware Hand Made Pottery by Wadeheath, England" with impressed "11"

No.	Description	Colourways	Size	U.S.$	Can.$	U.K.£
V-1a	Flaxman 11	Cream; green foliage; orange/blue flowers; brown outline of bird	150	120.00	160.00	60.00
V-1b	Flaxman 11	Green streaked top, base; orange streaked middle	150	120.00	160.00	60.00

SHAPE 17

Orcadia Ware Vases, 1933-1934

Orcadia Ware was produced in vivid streaked glazes that were allowed to run over the rims and down the inside and the outside of the vases. This vase is tall with a long neck and is round at the base.

Photograph not available
at press time

Backstamp: Orange ink stamp "Wadeheath Orcadia Ware"

No.	Description	Colourways	Size	U.S.$	Can.$	U.K.£
V-2	Orcadia 17	Orange/green/yellow	230	150.00	200.00	75.00

Vase, 1934-1935

Photograph not available
at press time

Backstamp: Black ink stamp "WadeHeath England" with a lion and impressed "17"

No.	Description	Colourways	Size	U.S.$	Can.$	U.K.£
V-3	Shape 17	Green; yellow flowers	230	150.00	200.00	75.00

SHAPE 19

Vases, 1933-1937

Orcadia ware vases were produced between 1933 and 1935.

Orcadia Ware (V-4h)   Tube line design (V-4f)

Backstamp: **A.** Orange ink stamp "Wade's Orcadia Ware" with a lion, 1933
B. Orange ink stamp "Wadeheath Orcadia Ware," 1933-1934
C. Black ink stamp "WadeHeath England" with a lion and impressed "19," 1933-1935
D. Black ink stamp "Flaxman Ware Hand Made Pottery by Wadeheath, England" with impressed "19," 1935-1937

No.	Description	Colourways	Size	U.S.$	Can.$	U.K.£
V-4a	Flaxman 19	Cream; brown rim, handles, tree stump; orange bird; blue flowers	120	110.00	145.00	55.00
V-4b	Flaxman 19	Green/cream; orange/mauve flowers; brown bird	120	110.00	145.00	55.00
V-4c	Flaxman 19	Green handles; brown flecks; pink flowers; green leaves	120	110.00	145.00	55.00
V-4d	Flaxman 19	Mottled orange	120	70.00	95.00	35.00
V-4e	Flaxman 19	Mustard; brown leaves	120	70.00	95.00	35.00
V-4f	Flaxman 19	Yellow; brown bird; blue flower (tube lined)	120	110.00	145.00	55.00
V-4g	Orcadia 19	Orange/yellow	120	90.00	120.00	45.00
V-4h	Orcadia 19	Green/orange	120	90.00	120.00	45.00
V-4i	Shape 19	Turquoise; brown/turquoise/green design	120	110.00	145.00	55.00
V-4j	Shape 19	Orange top, handles; bright blue/orange/green/ yellow/purple stripes	120	110.00	145.00	55.00
V-4k	Shape 19	Brown; orange/yellow flowers	120	90.00	120.00	45.00
V-4l	Shape 19	Orange/yellow/brown streaks	120	70.00	95.00	35.00
V-4m	Shape 19	Orange; blue flowers; green leaves	120	90.00	120.00	45.00

SHAPE 69

Vases, 1935-c.1952

The Flaxman vases were produced from 1935 to 1939. The peony design vases were produced between the late 1940s and the early 1950s.

Backstamp: **A.** Black ink stamp "Harvest Ware Wade England" with impressed "69," late 1940s-early 1950s
B. Black ink stamp "Flaxman Ware Hand Made Pottery by Wadeheath England" with impressed "69," 1935-1937
C. Black ink stamp "Flaxman Wade Heath England" with impressed "69," 1937-1939

No.	Description	Colourways	Size	U.S.$	Can.$	U.K.£
V-5a	Flaxman 69	Green/brown/yellow streaks; dark brown base	125	80.00	110.00	40.00
V-5b	Flaxman 69	Blue/yellow brown speckles	205	90.00	120.00	45.00
V-5c	Peony 69	Cream; multi-coloured flowers	200	70.00	95.00	35.00

SHAPE 94

Richmond Vases with Handle, 1934-1935, 1937-1939

These vases have horizontal ribs on the neck.

Backstamp: A. Black ink stamp "WadeHeath England" with a lion and embossed "94 Richmond," 1934-1935
B. Black ink stamp "Flaxman Wade Heath England," 1937-1939

No.	Description	Colourways	Size	U.S.$	Can.$	U.K.£
V-6a	Flaxman 94	Blue/green with chevron, flowers	160	80.00	110.00	40.00
V-6b	Richmond 94	Green/yellow; brown streaks at base	160	80.00	110.00	40.00
V-6c	Richmond 94	Yellow; orange bands; blue/orange streaks; blue dots, cross lines	160	80.00	110.00	40.00
V-6d	Richmond 94	Off white; pink/blue/yellow flowers	160	80.00	110.00	40.00
V-6e	Richmond 94	Yellow; orange rim, handle, base, circles; blue/green leaves	160	80.00	110.00	40.00
V-6f	Richmond 94	Blue/green; blue handle, flower; golden brown triangles	160	80.00	110.00	40.00
V-6g	Richmond 94	Green/blue; brown fan; blue/brown squares	160	80.00	110.00	40.00

SHAPE 95
Richmond Vase without Handle, 1934-1935

Photograph not available
at press time

Backstamp: Black ink stamp "WadeHeath England" with a lion and embossed "95 Richmond"

No.	Description	Colourways	Size	U.S.$	Can.$	U.K.£
V-7	Richmond 95	Green; green/yellow top stripe; brown bottom stripe	Unknown	Unknown		

SHAPE 107
Vase, 1934-1935

This vase has two handles that end on the round footed base.

Photograph not available
at press time

Backstamp: Black ink stamp "Wadeheath England" with a lion and embossed "107"

No.	Description	Colourways	Size	U.S.$	Can.$	U.K.£
V-8a	Shape 107	Cream; pink flower; green leaves; grey trees	225	95.00	130.00	50.00
V-8b	Shape 107	Yellow/brown/orange	225	70.00	95.00	35.00

SHAPE 212
Vases, 1934-1935

Backstamp: Black ink stamp "WadeHeath England" with a lion and impressed "212"

No.	Description	Colourways	Size	U.S.$	Can.$	U.K.£
V-9a	Shape 212	Cream; grey rim; yellow turrets; mauve/purple flowers	165	120.00	160.00	60.00
V-9b	Shape 212	Brown; orange/yellow flowers; green leaves	165	120.00	160.00	60.00

SHAPE 213
Vases, 1934-1935

Backstamp: Black ink stamp "WadeHeath England" with a lion and impressed "213"

No.	Description	Colourways	Size	U.S.$	Can.$	U.K.£
V-10a	Shape 213	Cream/brown; brown/green tree; brown rocks; green grass	184	120.00	160.00	60.00
V-10b	Shape 213	Fawn; orange leaves; blue/red flowers	184	110.00	145.00	55.00

SHAPE 214
Vases, 1934-1935

Backstamp: Black ink stamp "WadeHeath England" with a lion and impressed "214"

No.	Description	Colourways	Size	U.S.$	Can.$	U.K.£
V-11	Shape 214	Mottled cream/brown; yellow leaves; orange/blue flowers	184	110.00	145.00	55.00

SHAPE 217
Vases, 1934-1937

There are several holes for flowers on top of the scalloped ledge in the middle of the vase.

Backstamp: A. Black ink stamp "WadeHeath England" with a lion and impressed "217," 1934-1935
B. Black ink stamp "Flaxman Ware Hand Made Pottery by Wadeheath England" with impressed "217," 1935-1937

No	Description	Colourways	Size	U.S.$	Can.$	U.K.£
V-12a	Flaxman 217	Mottled grey/pale blue	225	110.00	145.00	55.00
V-12b	Flaxman 217	Mottled blue	225	110.00	145.00	55.00
V-12c	Shape 217	Cream; yellow/mauve/orange flowers; green handles, shields; orange rim	225	130.00	175.00	65.00
V-12d	Shape 217	Cream; orange flowers; grey shields; orange rim	225	130.00	175.00	65.00

SHAPE 243
Vases, 1937-1939

Four sides of these flower holders have stepped pillars on them. There is a flower frog inserted in the mouth.

Backstamp: **A.** Black ink stamp "Wade Heath England," 1936-1940s
B. Black ink stamp "Flaxman Wade Heath England" with impressed "243"

No.	Description	Colourways	Size	U.S.$	Can.$	U.K.£
V-13a	Flaxman 243	Pale blue	140	100.00	145.00	55.00
V-13b	Shape 243	Off white; yellow pillars; pink flowers	140	120.00	165.00	60.00
V-13c	Shape 243	Off white	140	100.00	145.00	55.00

SHAPE 244
Flaxman Ware Vase, 1937-1939

This art nouveau flower holder has a flower frog inserted in the mouth.

Backstamp: Black ink stamp "Flaxman Wade Heath England"

No.	Description	Colourways	Size	U.S.$	Can.$	U.K.£
V-14	Flaxman 244	Mottled yellow/brown/green	140	150.00	200.00	75.00

SHAPE 313
Peony Series Vase, c.1948-c.1952

This vase was underglazed with large hand-painted peonies, so no two are identical.

Backstamp: Black ink stamp "Harvest Ware Wade England" with impressed "313"

No.	Description	Colourways	Size	U.S.$	Can.$	U.K.£
V-15	Harvest Ware 313	Cream; multi-coloured flowers	225	70.00	95.00	35.00

SHAPE 316
Flaxman Ware Vase, 1937-1939

Photograph not available
at press time

Backstamp: Black ink stamp "Flaxman Wade Heath England"

No.	Description	Colourways	Size	U.S.$	Can.$	U.K.£
V-16	Flaxman 316	Mottled beige	Unknown	100.00	135.00	50.00

SHAPE 332

Vases, c.1948–c.1953

Backstamp: **A.** Black ink stamp "Harvest Ware Wade England" with impressed "332"
B. Black ink stamp "Wade England" with impressed "332"

No.	Description	Colourways	Size	U.S.$	Can.$	U.K.£
V-17a	Peony 332	Cream; multi-coloured flowers	225	70.00	95.00	35.00
V-17b	Shape 332	Cream; brown leaves, bands	225	70.00	95.00	35.00

SHAPE 333

Peony Series Vase, c.1948–c.1952

This vase was underglazed with large hand-painted peonies, so no two are identical.

Backstamp: Black ink stamp "Harvest Ware Wade England" with impressed "333"

No.	Description	Colourways	Size	U.S.$	Can.$	U.K.£
V-18	Harvest Ware 333	Cream; multi-coloured flowers	225	70.00	95.00	35.00

SHAPE 342
Peony Series Vase, c.1948-c.1952

This vase was underglazed with large hand-painted peonies, so no two are identical.

Backstamp: Black ink stamp "Harvest Ware Wade England" with impressed "342"

No.	Description	Colourways	Size	U.S.$	Can.$	U.K.£
V-19	Harvest Ware 342	Cream; multi-coloured flowers	280	90.00	120.00	45.00

SHAPE 343

Vases, 1937-c.1952

The aqua vase was in production between 1937 and 1938, and the peony series vase between the late 1940s and early 1950s.

Backstamp: A. Black ink stamp "Wade Heath England," 1936-1940s
B. Black ink stamp "Harvest Ware Wade England" with impressed "343," late 1940s-early 1950s

No.	Description	Colourways	Size	U.S.$	Can.$	U.K.£
V-20a	Aqua 343	Pale green; orange leaves	260	170.00	225.00	85.00
V-20b	Harvest Ware 343	Cream; multi-coloured flowers	225	90.00	120.00	45.00

SHAPE 359

Gothic Ware Vases, 1937-1939, c.1948-c.1952

The 1937-1939 issue was produced in matt colours. It was reissued from the late 1940s to early 1950s in new gloss colours, with the embossed design highlighted in pastel colours and gold lustre.

Shape 359, matt (V-21a)   Shape 359, gloss (V-21c)

Backstamp: **A.** Black ink stamp "Gothic Wade Heath England" with impressed "359"
B. Green ink stamp "Wade England Gothic" with impressed "359"

No.	Description	Colourways	Size	U.S.$	Can.$	U.K.£
V-21a	Gothic 359	Orange; matt	170	110.00	145.00	55.00
V-21b	Gothic 359	Pale orange; pale pink flowers; pale green leaves; gloss	170	110.00	145.00	55.00
V-21c	Gothic 359	Cream; pink/yellow flowers; blue green leaves; gold lustre; gloss	170	110.00	145.00	55.00
V-21d	Gothic 359	Cream; lilac/pink flowers; green/gold leaves; gloss	160	110.00	145.00	55.00

Derivative

Gothic Ware Lamp, c.1948-1953

The shape-359 vase, above, was also made into a table lamp, with a hole in the base for the electrical cord.

Backstamp: Green ink stamp "Wade England Gothic" with impressed "359"

No.	Description	Colourways	Size	U.S.$	Can.$	U.K.£
V-21c1	Gothic 359 lamp	Cream; pink/yellow flowers; blue/green leaves; gloss	170	130.00	175.00	65.00

SHAPE 360
Gothic Ware Vase, c.1948-1953

Backstamp: Green ink stamp "Wade England Gothic" with impressed"360"

No.	Description	Colourways	Size	U.S.$	Can.$	U.K.£
V-22	Gothic 360	Cream; lilac/pink flowers; green/gold leaves; gloss	215	110.00	145.00	55.00

SHAPE 362
Peony Series Vase, c.1948-c.1952

Backstamp: Black ink stamp "Harvest Ware Wade England" with impressed "362"

No.	Description	Colourways	Size	U.S.$	Can.$	U.K.£
V-23	Harvest Ware 362	Cream; multi-coloured flowers	225	90.00	125.00	45.00

SHAPE 366
Gothic Ware Vase, c.1948-1953

Backstamp: Green ink stamp "Wade England Gothic" with impressed "366"

No.	Description	Colourways	Shape/Size	U.S.$	Can.$	U.K.£
V-24	Gothic 366	Cream; lilac/pink flowers; green/gold leaves	Ball shape/230	150.00	195.00	75.00

SHAPE 394
Peony Series Vase, c.1948-c.1952

Backstamp: Black ink stamp "Harvest Ware Wade England" with impressed "394"

No.	Description	Colourways	Size	U.S.$	Can.$	U.K.£
V-25	Harvest Ware 394	Cream; multi-coloured flowers	225	70.00	95.00	35.00

SHAPE 400

Empress Series Vases, c.1948-1953

In the late 1940s the Wadeheath Pottery produced these vases in mottled glazes. In the early 1950s, they were issued in matt white, and from 1952 to 1953, they were glazed in bright colours.

Photograph not available
at press time

Backstamp: A. Circular ink stamp "Royal Victoria Pottery Wade England," late 1940s
B. Black ink stamp "Wade England" with impressed "400," early 1950s
C. Black ink stamp "Wade Empress England" with impressed "400," 1952-1953

No.	Description	Colourways	Size	U.S.$	Can.$	U.K.£
V-26a	Empress 400	Mottled green	215	80.00	110.00	40.00
V-26b	Empress 400	White	215	80.00	110.00	40.00
V-26c	Empress 400	Blue; gold stripes	215	130.00	175.00	65.00
V-26d	Empress 400	Green; gold stripes	215	130.00	175.00	65.00
V-26e	Empress 400	Maroon; gold stripes	215	130.00	175.00	65.00

SHAPE 402

Empress Series Vases, c.1948-1953

In the late 1940s the Wadeheath Pottery produced these vases in mottled glazes. In the early 1950s, they were issued in matt white, and from 1952 to 1953, they were glazed in bright colours.

Backstamp: A. Circular ink stamp "Royal Victoria Pottery Wade England," late 1940s
B. Black ink stamp "Wade England" with impressed "402," early 1950s
C. Black ink stamp "Wade Empress England" with impressed"402," 1952-1953

No.	Description	Colourways	Size	U.S.$	Can.$	U.K.£
V-27a	Empress 402	Mottled green	225	80.00	110.00	40.00
V-27b	Empress 402	White	225	80.00	110.00	40.00
V-27c	Empress 402	Blue; gold stripes	225	130.00	175.00	65.00
V-27d	Empress 402	Green; gold stripes	225	130.00	175.00	65.00
V-27e	Empress 402	Maroon; gold stripes	225	130.00	175.00	65.00

SHAPE 403
Empress Series Vases, c.1948-1953

In the late 1940s the Wadeheath Pottery produced these vases in mottled glazes. In the early 1950s, they were issued in matt white, and from 1952 to 1953, they were glazed in bright colours. The variation in sizes is due to the replacement of worn dies.

Backstamp: A. Circular ink stamp "Royal Victoria Pottery Wade England," late 1940s
B. Black ink stamp "Wade England" with impressed "403," early 1950s
C. Black ink stamp "Wade Empress England" with impressed "403," 1952-1953

No.	Description	Colourways	Size	U.S.$	Can.$	U.K.£
V-28a	Empress 403	Mottled green	180	80.00	110.00	40.00
V-28b	Empress 403	White	180	80.00	110.00	40.00
V-28c	Empress 403	Blue; gold stripes	170	130.00	175.00	65.00
V-28d	Empress 403	Green; gold stripes	170	130.00	175.00	65.00
V-28e	Empress 403	Maroon; gold stripes	170	130.00	175.00	65.00

SHAPE 404
Empress Series Vases, c.1948-1953

In the late 1940s the Wadeheath Pottery produced these vases in mottled glazes. In the early 1950s, they were issued in matt white, and from 1952 to 1953, they were glazed in bright colours.

Photograph not available
at press time

Backstamp: A. Circular ink stamp "Royal Victoria Pottery Wade England," late 1940s
B. Black ink stamp "Wade England" with impressed "404," early 1950s
C. Black ink stamp "Wade Empress England" with impressed"404," 1952-1953

No.	Description	Colourways	Size	U.S.$	Can.$	U.K.£
V-29a	Empress 404	Mottled green	255	90.00	125.00	45.00
V-29b	Empress 404	White	255	90.00	125.00	45.00
V-29c	Empress 404	Blue; gold stripes	255	140.00	195.00	75.00
V-29d	Empress 404	Green; gold stripes	280	140.00	195.00	75.00
V-29e	Empress 404	Maroon; gold stripes	280	140.00	195.00	75.00

SHAPE 434
Harmony Ware Vases, 1957–c.1962

Backstamp: **A.** Red transfer print "Wade England" with impressed "England" and "434"
B. Red transfer print "Wade England Fern" with impressed "England" and "434"
C. Black transfer print "Wade England Parasol" with impressed "England" and "434"
D. Black print "Wade England," green shooting stars and impressed "England" and "434"
E. Impressed "Wade England" and "434"

No	Description	Colourways	Size	U.S.$	Can.$	U.K.£
V-30a	Carnival	White; yellow/red/green flower	220	80.00	110.00	40.00
V-30b	Fern	White; red/black ferns	220	80.00	110.00	40.00
V-30c	Parasols	White; multi-coloured parasols	220	80.00	110.00	40.00
V-30d	Shooting stars	White; multi-coloured stars	220	80.00	110.00	40.00
V-30e	Solid colour	Black	220	50.00	70.00	25.00
V-30f	Solid colour	White	220	50.00	70.00	25.00
V-30g	Solid colour	Green	220	50.00	70.00	25.00
V-30h	Solid colour	Yellow	220	50.00	70.00	25.00
V-30i	Two tone	Grey outside; pink inside	220	50.00	70.00	25.00
V-30j	Two tone	Green outside; peach inside	220	50.00	70.00	25.00

SHAPE 452

Harmony Ware Vases, 1957-c.1962

Shape 452 is a miniature bud vase with a deep V-shaped mouth.

Photograph not available
at press time

Backstamp: **A.** Red transfer print "Wade England" with impressed "England" and "452"
B. Red transfer print "Wade England Fern" with impressed "England" and "452"
C. Black transfer print "Wade England Parasol" with impressed "England" and "452"
D. Black print "Wade England," green shooting stars and impressed "England" and "452"
E. Impressed "Wade England" and "452"

No.	Description	Colourways	Size	U.S.$	Can.$	U.K.£
V-31a	Carnival	White; yellow/red/green flower	126	20.00	30.00	10.00
V-31b	Fern	White; black/red ferns	126	20.00	30.00	10.00
V-31c	Parasols	White; multi-coloured parasols	126	20.00	30.00	10.00
V-31d	Shooting stars	White; multi-coloured stars	126	20.00	30.00	10.00
V-31e	Solid colour	Black	126	10.00	15.00	5.00
V-31f	Solid colour	White	126	10.00	15.00	5.00
V-31g	Solid colour	Green	126	10.00	15.00	5.00
V-31h	Solid colour	Yellow	126	10.00	15.00	5.00
V-31i	Two tone	Grey outside; pink inside	126	10.00	15.00	5.00
V-31j	Two tone	Green outside; peach inside	126	10.00	15.00	5.00

SHAPE 458

These vases are similar to shape 434.

Ballet Series Vase, 1957-1958

Backstamp: A. Black and red transfer print "Ballet Wade of England" and impressed "England" with "458"
B. Black and red transfer print "Ballet Wade of England" with impressed "England"

No.	Description	Colourways	Size	U.S.$	Can.$	U.K.£
V-32	Ballet	White; black mouth; black/yellow print	185	130.00	175.00	65.00

Harmony Ware Vases, 1957-c.1962

Photograph not available
at press time

Backstamp: A. Red transfer print "Wade England" with impressed "England" and "458"
B. Red transfer print "Wade England Fern" with impressed "England" and "458"
C. Black transfer print "Wade England Parasol" with impressed "England" and "458"
D. Black print "Wade England," green shooting stars and impressed "England" and "458"
E. Impressed "Wade England" and "458"

No.	Description	Colourways	Size	U.S.$	Can.$	U.K.£
V-33a	Carnival	White; yellow/red/green flower	177	50.00	70.00	25.00
V-33b	Fern	White; black/red ferns	177	50.00	70.00	25.00
V-33c	Parasols	White; multi-coloured parasols	177	50.00	70.00	25.00
V-33d	Shooting stars	White; multi-coloured stars	177	50.00	70.00	25.00
V-33e	Solid colour	Black	177	30.00	45.00	15.00
V-33f	Solid colour	White	177	30.00	45.00	15.00
V-33g	Solid colour	Green	177	30.00	45.00	15.00
V-33h	Solid colour	Yellow	177	30.00	45.00	15.00
V-33i	Two tone	Grey outside; pink inside	177	30.00	45.00	15.00
V-33j	Two tone	Green outside; peach inside	177	30.00	45.00	15.00

SHAPE 459
Zamba Series Vase, 1957

This vase features black dancers in rhythmic poses silhouetted on a white glazed background. Care has to be taken when washing as the black paint inside flakes off.

Backstamp: **A.** Red transfer print "Wade England" with impressed "England" and "459"
B. Black transfer print "Wade England" with impressed "England" and "459"
C. Red transfer print "Wade England"
D. Black transfer print "Wade England"
E. Red transfer print "Wade England" with impressed "England"
F. Black transfer print "Wade England" with impressed "England"

No.	Description	Colourways	Size	U.S.$	Can.$	U.K.£
V-34	Zamba 459	White; black print	285	200.00	265.00	100.00

SHAPE 460

Ballet Series Vase, 1957-1958

Backstamp: A. Black and red transfer print "Ballet Wade of England" and impressed "England" with "460"
   B. Black and red transfer print "Ballet Wade of England" with impressed "England"

No.	Description	Colourways	Size	U.S.$	Can.$	U.K.£
V-35	Ballet 460	White; black mouth; black/yellow print	185	130.00	175.00	65.00

Fantasia Series Vase, 1961

Photograph not available
at press time

Backstamp: Black transfer print "Fantasia by Wade of England - copyright Walt Disney Productions"
   with impressed "England 460"

No.	Description	Colourways	Size	U.S.$	Can.$	U.K.£
V-36	Fantasia 460	Grey outside; pink inside; black, white, pink print	185	130.00	175.00	65.00

Zamba Series Vase, 1957

   This vase features black dancers in rhythmic poses silhouetted on a white glazed background. Care has to be taken when washing as the black paint inside flakes off.

Photograph not available
at press time

Backstamp: A. Red transfer print "Wade England" with impressed "England" and "460"
   B. Black transfer print "Wade England" with impressed "England" and "460"
   C. Red transfer print "Wade England"
   D. Black transfer print "Wade England"
   E. Red transfer print "Wade England" with impressed "England"
   F. Black transfer print "Wade England" with impressed "England"

No.	Description	Colourways	Size	U.S.$	Can.$	U.K.£
V-37	Zamba 460	White; black print	180	160.00	215.00	80.00

SHAPE 464

Zamba Series Vase, 1957

This vase features black dancers in rhythmic poses silhouetted on a white glazed background. Care has to be taken when washing as the black paint inside flakes off.

Backstamp: **A.** Red transfer print "Wade England" with impressed "England" and "464"
B. Black transfer print "Wade England" with impressed "England" and "464"
C. Red transfer print "Wade England"
D. Black transfer print "Wade England"
E. Red transfer print "Wade England" with impressed "England"
F. Black transfer print "Wade England" with impressed "England"

No.	Description	Colourways	Size	U.S.$	Can.$	U.K.£
V-38	Zamba 460	White; black print	235	160.00	215.00	80.00

SHAPE 467

Vases, 1957-1958

The Ballet Series vase was issued between 1957 and 1958 and the Zamba Series vase in 1957.

Backstamp: **A.** Red transfer print "Wade England"
B. Black transfer print "Wade England"
C. Red transfer print "Wade England" with impressed "England"
D. Black transfer print "Wade England" with impressed "England"
E. Red transfer print "Wade England" with impressed "England" and "467"
F. Black transfer print "Wade England" with impressed "England" and "467"
G. Black and red transfer print "Ballet Wade of England" and impressed "England" with "467"
H. Black and red transfer print "Ballet Wade of England" with impressed "England"

No.	Description	Colourways	Size	U.S.$	Can.$	U.K.£
V-39a	Ballet Series	White; black mouth; black/yellow print	105	90.00	125.00	45.00
V-39b	Zamba Series	White; black mouth; black print	105	90.00	125.00	45.00

SHAPE 468

Ballet Series Vase, 1957-1958

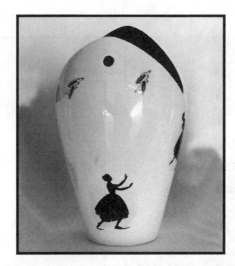

Backstamp: A. Black and red transfer print "Ballet Wade of England" and impressed "England" with "468"
B. Black and red transfer print "Ballet Wade of England" with impressed "England"

No.	Description	Colourways	Size	U.S.$	Can.$	U.K.£
V-40	Ballet 468	White; black mouth; black/yellow print	245	150.00	200.00	75.00

Fantasia Series Vase, 1961

Backstamp: Black transfer print "Fantasia by Wade of England - copyright Walt Disney Productions" with impressed "England 468"

No.	Description	Colourways	Size	U.S.$	Can.$	U.K.£
V-41	Fantasia 468	Grey outside; pink inside; black/white/pink print	228	160.00	215.00	80.00

SHAPE 469
Zamba Series Miniature Vase, 1957

Backstamp: A. Red transfer print "Wade England" with impressed "England" and "469"
B. Black transfer print "Wade England" with impressed "England" and "469"
C. Red transfer print "Wade England"
D. Black transfer print "Wade England"
E. Red transfer print "Wade England" with impressed "England"
F. Black transfer print "Wade England" with impressed "England"

No.	Description	Colourways	Size	U.S.$	Can.$	U.K.£
V-42	Zamba 469	White; black print	125	40.00	55.00	20.00

SHAPE 477

Vases, 1957-1961

The Ballet series was produced between 1957 and 1958 and the Fantasia series was available during 1961 only.

Photograph not available
at press time

Backstamp: A. Black and red transfer print "Ballet Wade Of England" and impressed "England" with "477"
B. Black and red transfer print "Ballet Wade Of England" with impressed "England"
C. Black transfer print "Fantasia by Wade of England - copyright Walt Disney Productions," impressed "England 477"

No.	Description	Colourways	Size	U.S.$	Can.$	U.K.£
V-43	Ballet 477	White; red mouth; black/yellow print	228	100.00	135.00	50.00
V-44a	Fantasia 477	Grey outside; pink inside; black/white/pink print	228	100.00	135.00	50.00
V-44b	Fantasia 477	Pink outside; grey inside; black/white/pink print	228	100.00	135.00	50.00

SHAPE 478

Ballet Series Vase, 1957-1958

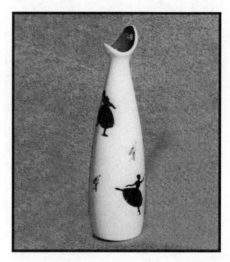

Backstamp: A. Black and red transfer print "Ballet Wade of England" and impressed "England" with "478"
B. Black and red transfer print "Ballet Wade of England" with impressed "England"

No.	Description	Colourways	Size	U.S.$	Can.$	U.K.£
V-45	Ballet 478	White; red mouth; black/yellow print	300	100.00	135.00	50.00

Zamba Series Vase, 1957

This vase features black dancers in rhythmic poses silhouetted on a white glazed background. Care has to be taken when washing as the paint flakes off.

Backstamp: A. Red transfer print "Wade England" with impressed "England" and "478"
B. Black transfer print "Wade England" with impressed "England" and "478"
C. Red transfer print "Wade England"
D. Black transfer print "Wade England"
E. Red transfer print "Wade England" with impressed "England"
F. Black transfer print "Wade England" with impressed "England"

No.	Description	Colourways	Size	U.S.$	Can.$	U.K.£
V-46	Zamba 478	White; red mouth; black print	300	100.00	135.00	50.00

SHAPE 483

Ballet Series Vase, 1957-1958

Photograph not available
at press time

Backstamp: A. Black and red transfer print "Ballet Wade of England" and impressed "England" with "483"
B. Black and red transfer print "Ballet Wade of England" with impressed "England"

No.	Description	Colourways	Size	U.S.$	Can.$	U.K.£
V-47	Ballet 483	White; black mouth; black/yellow print	110	30.00	40.00	15.00

Black Frost Series Vase, 1957-c.1962

Photograph not available
at press time

Backstamp: Red print "Wade England"

No.	Description	Colourways	Size	U.S.$	Can.$	U.K.£
V-48	Black Frost 483	Black; white flowers; gold rim	110	20.00	30.00	10.00

Souvenir Bud Vases, c.1958-c.1962

Backstamp: A. Red transfer print "Wade England"
B. Red transfer print "Wade England" with impressed "483"

No.	Description	Colourways	Size	U.S.$	Can.$	U.K.£
V-49a	Balmoral stag's head	White; multi-coloured print	110	20.00	30.00	10.00
V-49b	Big Ben	White/black; black/blue print	110	20.00	30.00	10.00
V-49c	Eastbourne	White/black; red/green pixie	110	20.00	30.00	10.00
V-49d	Eros, Piccadilly Circus	White/black; black/blue print	110	20.00	30.00	10.00
V-49e	London arms	White/gold; multi-coloured print	110	20.00	30.00	10.00
V-49f	New Brunswick shield	White/gold; multi-coloured print	115	20.00	30.00	10.00
V-49g	Prince Edward Island	White/gold; multi-coloured print	115	20.00	30.00	10.00
V-49h	Tower Bridge	White/black; black/blue print	110	20.00	30.00	10.00
V-49i	Trafalgar Square	White/black; black/blue print	110	20.00	30.00	10.00
V-49j	Trafalgar Square	Black; white print	110	20.00	30.00	10.00

Vases, c.1958-c.1965

The rim of these vases is coloured in 22-karat gold.

Backstamp: **A.** Red transfer print "Wade England"
B. Black transfer print "Wade England"

No.	Description	Colourways	Size	U.S.$	Can.$	U.K.£
V-50a	Pink rose	White; gold mouth; pink flower	110	20.00	30.00	10.00
V-50b	Pixie on mushroom	White; gold mouth; green/red pixie	110	20.00	30.00	10.00
V-50c	Red rose	White; gold mouth; red flower	110	20.00	30.00	10.00
V-50d	Wild violet	White; gold mouth; violet flowers	110	20.00	30.00	10.00
V-50e	Yellow rose	White; gold mouth; yellow flower	110	20.00	30.00	10.00

SHAPE 484

Ballet Series Vase, 1957-1958

Photograph not available
at press time

Backstamp: A. Black and red transfer print "Ballet Wade of England" and impressed "England" with "484"
B. Black and red transfer print "Ballet Wade of England" with impressed "England"

No.	Description	Colourways	Size	U.S.$	Can.$	U.K.£
V-51	Ballet 484	White; red mouth; black/yellow print	110	30.00	40.00	15.00

Souvenir Bud Vases, c.1958-c.1962

Photograph not available
at press time

Backstamp: A. Red transfer print "Wade England"
B. Red transfer print "Wade England" with impressed "484"

No.	Description	Colourways	Shape/Size	U.S.$	Can.$	U.K.£
V-52a	New Brunswick	White/gold; multi-coloured print	110	20.00	30.00	10.00
V-52b	Paignton pixie	White/gold; red/green pixie	110	20.00	30.00	10.00
V-52c	Prince Edward Island	White/gold; multi-coloured print	110	20.00	30.00	10.00
V-52d	Remember London	White; gold mouth; multi-coloured print	110	20.00	28.00	8.00

Vases, c.1958-c.1965

Backstamp: A. Red transfer print "Wade England"
B. Black transfer print "Wade England"

No.	Description	Colourways	Size	U.S.$	Can.$	U.K.£
V-53a	Pearlised	Pearlised orange; gold mouth	110	20.00	30.00	10.00
V-53b	Pink rose	White; gold mouth; pink flower	110	20.00	30.00	10.00
V-53c	Red rose	White; gold mouth; red flower	110	20.00	30.00	10.00
V-53d	Yellow rose	White; gold mouth; yellow flower	110	20.00	30.00	10.00

SHAPE 513
Black Frost Series Vase, 1957-c.1962

The Black Frost design used on these vases is the same as that used by Wade Heath in the 1930s.

Backstamp: Red print "Wade England"

No.	Description	Colourways	Size	U.S.$	Can.$	U.K.£
V-54	Black Frost 513	Black; white flowers; gold rim	143	50.00	70.00	25.00

SHAPE C.345
Mourne Series, 1971-1976

This series of porcelain vases is completely different from previously produced Irish Wade.

Backstamp: Embossed "Made in Ireland Porcelain Wade eire tira dheanta"

No.	Description	Colourways	Size	U.S.$	Can.$	U.K.£
V-55	Mourne C.345	Grey/green; orange sunflower	95	60.00	80.00	30.00

SHAPE C.346
Mourne Series Vase, 1971-1976

Backstamp: Embossed "Made in Ireland Porcelain Wade eire tira dheanta"

No.	Description	Colourways	Size	U.S.$	Can.$	U.K.£
V-56	Mourne C.346	Grey/green; yellow flower	100	60.00	80.00	30.00

SHAPE C.347
Mourne Series Vase, 1971-1976

Backstamp: Embossed "Made in Ireland Porcelain Wade eire tira dheanta"

No.	Description	Colourways	Size	U.S.$	Can.$	U.K.£
V-57	Mourne C.347	Brown/green; orange rose	190	70.00	95.00	35.00

SHAPE C.350
Mourne Series Vase, 1971-1976

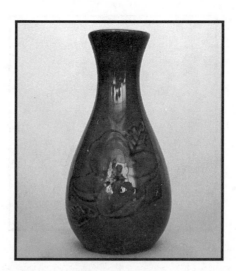

Backstamp: Embossed "Made in Ireland Porcelain Wade eire tira dheanta"

No.	Description	Colourways	Size	U.S.$	Can.$	U.K.£
V-58	Mourne C.350	Brown/green; orange flower	170	60.00	80.00	30.00

SHAPE C.K.3
Celtic Porcelain Urn, 1965

Backstamp: A. Embossed "Celtic Porcelain by Wade Ireland" in an Irish knot wreath
B. Black transfer print "Celtic Porcelain made in Ireland by Wade Co. Armagh"

No.	Description	Colourways	Size	U.S.$	Can.$	U.K.£
V-59	Celtic C.K.3	Mottled blue-green	Large/293	100.00	135.00	50.00

SHAPE C.K. 5
Celtic Porcelain Urn, 1965

Backstamp: A. Embossed "Celtic Porcelain by Wade Ireland" in an Irish knot wreath
B. Black transfer print "Celtic Porcelain made in Ireland by Wade Co. Armagh"

No.	Description	Colourways	Size	U.S.$	Can.$	U.K.£
V-60	Celtic C.K.5	Mottled blue-green	Small/146	90.00	120.00	45.00

SHAPE DON
1933-1934

These round flower holders have a flared, wavy rim and a flower frog in the neck.

Photograph not available
at press time

Backstamp: Red ink stamp "Wadeheath England" with a lion

No.	Description	Colourways	Size	U.S.$	Can.$	U.K.£
V-61a	Don	Cream; red/blue/orange jigsaw design	141	190.00	255.00	95.00
V-61b	Don	Cream; brown/orange rings	141	190.00	255.00	95.00

SHAPE I.P.93
Barrel Vases, 1950-c.1985

The style V-62a vase has two rows of knurls and a row of shamrock leaves around the centre. It was first produced in the 1950s, then again in the 1970s and 1980s. Version V-62b, produced from the early 1960s to the 1980s, has a transfer print of the giant Finn McCaul on the front.

Backstamp: A. Impressed "Irish Porcelain" curved over a shamrock with "Made in Ireland" impressed in a straight line underneath
        B. Black print "Irish Porcelain" over a shamrock with "Wade County Armagh"

No.	Description	Colourways	Size	U.S.$	Can.$	U.K.£
V-62a	Barrel I.P.93	Blue/green	101	20.00	30.00	10.00
V-62b	Barrel I.P.93	Blue-grey; multi-coloured print	101	40.00	55.00	20.00

SHAPE S.R.09
Shamrock Range Vase, 1983-1986

Wade Ireland produced this vase with a design of shamrock leaves on it. It was from the same mould as the 1981 Royal Wedding vase.

For an illustration of this vase
see page 208

Backstamp: Unknown

No	Description	Colourways	Size	U.S.$	Can.$	U.K.£
V-63	Shamrock S.R.09	White; green shamrocks	220	30.00	40.00	15.00

SHAPE S.R.10
Shamrock Range Vase, 1983-1986

Wade Ireland produced this vase with a design of shamrock leaves on it.

For an illustration of this vase
see page 208

Backstamp: Unknown

No	Description	Colourways	Size	U.S.$	Can.$	U.K.£
V-64	Shamrock S.R.10	White; green shamrocks	Unknown	30.00	40.00	15.00

SHAPE S.R.11
Shamrock Range Vase, 1983-1986

Wade Ireland produced this vase with a design of shamrock leaves on it.

For an illustration of this vase
see page 208

Backstamp: Unknown

No	Description	Colourways	Size	U.S.$	Can.$	U.K.£
V-65	Shamrock S.R.11	White; green shamrocks	Unknown	30.00	40.00	15.00

SHAPE S.R.19
Shamrock Range Urn, 1983-1986

Wade Ireland produced this urn with a design of shamrock leaves on it.

For an illustration of this vase
see page 208

Backstamp: Unknown

No	Description	Colourways	Size	U.S.$	Can.$	U.K.£
V-66	Shamrock S.R.19	White; green shamrocks	202	30.00	40.00	15.00

BLACK FROST VASES, 1957-c.1962

The Black Frost design used on these vases is the same as that used by Wade Heath in the 1930s.

Backstamp: Red print "Wade England"

No.	Description	Colourways	Size	U.S.$	Can.$	U.K.£
V-67	Boat shape	Black; white flowers; gold rim	113	80.00	110.00	40.00
V-68	Cylindrical/ pierced lid	Black; white flowers; gold rim	165	90.00	120.00	45.00
V-69	Tapered neck	Black; white flowers; gold rim	170	70.00	95.00	35.00
V-70	Small bulbous	Black; white flowers; gold rim	112	50.00	70.00	25.00

BLUE-RIMMED MINIATURE BUD VASES, 1959-c.1965

These footed vases are the same shapes as styles V-73 and V-74 of the Charles Dickens miniature bud vases, with different transfer prints on the front.

Backstamp: A. Red print "Wade England"
B. Black print "Wade England"

No.	Description	Colourways	Shape/Size	U.S.$	Can.$	U.K.£
V-71a	Crinoline lady	White; blue rim; multi-coloured print	Footed, sloping/115	20.00	30.00	10.00
V-71b	Flower spray	White; blue rim; multi-coloured flowers	Footed, sloping/115	20.00	30.00	10.00
V-72a	Flower	White; orange rim; pink flower	Footed, round/115	20.00	30.00	10.00
V-72b	Flower	White; yellow rim; pink flower	Footed, round/115	20.00	30.00	10.00
V-72c	Wild violets	White; blue rim; violet flowers	Footed, round/115	20.00	30.00	10.00

CHARLES DICKENS MINIATURE BUD VASES, 1959-1960

These vases are decorated with transfer prints of characters from Charles Dickens's novels. See also the Charles Dickens dishes.

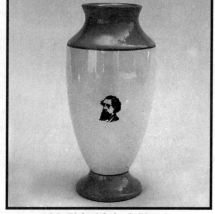

Mr. Pickwick, face (V-74c)   Mr. Pickwick, back (V-74c)

Backstamp: Red transfer print "Wade England" on base, with a silhouette of Dickens's head on the back of the vase

No.	Description	Colourways	Shape/Size	U.S.$	Can.$	U.K.£
V-73	Uriah Heep	White; blue rim, base; multi-coloured print	Footed, sloping/115	20.00	30.00	10.00
V-74a	Little Nell	White; blue rim, base; multi-coloured print	Footed, round/115	20.00	30.00	10.00
V-74b	Mr. Micawber	White; blue rim, base; multi-coloured print	Footed, round/115	20.00	30.00	10.00
V-74c	Mr. Pickwick	White; blue rim, base; multi-coloured print	Footed, round/115	20.00	30.00	10.00
V-75	Mr. Pickwick	White; blue rim, base; multi-coloured print	No foot/round/115	20.00	30.00	10.00

CHELSEA SERIES VASE, 1962

This vase is similar in style to the Empress vases.

Photograph not available
at press time

Backstamp: Red transfer print "Wade England"

No	Description	Colourways	Size	U.S.$	Can.$	U.K.£
V-76	Chelsea	Black matt; gold highlights	171	60.00	85.00	30.00

CLARENCE AND CLARA BUD VASES

These miniature bud vases, which were called "Buddies" on the package, were painted to look like cats.

Backstamp: Red transfer print "Wade England"

No.	Description	Colourways	Size	U.S.$	Can.$	U.K.£
V-77a	Clarence	White; red inside; black/blue/red face; eyes open	110	40.00	55.00	20.00
V-77b	Clara	White; red inside; black/red face; eyes closed	110	40.00	55.00	20.00

DIAMOND-SHAPED FLOWER HOLDER, 1936-1940s

This diamond-shaped flower holder has fins on each side and a fitted flower frog in the top.

Photograph not available
at press time

Backstamp: Black ink stamp "Wadeheath England" with a lion

No.	Description	Colourways	Size	U.S.$	Can.$	U.K.£
V-78	Diamond	Cream; black fins; orange base, flower; orange/black/yellow bands	171	150.00	200.00	75.00

EDWARDIAN VASES, 1986-1990

These vases have a flared neck and a wavy rim.

Backstamp: Red "Wade England" with two red lines

No.	Description	Colourways	Size	U.S.$	Can.$	U.K.£
V-79a	Floral fayre	White; pink/green print	Small/153	20.00	30.00	10.00
V-79b	Fuchsia	White; pink/yellow/grey print	Small/153	20.00	30.00	10.00
V-80a	Floral fayre	White; pink/green print	Medium/190	30.00	40.00	15.00
V-80b	Fuchsia	White; pink/yellow/grey print	Medium/190	30.00	40.00	15.00

FANTASIA SERIES VASES, 1961

Round/short neck

Round/long neck

Backstamp: Black transfer print "Fantasia by Wade of England - copyright Walt Disney Productions"

No.	Description	Colourways	Size	U.S.$	Can.$	U.K.£
V-81	Round/short neck	Pale blue; black, white, pink print; gold rim	225	150.00	200.00	75.00
V-82	Round/long neck	Pale blue; black, white, pink print; gold rim	185	150.00	200.00	75.00

FLOWER HOLDER WITH FINS, 1936-c.1940

Backstamp: Green ink stamp "Wade Heath England"

No.	Description	Colourways	Size	U.S.$	Can.$	U.K.£
V-83	Flower holder	Cream; brown fins, base; blue/pink flowers	130	150.00	200.00	75.00

JACOBEAN AND KAWA VASES, 1990-1992

The Jacobean design consists of enamelled exotic flowers, and Kawa is a Japanese design of peonies and bamboo stems.

Photograph not available at press time

Backstamp: A. Red print "Wade England" with two red lines and "Jacobean"
B. Gold print "Wade England" with two gold lines and "Kawa"

No.	Description	Colourways	Size	U.S.$	Can.$	U.K.£
V-84a	Jacobean	White; red/black print	Small/Unknown	30.00	40.00	15.00
V-84b	Kawa	White; pastel pink/green print; gold highlights	Small/Unknown	30.00	40.00	15.00
V-85a	Jacobean	White; red/black print	Medium/Unknown	40.00	55.00	20.00
V-85b	Kawa	White; pastel pink/green print; gold highlights	Medium/Unknown	40.00	55.00	20.00
V-86a	Jacobean	White; red/black print	Large/Unknown	50.00	70.00	25.00
V-86b	Kawa	White; pastel pink/green print; gold highlights	Large/Unknown	50.00	70.00	25.00

MINIATURE-HANDLES VASE, 1937

This round vase has miniature handles near the top and a rolling scroll design around the base.

Photograph not available at press time

Backstamp: Black ink stamp "Flaxman Ware Hand Made Pottery by Wadeheath England," 1935-1937

No.	Description	Colourways	Size	U.S.$	Can.$	U.K.£
V-87	Miniature handles	Mottled green/grey	229	70.00	95.00	35.00

ORCADIA WARE VASES, 1933-1935

Orcadia Ware was produced in vivid streaked glazes that were allowed to run over the rims and down the inside and the outside of the vases.

Style V-88 is an art nouveau style with high shoulders that narrow to a flared foot. The style V-89 flower holder has a flared, wavy rim and a flower frog which sits in the neck. Styles V-91 and 92 are round with a wide mouth and two ribs around the shoulder. The square-topped flower holder, style V-93, has fins on each side and a flower frog in the neck. Style V-95 has a wide mouth and a waist.

| Round (V-90) | Square flower holder (V-93) | Straight sides (V-94b) |

Backstamp: Orange ink stamp "Wadeheath Orcadia Ware"

No.	Description	Colourways	Size	U.S.$	Can.$	U.K.£
V-88	Art nouveau	Orange/green	180	150.00	200.00	75.00
V-89	Don flower holder	Orange/brown	141	190.00	255.00	95.00
V-90	Round	Green/orange streaks; blue base	175	150.00	200.00	75.00
V-91a	Shoulders	Green/orange	170	150.00	200.00	75.00
V-91b	Shoulders	Grey blue/orange/yellow	170	150.00	200.00	75.00
V-91c	Shoulders	Yellow/orange	170	150.00	200.00	75.00
V-92	Square flower holder	Orange/green	170	190.00	255.00	95.00
V-93a	Straight sides	Orange/yellow	190	150.00	200.00	75.00
V-93b	Straight sides	Green/orange streaks; blue base	190	150.00	200.00	75.00
V-94	Waisted	Orange/green	145	150.00	200.00	75.00

REGENCY SERIES MINIATURE VASE, 1959-1961

Backstamp: A. Red transfer print "Wade England"
B. Black transfer print "Wade England"

No.	Description	Colourways	Size	U.S.$	Can.$	U.K.£
V-95	Regency	White; gold highlights	Miniature/110	30.00	40.00	15.00

ROMAN AMPHORA VASES, 1937-1939

| Impressed flower handles (V-96) | Ribbed handles (V-97) | Three-ring handles (V-98a) |

Backstamp: Black ink stamp "Flaxman Wade Heath England"

No.	Description	Colourways	Size	U.S.$	Can.$	U.K.£
V-96	Impressed flower handles	Pale mottled green/grey	Miniature/100	70.00	95.00	35.00
V-97	Ribbed handles	Mottled orange/grey	Miniature/100	70.00	95.00	35.00
V-98a	Three-ring handles	Light brown	Miniature/95	70.00	95.00	35.00
V-98b	Three-ring handles	Pale blue	Miniature/95	70.00	95.00	35.00

ROSE TRELLIS VASES, 1986-1990

Backstamp: Red print "Wade England" with two red lines

No.	Name	Description	Size	U.S.$	Can.$	U.K.£
V-99	Rose trellis	White; dark pink/green print	159	20.00	30.00	10.00
V-100	Rose trellis	White; dark pink/green print	190	40.00	55.00	20.00

SHOULDERED, POT-SHAPED VASES, 1933-1935

These vases are the same shapes as style V-91 of the Orcadia Ware vases.

Backstamp: Black ink stamp "Wadeheath England" with a lion

No.	Description	Colourways	Size	U.S.$	Can.$	U.K.£
V-101	Pot shape	Pale yellow; black square; large mauve/orange/ blue flowers; green leaves	Small/165	110.00	145.00	55.00
V-102	Pot shape	Pale yellow; large orange flower; green leaves	Large/170	110.00	145.00	55.00

SILHOUETTE SERIES VASES, 1962

First issued in January 1962, these unusual-shaped vases have two blue panels and two matt-black panels with either a giraffe or a lion on them. The giraffe vase was introduced in January 1962, the lion vases in summer 1962. The original price was 5/6d.

Backstamp: Embossed "Wade Porcelain made in England"

No.	Description	Colourways	Size	U.S.$	Can.$	U.K.£
V-103a	Giraffe	Blue/black; blue giraffe	108	60.00	80.00	30.00
V-103b	Lion	Blue/black; blue lion	108	60.00	80.00	30.00
V-103c	Lion	Blue/black; white lion	108	60.00	80.00	30.00

SOUVENIR BUD VASES, c.1958–c.1962

This is the same shape vase as the blue-rimmed miniature bud vases, although a new mould made these vases slightly smaller.

Backstamp: Red transfer print "Wade England"

No.	Description	Colourways	Shape/Size	U.S.$	Can.$	U.K.£
V-104a	New Brunswick shield	White; gold foot; multi-coloured print	Round/112	20.00	30.00	10.00
V-104b	Nova Scotia shield	White; gold foot; multi-coloured print	Round/112	20.00	30.00	10.00

TOPLINE VASES, 1963

The designs on the Topline vases were created by freelance designer Michael Caddy. They are all cylindrical in shape.

Backstamp: Red print "Wade England"

No.	Description	Colourways	Size	U.S.$	Can.$	U.K.£
V-105	Cylindrical	White; purple abstract panels	108	60.00	80.00	30.00
V-106a	Foot	White; black leaf medallion; gold foot	108	50.00	70.00	25.00
V-106b	Foot	White; multi-coloured print; black foot	108	50.00	70.00	25.00
V-106c	Foot	White; purple/gold abstract panels; black foot	108	60.00	80.00	30.00
V-106d	Foot	Black; white feather medallion; gold foot	108	50.00	70.00	25.00
V-106e	Foot	White; black bands, foot; gold abstract panels	108	60.00	80.00	30.00
V-107a	Foot	White; broad black band; purple abstract panels; gold foot	157	60.00	80.00	30.00
V-107b	Foot	White; multi-coloured print; black foot	157	50.00	70.00	25.00
V-107c	Foot	White; purple/gold abstract panels; black foot	157	60.00	80.00	30.00
V-107d	Foot	Black; white leaf medallions; gold foot	157	50.00	70.00	25.00
V-107e	Foot	White; black bands, foot; gold abstract panels	157	60.00	80.00	30.00
V-108a	Foot/short neck	White; black/silver-grey leaf medallion; black neck; gold foot	98	40.00	55.00	20.00
V-108b	Foot/short neck	White; purple abstract panels; black neck; gold foot	98	50.00	70.00	25.00
V-108c	Foot/short neck	White; multi-coloured print; black neck, foot	98	40.00	55.00	20.00
V-108d	Foot/short neck	White; purple/gold abstract panels; black neck, foot	98	50.00	70.00	25.00
V-108e	Foot/short neck	White; gold abstract panels; black neck, foot	98	50.00	70.00	25.00
V-109a	Long neck	White; black/silver-grey leaf medallion; black neck; gold rim	165	60.00	80.00	30.00
V-109b	Long neck	White; purple abstract panels; black neck; gold rim	165	70.00	95.00	35.00
V-109c	Long neck	White; multi-coloured print; black neck; gold rim	165	60.00	80.00	30.00
V-109d	Long neck	White; purple/gold abstract panels; black neck; white rim	165	70.00	95.00	35.00
V-109e	Long neck	White; white feather medallion; gold neck; black rim	165	60.00	80.00	30.00
V-109f	Long neck	White; gold abstract panels, rim; black neck	165	70.00	95.00	35.00
V-110	Flower holder/lid	White; black leaf medallion, neck; gold rim	165	80.00	110.00	40.00

TROPICAL FRUIT GATHERER VASES, 1961

The large vase has ribs running down the body, whereas the small vase does not.

Backstamp: Red transfer print "Wade England"

No.	Description	Colourways	Shape/Size	U.S.$	Can.$	U.K.£
V-111a	Banana gatherer	White; multi-coloured print	Bud/112	20.00	30.00	10.00
V-111b	Coconut gatherer	White; multi-coloured print	Bud/112	20.00	30.00	10.00
V-111c	Date gatherer	White; multi-coloured print	Bud/112	20.00	30.00	10.00
V-111d	Pineapple gatherer	White; multi-coloured print	Bud/112	20.00	30.00	10.00
V-111e	Prickly pear gatherer	White; multi-coloured print	Bud/112	20.00	30.00	10.00
V-111f	Sugar cane cutter	White; multi-coloured print	Bud/112	20.00	30.00	10.00
V-112	Banana gatherer	Cream; gold rim, foot; multi-coloured print	Large/242	70.00	95.00	35.00

VIKING VASES, 1959-1965, 1976-1982

First issued in September 1959, these vases were produced in a Scintillite, high-gloss finish. The unusual Flaxman Ware mottled-green model may have been a prototype. These vases were produced both in England and Ireland. The original price was 4/11d each. Versions V-114c and 114d were reissued from 1976 to 1982.

Backstamp: A. Embossed "Wade Porcelain Made in England"
B. Embossed "Wade Porcelain Made in Ireland"

No.	Description	Colourways	Size	U.S.$	Can.$	U.K.£
V-113a	Viking vase	Mottled green	80	70.00	95.00	35.00
V-113b	Viking vase	Brown/blue/grey	80	40.00	55.00	20.00
V-113c	Viking vase	Honey brown/grey green	80	40.00	55.00	20.00
V-113d	Viking vase	Dark brown/grey blue	80	40.00	55.00	20.00

SHAPE INDEX
AND DESIGNS

SHAPE NUMBER INDEX

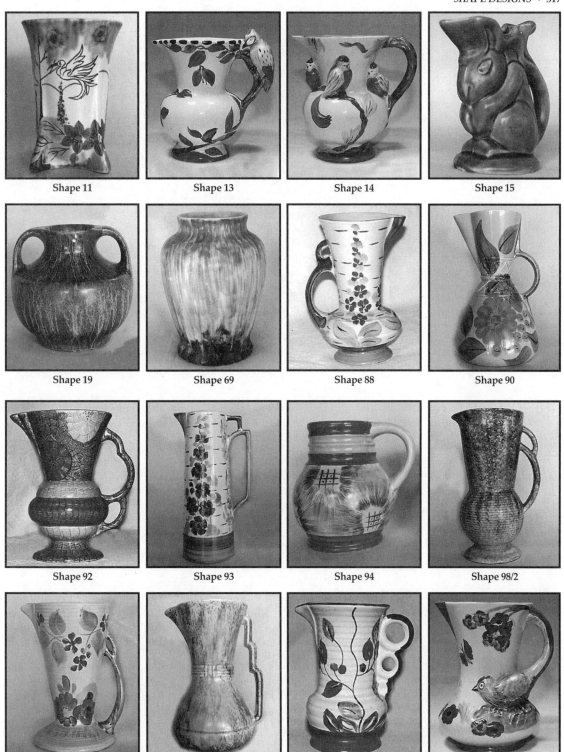

Shape 11	Shape 13	Shape 14	Shape 15
Shape 19	Shape 69	Shape 88	Shape 90
Shape 92	Shape 93	Shape 94	Shape 98/2
Shape 106	Shape 110	Shape 113	Shape 114

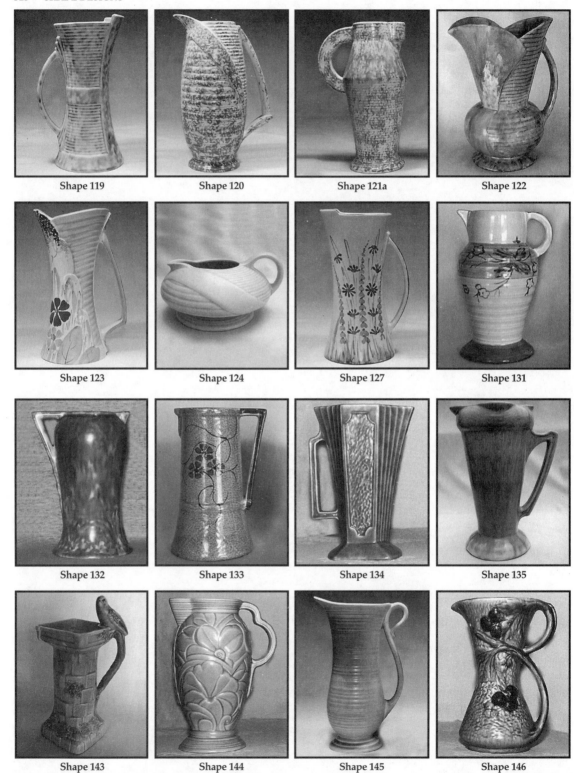

Shape 119

Shape 120

Shape 121a

Shape 122

Shape 123

Shape 124

Shape 127

Shape 131

Shape 132

Shape 133

Shape 134

Shape 135

Shape 143

Shape 144

Shape 145

Shape 146

Shape 147

Shape 148

Shape 149

Shape 154

Shape 155

Shape 157

Shape 159

Shape 161

Shape 168

Shape 169

Shape 173

Shape 212

Shape 213

Shape 214

Shape 216

Shape 217

Shape 224

Shape 225

Shape 226

Shape 242

Shape 243

Shape 244

Shape 246

Shape 247

Shape 248

Shape 249

Shape 250

Shape 301

Shape 302

Shape 313

Shape 332

Shape 333

Shape 334

Shape 342

Shape 343

Shape 359

Shape 360

Shape 362

Shape 366

Shape 369

Shape 371

Shape 394

Shape 398

Shape 400

Shape 401

Shape 402

Shape 403

Shape 404

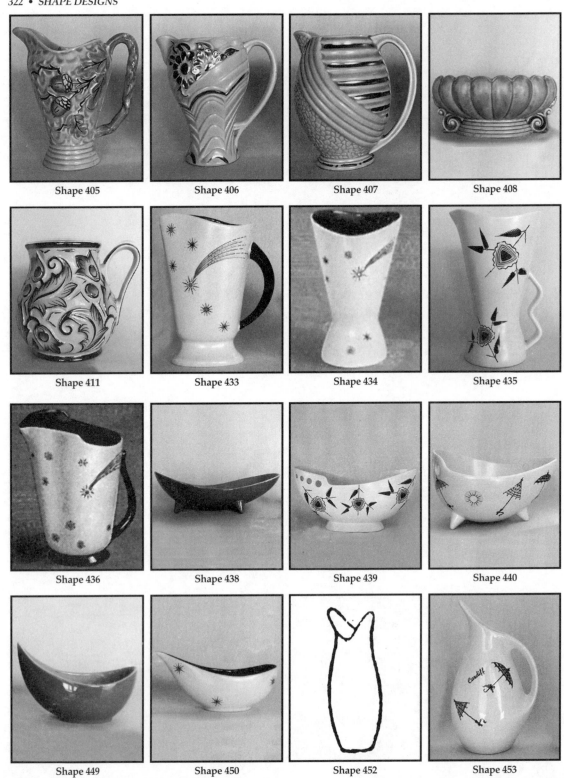

Shape 405	Shape 406	Shape 407	Shape 408
Shape 411	Shape 433	Shape 434	Shape 435
Shape 436	Shape 438	Shape 439	Shape 440
Shape 449	Shape 450	Shape 452	Shape 453

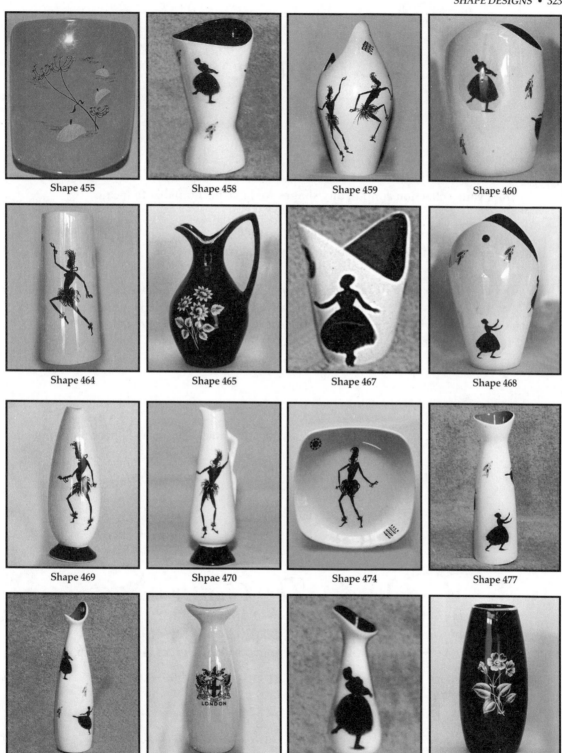

Shape 455

Shape 458

Shape 459

Shape 460

Shape 464

Shape 465

Shape 467

Shape 468

Shape 469

Shpae 470

Shape 474

Shape 477

Shape 478

Shape 483

Shape 484

Shape 513

The Charlton Press

Dear Collector:

Does your collection contain any shapes we have been unable to locate?

While we have searched as thoroughly as possible, we realize that some of you have collections that may include those obscure shapes that have eluded us.

Our goal is to make our *Charlton Standard Catalogues of Wade* as complete and useful as they can possibly be. The shape index we have provided here is just one example. If you have a shape which you do not see in *The Charlton Standard Catalogue of Wade, Vol.2 Decorative Ware* we would greatly appreciate a photograph of it. Black and white, unscreened photos are best, but colour is also suitable.

Please send your contributions together with your name, address and phone number to:

The Charlton Press
Editorial Office
2010 Yonge Street
Toronto, Ontario M4S 1Z9 Fax (416) 488-4656

NAME INDEX

NAME INDEX

Temple vase (with flowers), 116
Thistle ashtrays, 7
Three-legged posy bowls, 260
Tyre dishes, 87
Topline:
  dishes, 87
  jars, 120
  vases, 312
Traditional posy bowls, 261
Treasure chest trinket box, 36
Triangle (with flowers), 110
Triangular vase, stepped base (with flowers), 116
Tropical fruit gatherers:
  dishes, 88
  vases, 313
Trumps dishes, 88
T.T. trays, 89
Tulip planter, 216

V

Valencia posy bowls, 262
Vases (with flowers), 114-116
Venetian flower pots, 216
Veteran cars and horse-drawn bus boxes, 37
Veteran Car Series:
  dishes, 90
  miniature oil funnels, 207
  oil jugs, 181
  peanut dishes, 90
  tire dishes, 91
  wall plates, 236

Victorian Ladies cameo portrait:
  plaques, 226
  trinket pots, 37
Victorian water jug and bowl, 186
Viking vases, 314
Vintage cars lamp, 196
Violet posy bowl, 262
Vulcan pots (with flowers), 107

W

Wagon Train dishes, 92
Wall masks, 230
Wee Willie Winkie nursery wall plaques, 227
Wellyphant wall plate, 236
Wide-mouth jug (with flowers), 113
Wide-mouth jugs, 186
Wildfowl wall plaques, 228
Windsor Castle pin tray, 92
Woven basket with roses, 14

Y

Yacht wall plaques, 229

Z

Zamba Series:
  dishes, 93
  jug, 172, 173
  vases, 284, 285, 286, 287, 289, 290
Zebra-striped jugs, 187
Zukuro lamps, 197

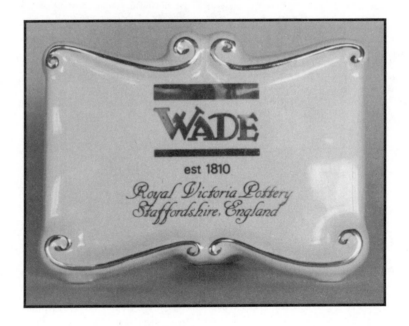

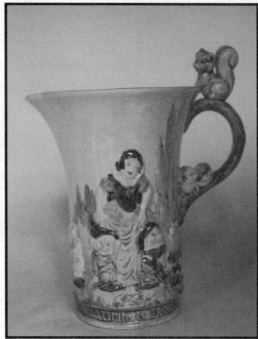

The Charlton Press

Dear Collector:

   The Charlton Press has an ongoing commitment to excellence and completeness in the production of all its Wade reference works.

   Our 1996 schedule will include:

   The Charlton Standard Catalogue of Wade, Volume 1, General Issues, 2nd Ed.
   The Charlton Standard Catalogue of Wade, Volume 2, Decorative Ware, 2nd Ed.
   The Charlton Standard Catalogue of Wade Whimsical Collectables, 3rd Ed.

   Our 1997 schedule will include:

   The Charlton Standard Catalogue of Wade, Volume 3, Tableware, 2nd Ed.
   The Charlton Standard Catalogue of Wade Whimsical Collectables, 4th Ed.

   We ask that collectors having information not included in any of our pricing references to please send it along to our editorial offices in Toronto.

   We will consider editorial additions or corrections regarding colourways, varieties, series, issue dates, designs and styles, as well as well as other information that would be of interest to collectors. Photos of models that were unavailable in previous issues are particularly welcome. Black and white, unscreened photos are best, but colour is also suitable.

   Your help in providing new or previously unobtainable data on any aspect of Wade models or collecting will be considered for inclusion in subsequent editions. Those providing information will be acknowledged in the contributor's section in the front of every catalogue.

The Charlton Press
Editorial Office
2010 Yonge Street
Toronto, Ontario M4S 1Z9 Fax (416) 488-4656